Modernism and Melancholia

Modernist Literature & Culture

Kevin J. H. Dettmar & Mark Wollaeger, Series Editors

Modernism and Melancholia

Writing as Countermourning

Sanja Bahun

OXFORD
UNIVERSITY PRESS

OXFORD
UNIVERSITY PRESS

Oxford University Press is a department of the University of Oxford.
It furthers the University's objective of excellence in research, scholarship,
and education by publishing worldwide.

Oxford   New York

Auckland   Cape Town   Dar es Salaam   Hong Kong   Karachi
Kuala Lumpur   Madrid   Melbourne   Mexico City   Nairobi
New Delhi   Shanghai   Taipei   Toronto

With offices in

Argentina   Austria   Brazil   Chile   Czech Republic   France   Greece
Guatemala   Hungary   Italy   Japan   Poland   Portugal   Singapore
South Korea   Switzerland   Thailand   Turkey   Ukraine   Vietnam

Oxford is a registered trademark of Oxford University Press
in the UK and certain other countries.

Published in the United States of America by
Oxford University Press
198 Madison Avenue, New York, NY 10016

© Oxford University Press 2014

Library of Congress Cataloging-in-Publication Data
Bahun, Sanja.
Modernism and melancholia : writing as countermourning / Sanja Bahun.
pages cm.—(Modernist Literature & Culture)
Includes bibliographical references and index.
ISBN 978-0-19-997795-6 (acid-free paper)   1. Modernism (Literature)
2. Depression, Mental, in literature.   I. Title.
PN56.M54B34 2013
809'.9112—dc23
2013009684

9 8 7 6 5 4 3 2 1
Printed in the United States of America
on acid-free paper

To Gordana Les, and to the memory of Dragutin Bahun, whose love and support made this book possible.

Contents

Series Editors' Foreword

How could relations between modernism and melancholia not already have received substantial attention? One senses intuitively their deep interconnection, whether in the meandering (failed) attempts to reconstruct distant traumas characteristic of so many modernist narratives or in the affective struggles of so many modern protagonists. But in *Modernism and Melancholia: Writing as Countermourning*, Sanja Bahun offers distinctly fresh contributions to both modernist studies and interdisciplinary studies of melancholia that open new perspectives on major works by Andrei Bely, Franz Kafka, and Virginia Woolf. Most broadly, Bahun's achievement lies in her integration of psychoanalytic and historical methodologies, but a great deal of pleasure and enlightenment also emerges from her richly detailed close readings of great writing.

Bahun believes that "the modernist engagement with history is both most poignant and most effective when it acknowledges the rarity of historical 'healing' and yet persists in its representation." The concept of non-closure here simultaneously invokes and thus links the aesthetic, the psychoanalytic, and the historical. Bahun's meticulous analysis interweaves these domains throughout her introduction and a lengthy methodological first chapter, as well as in chapters devoted to each of her three authors and a conceptually and historically expansive conclusion. But let me linger over each of the three strands for a moment.

Melancholia has of course been represented in art for many centuries—Bahun reminds us of Democritus in his garden, surrounded by the carcasses of dissected animals, writing a treatise on madness. What's new in modernism is that melancholia is not simply depicted in, say, the psychology of a central character; it is *textually performed*: lack of closure with respect to plot is thus in part a formal expression of melancholia's interminability. Bahun also studies linguistic enactments of melancholia on a more granular level, including syntax, diction, and tone, as well as at the level of subjectivity. Yet the broader aesthetic yield of her argument can only be grasped in relation to her intervention in psychoanalytic studies.

Such studies, following Freud's early work, have tended to oppose melancholia to mourning—melancholia simply results from the failure to mourn effectively. But Bahun, reading through the full spectrum of Freud's writings on the subject, from letters to Wilhelm Fliess to his late studies of group psychology, aims to displace that binary, in which melancholia is always the abjected half. Instead, taking her cue from Julia Kristeva, she wants to focus on the mutual implication of mourning and melancholia. Two advantages follow from this: first, melancholia's association with heightened creativity comes to the foreground, giving the concept a productive force that helps account for modernism's paradoxical investment in *performing* melancholia; second, "mourning," rather than serving as the successful opposite to melancholia's failed response to loss, can be reserved for its more properly anthropological meaning, namely, mourning rituals, group rites designed to console.

Mourning thus understood leads into the historical dimension of Bahun's argument. Treated at length in her first chapter, the waning of mourning rites over the course of the nineteenth century, as explored by Philippe Ariès and others, provides a key historical narrative for Bahun's account of the particular way modernism mediates an increasingly inescapable fact of modernity. Modernist literature, she argues, can be understood as "an alternative mourning rite directed at a specific 'climate of loss,'" one distinguished by "the unusual tendency to give form to the very impossibility of mourning." Hence the aesthetic, psychoanalytic, and historical force of Bahun's subtitle: "writing as countermourning." Countermourning for Bahun names a practice of writing in which "the new content of historical experience"—call it the inability to mourn—is "represented, enacted, and/or induced in the reader in such a way that interpretive closure and the affective attitudes of acceptance and resignation...are suspended." "Questioning the efficacy of mourning rites as it performs them," modernist countermourning, one might say, offers a non-consoling form of consolation

But to what end? In recent years modernist scholarship has sought to highlight forms of historical agency whose lack Marxist and postmodern critique often understood as constitutive of modernism; but Bahun argues that melancholia provides a template for understanding modernism's profoundly ambivalent efforts to engage with history. Given that clinical, anthropological, sociological, and psychoanalytic studies tend to overlook melancholia's historicity, Bahun wants to redirect focus to specific meanings of the concept-condition as defined by its particular historical and cultural contexts. Bahun's project thus benefits enormously from her comparative approach: Bely's *Petersburg* tracks the tumultuous movement from imperial Russia to the early Soviet Union; Kafka's *The Castle* performs melancholia within a Czech-German-Jewish narrative enmeshed in issues of national and subnational identities; Woolf's *Between the Acts* provides an English exploration of "mourning in advance" on the verge of World War II. Always attentive to the historical and cultural specificity of each, Bahun also shows these texts share a sense that their particular affective posture requires "a comparable reshaping of the novel by the kind of representation that makes use of inconsistency, incoherence, over-determination, and other markers of 'symbolic collapse.'"

This foreword can only sketch out the riches to follow. *Modernism and Melancholia* will be of great interest not only to students of modernism, psychoanalysis, and trauma, but also to anyone interested in the rapidly developing field of affect theory and also to postcolonial and transnational critics in search of a flexible model for comparative study.

—Mark Wollaeger and Kevin J. H. Dettmar

Acknowledgments

Modernism and Melancholia: Writing as Countermourning has been gestating for nearly a decade, and it has accumulated many debts. I first thank my Oxford University Press commissioning editor, Mark Wollaeger, for his belief in and support of the book, and Stephen Bradley for his editorial help. For their intellectual generosity and invaluable advice in the early stages of the production of this book I am grateful to Jerry Aline Flieger, Maria DiBattista, Gerald Pirog, and Janet Walker. For their incisive readings of selected drafts I thank Leon Burnett, Jeffrey Geiger, John Gillies, Jane Goldman, and Guido Snel. I owe special thanks to Elin Diamond, Josephine Diamond, Caryl Emerson, Michael McKeon, and Steven Walker. For the rewarding intellectual exchanges that influenced the project in indirect ways, I am indebted to Joshua Beall, Leslie Dovale, Yianna Ioannou, Chad Loewen-Schmidt, Marinos Pourgouris, V. G. Julie Rajan, and JaeEun Yoo.

I am grateful to the Metropolitan Museum of Art for granting me the permission to reproduce their image of Albrecht Dürer's *Melancolia I* (1514), and to the Israel Museum, Jerusalem, for the permission to reproduce their image of Paul Klee's *Angelus Novus* (1920).

The completion of this book would have been impossible without, first, the Fellowship from the Graduate School of Rutgers University, and, then, generous sabbatical allowance from the Department of Literature, Film, and Theatre Studies, University of Essex. I am most grateful to these institutions for their support.

As always, my main interlocutors have been Dušan and Jakov Radunović.

List of Abbreviations

BTA = Virginia Woolf. *Between the Acts*. San Diego, New York, and London: Harvest Book and Harcourt Brace Jovanovich, 1970.

KW = Søren Kierkegaard. *Kierkegaard's Writings*. 26 vols. Ed. and trans. Edna H. Hong and Howard V. Hong. Princeton: Princeton University Press, 1980-2000.

PH = Virginia Woolf. *Pointz Hall: The Earlier and Later Transcripts of* Between the Acts. Ed. Mitchell A. Leaska. New York: The John Jay Press, University Publications, 1983.

SE = Sigmund Freud. *The Standard Edition of the Complete Works of Sigmund Freud*. Ed. James Strachey. London: Hogarth Press, 1957; New York: W. W. Norton, 1961.

SW = Walter Benjamin. *Selected Writings*. 4 vols. Cambridge, Mass. and London: Harvard University Press, 1996-2003.

TG = Virginia Woolf. *Three Guineas*. London: Hogarth Press, 1938.

WMK = Klein, Melanie. *The Writings of Melanie Klein*. 4 vols. Ed. Roger Money-Kyrle, Betty Joseph, Edna O'Shaughnessy, and Hanna Segal. New York: Free Press, 1975.

Modernism and Melancholia

Introduction

It was in 1845 that Søren Kierkegaard, the first "modernist melancholic," declared with uncanny resoluteness devoid of sentimentality: "That our age is an age of mental depression, there is no doubt and no question: the only question is what can be done about it and what the age demands in this respect, for the age is a fashionable patient who is not given orders but is asked what he wants" (*Journals and Papers* V: 264). Rather than professing a belated Romanticist sentiment, as it might be argued, this statement correctly identifies and names the pulse of an emerging epoch, an era of accelerated industrialization, urban growth, scientific inventions, and demographic, cultural, economic, and political commotions that we term "modernization;" the epoch that is not given orders but is asked what it wants.[1] In the light of Kierkegaard's commitment to the refashioning of philosophical discourse into a *performance* of semantic contradiction, however, this recognition of historical melancholia as the key feature of a modernist mental picture amounts to more than the detection of a Weltanschauung. The inverted structure of the sentence quoted above, with its repetition and gratuitous semantic accretion, enacts, as it were, the very historical melancholia the author is exposing. In other words, Kierkegaard's cumulative assessment of the modern age takes form of a respondent rhetorical, indeed aesthetic, practice. Bringing together material history, self-reflection, artistic innovation, and the symptom-concept of melancholia, this semiotic practice is, I argue, paradigmatic of the modernist project itself. The manifestations of this aesthetic performance in literary modernism are the subject of *Modernism and Melancholia: Writing as Countermourning*.

The critical endeavor that purports to elucidate the dynamics of historical mel-ancholia in modernist literature tantalizingly but productively rests upon a set of concepts whose definitions are everything but final. To open with those defini-tional ambiguities befits a study of two phenomena that celebrate incompleteness and symbolic raptures: modernism and melancholia. Notoriously amorphous, modernism, the intellectual period/mode of artistic expression with which this book is concerned, continues to attract descriptions that are both over-applicable and conflicting. Modernist literary texts, for example, have been variously described as hosting "uncompromising intellectuality" (Levin), "formalism" (Lukács), and "negation of form" (Simmel), and they have appeared to scholars as "open works" (Eco) as well as "closed systems" (Foster).[2] The chronological and geographical boundaries of modernism are no less a matter of dispute; any serious critical attempt to define modernism(s) today faces the question of differentiated cultural responses to variably paced modernities.[3] In this context *Modernism and Melancholia* argues for a long modernist century and a flexible "siting" of modern-ism as both a period in intellectual history and a mode of artistic expression. While the book espouses that Sigmund Freud's reworking of the concept of melancholia should be given the status of a modernist paradigm, it also activates discourses on the concept/condition by a number of his international precursors, co-travelers, and followers—Kierkegaard being the most important of them—thereby expand-ing the notion of paradigm itself into a vagrant and temporally open dominant. For this very reason, the discussion is focused through the lens of comparative literary criticism; through a close reading of Andrei Bely's *Petersburg* (1916/1922), Franz Kafka's *The Castle* (1922), and Virginia Woolf's *Between the Acts* (1941). Written in different languages, informed by dissimilar cultural locales (real and imagined: the pre- and post-Revolution Russia, Czechoslovakia/Germany/Zion, and the *Sitzkrieg* England), and advancing disparate strategies of representation, these novels offer a fruitfully variegated view of geographic, intellectual, ethnic, and gender contexts of modernism.

Whereas the identity of modernism and its geo-temporal scope are hard to isolate, the single thing that no approach to modernism has doubted is the move-ment's intrinsic link to modernization. This relationship is complex. While it is true that modernist art often reflects some vigorous aspects of urban modernity on the level of themes and motifs, modernist texts and artworks more frequently engage with modernization through an ambiguous representation or formal ten-sion. Such representation boomerangs: because modernists offer their articula-tions of contemporary changes as a product on the very market that they take as their subject matter, they, in effect, not only participate in, but also reconfigure the symbolic and economic networks of modern life. To represent this dialectic conceptually, one needs an interdisciplinary framework that would "oblique" the relationship between societal changes and their articulation in aesthetic practice. The conceptual framework of melancholia may serve this purpose well, since historical melancholia was both a reaction to and the very form of modernists' interaction with the maelstrom of modern life.

But this proposition leads us to the site of further ambivalences. Like modernism itself, the phenomenon of melancholia feeds on its own ambiguity: both over- and under-defined, melancholia siphons off its "content" across disciplines, eluding classification and defying grounding. Thus, with equal accuracy, melancholia could be defined as an affect or an affective disorder, a conceptual construction, a type of behavior (an imagined societal "mood" like Baudelairean "ennui"), and a mere descriptive, thence a discourse, perception, and interpretation. Philosophers have conventionally drawn attention to the protean nature of the concept-condition, and described melancholia with a range of inexplicables: as a sorrow without a cause, and a condition that mysteriously triggers the powers of imagination and cognition (pseudo-Aristotle; Galen; Burton). These powers are, then, traditionally seen as aides in the melancholic's pressured search for the source of/reason for the condition itself; the latter is perhaps best epitomized in that ancient image of Democritus in the garden, surrounded by carcasses of beasts, dissected and anatomized by him in the possibly hopeless but irrevocable, hence unyielding, search for the fount of melancholia (Burton 16-17). This melancholic search embraces its own unfinalizability as much as it lays claims to the validity of its drives and propositions, and it is in the crevices of such hermeneutic position that more recent philosophers, like Giorgio Agamben, found social agency. For sociologists, on the other hand, melancholia is a type of enunciation, or restored behavior, tangibly present in some identifiable historical moments like periods of transition (Lepenies 164-65). Sociologists and anthropologists tend not to concern themselves with the medical condition of melancholia but to analyze its discursive-declamatory effects such as ennui, spleen, and other modes of self-fashioning and public pronouncement. (These I shall subsume under the term "melancholy" in this book, availing myself of the opportunity—afforded only in English—to distinguish the denotational spectrums of "melancholy" and "melancholia.") In contrast, contemporary clinical research dissolves in long lists of melancholic symptoms, the most frequently evoked of which are apprehension, agitation, psychomotor retardation, refusal of nourishment, and, in severe cases, psychosis (Taylor and Fink 2; see, also, Goodwin and Jamison). Reliant on the examination of so varied clinical realities, psychiatric literature is entangled in nosological untidiness: melancholia sometimes appears in guises of "bipolar depression" or "complicated grief," or, indeed, as "melancholia" or a "melancholic specifier," and it is variably labeled an illness, a stage of illness, and an umbrella term for a cluster of illnesses. This variegation in use is further compounded by recognition that the manifestations of this mood disorder have to be gradated on the scale from mild (subclinical melancholia) to severe (major or clinical melancholia), with multiple "stops" in between.[4] What is commonly overlooked in all these approaches, however, is melancholia's actual historicity: that the specific meaning of the concept/condition of melancholia is defined by the historical and cultural context its users are traversing.

The disciplinary splits outlined above are symptomatic of a deeper problem: melancholia has become an exceedingly vague and easily misused concept. Characteristic, for example, is the insistence of some literary scholars on attributing to modernism an elusive melancholic Weltanschauung whose only identifiable characteristic seems to be the rejection of social engagement. In contrast, I suggest a view of melancholia as not simply an escapist frame of mind, but a dual phenomenon with specific resonances and repercussions in the public sphere: both a discourse that interprets, constitutes, and produces experiential reality—"a form of social action that creates effects in the world" (Lutz and Abu-Lughod 12)—and a distinct symptom determined by its historical moment and observable in contemporary artistic performance. Such designation allies *Modernism and Melancholia* with a range of readings in cultural studies—most visibly, postcolonial studies—that have approached melancholia as a phenomenon that is simultaneously place-and-time specific and transgenerational (Baucom; Gilroy; Eng and Kazanjian). But the present book is both less expansive and more focused in its claims. I approach "modernist melancholia" as a historically contingent mood-bending and an affect-trace of problematic relationship with what is, consciously or unconsciously, experienced as loss; a social index that, in literature, finds its strategic expression in the problem-reflecting use of language and formal devices that purport to both artistically instantiate the process of mourning and reveal its "failure." And I attribute a fundamental shift in the perception of melancholia to a specific moment in time, namely, the emergence and rise of psychoanalysis—a science-discourse that is at the same time a product and a symptom of cultural modernism.

In this line of thought I follow Esther Sánchez-Pardo, who recently explored Melanie Klein's "modernist" theory of melancholia and used it to illuminate (mostly Anglophone) modernist production, and Jonathan Flatley, who investigated the possibility of a politically engaged operation of melancholia in two novels and one social treatise produced in the late nineteenth and early twentieth century (Sánchez-Pardo; Flatley). While their volumes and the present book harbor many important differences—not the least among which concerns the status of melancholia as a symptom and a discourse—we all seem to agree about the hermeneutic advantage of the concept of melancholia over those of some other "pathologies" that have been invoked as constitutive of modernist aesthetics (e.g., hysteria, schizophrenia, and paranoia; see Shawalter, Sass, and Trotter, respectively). I shall summarize here my own reasons for this preference. As a border-bending mood disorder, melancholia possesses stronger descriptive and self-descriptive force than the psychopathologies that entail more pronounced disturbances in behavior, and its critical use in modernist studies neither pathologizes modernist artists nor artificially isolates them from other groups in society. Discursively omnipresent and compulsively reconceptualized in modernism, melancholia also truly functioned as the psychoanalytic and symbolic emblem of the period. Modernists, of course, did not collectively suffer from melancholia (although some modernist writers were manic-depressive, and some others fashioned themselves as such) and not all of them took on a "melancholic" view of contemporary history. Yet, the discursive prominence of melancholia between 1850 and 1950 and the self-conscious employment of the "melancholic symptom" in art and literature of the period suggest heightened awareness of this borderline condition. Socially, this interest coincided with the attenuation of mourning practices and the attempts to find alternatives to normative mourning; and the search for alternative expression was a modernist hunt.[5] Not surprisingly, then, the "modernist" psychoanalytic descriptions of melancholia match the particular structure of affective experience that we associate with modernism—the synthesis of despair and revolt. The contemporaneously described symptomatology of melancholia furthermore corresponds both thematically and structurally to a whole plethora of societal and symbolic tremors in modernism. In particular, the three features of the psychic life that dominate the clinical picture of melancholia—struggles of ambivalence, experience of dislocation, and feelings of fragmentation in the face of an unacknowledged, cognitively inaccessible loss (or losses)—could be seen as modernist marker-sentiments, compulsively transcribed in modernist texts. For all these reasons, the concept of melancholia vividly captures both the subversive and the conservative side of modernist aesthetic intervention, and is methodologically wide enough to be activated in the assessment of markedly different texts and practices that we now recognize as modernist. Finally, it productively interacts with a number of interpretative frameworks recently activated in modernist scholarship: inquiries in modernist epistemology and ethics, modernism and medicine, and the modernists' political-affective postures such as nationalism, cosmopolitanism, and exilement. This width of notional scope is an exclusive privilege of the concepts-conditions that operate between normalcy and irregularity, commonality and exceptionality, specificity and generality.

Approaching the subject from an uneasy interdisciplinary position, early twentieth century psychoanalysis offers a profitably diversified set of categories to interrogate the phenomenon of "modernist historical melancholia." The psychoanalytic approach to melancholia that grounds my inquiry was first diagrammed by Sigmund Freud, a "modernist" personally, culturally, and historically imprinted by the condition. Freud's reconceptualization of melancholia serves as both the first in a series of case studies and the general critical framework for the present volume. His "modernist" reflections on melancholia, it is worth noting at the outset, are more diverse and more equivocal than their usual exploitation in literary and cultural studies might indicate: they span the thinker's early attempts to explain melancholia in neurological-psychological terms, as a "hole [...] in the psychic sphere" (*Freud to Fliess* 103-4); the First World War essays where Freud contemplates the links between contemporary history, melancholia, and sublimation, and differentiates between mourning and melancholia; his writings of the 1920s where he reassesses melancholia as a universal formative experience-condition; and his cultural texts of the 1930s where all these diverse cogitations are once again summoned and reapplied to group behavior. These varied assessments have served as an interlocutor for further investigations, at least two of which—Karl Abraham's positioning of melancholia as a recourse to the oral or "cannibalistic" stage of libidinal development, and Melanie Klein's cogitations on the ubiquity and creative power of the depressive position—shared the cultural and historical vicissitudes with modernist authors. Various (post-) Freudian approaches to mourning and melancholia, however, could also be helpful in assessing modernist aesthetic production—in particular, Jacques Lacan's relating of mourning to the coordinates of desire and language, Nicolas Abraham and Marie Torok's phenomenological contrasting of the creative expressiveness of language and its dysfunctions in melancholia, and Julia Kristeva's postulation of the mother as the primeval lost object—insofar as they all foreground, theoretically and clinically, the issues of language and expression. These questions are vital for any study of aesthetic melancholia because they target that mysterious link between melancholia and creativity, glossed by all commentators since pseudo-Aristotle. And the recognition of continuity between melancholia and sublimatory mourning rites such as writing is crucial for my own reclaiming of the concept of melancholia for modernist studies.

While the kind of psychoanalytic (and, more generally, disciplinary) eclecticism that I propose may seem problematic from the perspective of therapeutic practice, a guarded conceptual heterogeneity is beneficial when investigating cultural products such as literary texts; this is so because creative writers are not governed by, and even heedful of, disciplinary divisions. Modernist writers are in fact exemplary in their defiance of narrow disciplinary or sub-disciplinary readings, since their texts and practices tend to question precisely the hermeneutics of separation, distinctness, and classification—intellectually-politically validated and promulgated in nineteenth-century Western Europe—on which such interpretative practices rely. By opting for a deliberately, if cagily, creolized methodology, *Modernism and Melancholia* is able to address diverse international texts and artistic strategies, and to substantiate the claim that the rich conceptual framework of melancholia provides one with a fresh look on modernist writers' attitude toward history, or histories. This strategy has hidden benefits: by traversing the modernist reframing of melancholia in interdisciplinary fashion, the book contributes to the ongoing debates on the nature of the concept-condition itself. The most important of these conceptual interventions concerns the common practice of defining melancholia through an opposition to a normative response to grief—mourning. Prevalent in sociological and clinical discussions, this contradistinction is, then, replicated in literary studies that utilize these concepts—a tactic that more often than not results in strained interpretations. Rather than maintaining a strict differentiation between melancholia and mourning, I propose an understanding of melancholia/mourning as a bifacial dynamic whose common features are the ideal or real object-loss and the discord felt in language and personal and group self-fashioning. As we shall see, this approach is actually commensurate with the early psychoanalysts' own accounts of melancholia/mourning. For early psychoanalysts and modernist self-reflexive writers alike, a melancholic text is (by virtue of being a text and an attempt to *symbolize*) simultaneously a text of mourning.

Evoking this relativization of the borders between mourning and melancholia in *Black Sun*, Julia Kristeva usefully identifies "intolerance for object loss" and "modification of symbolic bonds" as characteristic features of both mourning and melancholia (10). To explain the tight intertwine between the two, she uses an age-old enigma. Because our coming to terms with any kind of absence relies so heavily on the development of creative means to compensate for it, melancholia has traditionally been perceived as a state subjacent to creativity.[6] While the exact nature of this link remains unresolved in both clinical and philosophical studies of melancholia, it is useful for literary critics to think about creative writing in particular as a boundary condition, a process emerging at the very moment in which the melancholic affect slips into the mourning effect. Whereas there is no doubt for Kristeva (or for Klein, from whom she inherited this train of thought) that the melancholic acting out of the death drive may easily freeze its subjects in a silent asymbolia, she nevertheless highlights the important function of melancholia as both generator and sustenance of symbol-formation; "loss, bereavement, and absence," she writes, "trigger the work of the imagination and nourish it permanently as much as they threaten it and spoil it" (9). As a fetish, the work of art emerges only when—and at the exact moment when—the activating sorrow has been repudiated. Yet this slippage from emotion into action does not repress, or cancel, the melancholic affect itself. Rather, it suggests a sublimatory hold over absence without obliterating the lost object (217). As the artist weaves "a *hypersign* around and with the depressive void" (99), the imprints of loss become visible to a careful reader.

Serving Kristeva's larger purpose to postulate the impossible mourning (or, melancholia) for the maternal object as both source and content of sublimation, her discussion also challenges the strict separation of mourning and melancholia. Whereas the therapeutic advantages of this approach may be a matter of dispute, I would follow Kristeva's insightful lead and argue against the artificial severance of the two processes and the deprecation of melancholia specifically in the case of literary criticism. As my analysis of Bely's, Kafka's, and Woolf's "melancholic texts" demonstrates, the methodological move away from the binary understanding of melancholia and mourning and toward the reexamination of the melancholia-creativity intertwine is particularly beneficial for modernist studies because it may help us understand the paradox of self-consciously "melancholic" performance. At the same time, I believe it is sensible to reserve the term "mourning" for what it properly denotes in anthropology, namely, mourning rituals—those group rites whose importance for the everyday life of society is paramount but whose worth cannot be judged solely on the basis of their "therapeutic" efficacy. For this reason I open the book with an account of the waning of mourning rites since the mid-nineteenth century. This decline is interpreted as both expression and consequence of the modern "inability to mourn," a state that fueled not only the modernists' structure of feeling but also their artistic strategies. Insofar as modernist literature can be understood as an alternative mourning rite directed at a specific "climate of loss," it is distinguished by the unusual tendency to give form to the very impossibility to mourn. I term such response to history the *practice of countermourning*. The latter concept allows one to envision a memorial articulation of loss that is at the same time expressive and critical, that aims at "therapeutic" engagement yet nevertheless utilizes the symptomatology of melancholia, thereby retaining (rather than recalling) the lost object, in all its uncognizability, as an integral part of the text and the reader's experience thereof.

It is here that my reinterpretation of the melancholia-mourning intertwine partakes in the reevaluations of melancholia and its social function in contemporary critical theory.[7] My dual hypothesis is that melancholia, as both a symptom-cluster and a tool in the cultural practice of countermourning, may have a far more active social function than commonly perceived, and that modernists were acutely aware of this potential. Of course, to put forward an understanding of a modernist text as a melancholic, or, more generally, symptomatic text, means to engage with a set of disquieting questions—about the nature of the symptom, the relationship between individual and group symptoms, and, finally, about the relation of that symptom to aesthetic production—which I shall briefly outline here. In Freudian psychoanalysis the symptom is simultaneously an exteriorization of affliction and the very point at which "healing" commences. The same holds true for the melancholic utterance itself, which, however monologic it may appear, entails intricate strategies of social interaction (see Taylor and Fink 49). It is not surprising, since, from a sociological perspective, the symptom both speaks about times and bodies and presents an aberration to times and bodies. The modernists' complex attitude toward contemporary history and the artistic strategies they developed to express this stance in language testify to this folded nature of the symptom. As a means of expressing an inner (traumatic) response to exterior events, the melancholic symptom serves modernists as at once an emblem of the times and an exception to them, a cry for help and a powerful social corrective.

Melancholia, admittedly, has its traps. Most cases of melancholia belong to milder manifestations of illness and thus could be seen as allowing expression while curbing the dictates of reason (Jamison 9). Still, as Greg Forter has recently reminded us, the unguarded elevation of melancholia on the level of a paradigmatic subversive strategy may occlude the damaging sides of the condition that occur in grave forms of illness: the (possibly complete) foreclosure of expression and (possibly ultimate) disconnection from society/history, and a form of exclusionist identitarianism that rejects the possibility of relation, indeed any political commonality, among those who have and who have not experienced certain losses (139-43). While Forter's assessment of mourning and melancholia could be challenged on the grounds of its own essentialism, his objections should nevertheless be taken into account when discussing modernist fiction. Not incidentally, an awareness of the detrimental aspects of melancholia also resonates in modernist prose, including precisely those texts that are based on the strategic use of the melancholic utterance. The historical context of the late 1930s in particular gave momentum to inquiries into restitutive mourning. For reasons that are explored in chapter 4, it befell no one else but Virginia Woolf to probe the foreclosure of solidarity in melancholia: her last novel derives much of its contradictory interpretative potential precisely from the simultaneous espousal and questioning of the melancholic politics of community. Melancholia, such literary practices suggest, contravenes easy resolutions: it refuses its "subjects" social commonality but it also offers them political, hermeneutic, and aesthetic apertures.

To give justice to these convolutes I open my "matrix" discussion of modernism in chapter 1 by identifying the discursive prominence and conceptual reframing of melancholia in the period between 1850 and 1950s.[8] Zooming in on the modernist artists and writers' use of the melancholic symptom I propose that two general traits differentiate their practice from all previous "aesthetic" melancholias. First, modernist melancholia is inextricably bound to contemporaneous social history: it is informed by and almost obsessively concerned with the psycho-social rifts and lacunae generated by what Benjamin terms "a change in structure of experience" (SW IV: 314). More importantly, perhaps, modernist melancholia distinguishes itself by representing the historical content through formal inflection rather than description. For the first time in the history of representational arts, the melancholic dynamics are not—or not only—depicted (through characters, their meditation, and their relations), but *performed*. Modernism finds a therapeutic "container" in the form itself, and it is the latter that now speaks out a "melancholic" history: the "fleeing" of the self, the troublesome father-son relation, anxiety of origin, mourning for the mother, the simultaneous exaltation and mistrust of language, and other dynamics that psychoanalysts customarily ally with the symptomatology of melancholia and modernist scholars recognize as the *differentiae specificae* of modernism. Melancholia therefore operates as both a propeller and a sustainer of the modernist project: it permeates modernist epistemology, but also gives a distinctive shape to modernist art.[9]

Modernists used the melancholic symptom not only to relay the complex history of the late nineteenth and early twentieth centuries but also to articulate a need for an alternative to such history; it is not difficult to identify in modernist "melancholic" artworks an emphatic call for a transformation of the methods that we use to select, archive, reference, and interpret historical data. As a genre that has a particularly intimate relationship to history and the practices of its record, the novel is an apt case study for probing the inscriptions of historical melancholia in the modernist aesthetic body. Both cannibalistically appropriative and compulsively exportive of formal features and discursive strategies, the novel tends to address the entangled relationship between historical dynamics and literature in more immediate ways than other genres. The discussion in *Modernism and Melancholia* concentrates on what I identify as the three vital elements of the novel, particularly serviceable in the context of modernist commitment to representing relays between the external world and the subjective experience: the character, the chronotope, and language. All three have undergone a substantial transformation in modernism. Hence these aspects of the novel, together with the relevant conceptual and clinical features of melancholia, focus the discussion in all chapters. But the character, the chronotope, and language are not only the artistic tools of modernist fiction. They are also the concepts of considerable weight for modernist writers, and, as such, they establish both independent and shared links with the symptomatology of melancholia. For this reason, they are provisionally treated as discrete components in chapter 1, and their essential interrelatedness is rendered visible and critically workable in chapters 2 to 4, dedicated to Bely's *Petersburg*, Kafka's *The Castle*, and Woolf's *Between the Acts*, respectively.

Melancholic performance naturally striates these texts in different ways. Although separate in time-space and the mode of writing, all three novels are, however, expressly concerned with history and transformation in the experience of reality. Serialized in 1913, first published as a book in 1916, and substantially revised between 1916 and 1922, in the years that saw a most thorough makeover of Russian society, Andrei Bely's *Petersburg* is a text in which socio-historical reality operates vigorously amidst metaphysical questioning. It is particularly apposite to open my series of close readings with *Petersburg* because, in terms of history of melancholia in modernist fiction, Bely's novel is a paradigm shifter: it stages a self-conscious move from the psychology-of-character-based representation of "melancholy" (typical of the Russian nineteenth-century novel) toward an avant-garde *textual performance* of "melancholia." Bely's tale of failed patricide narrates the psycho-social dynamics attending the abortive revolution of 1905: struggle between fathers and sons, mourning for the mother(land), issues of the decline of the West and the rise of the East, and the uncertain fate of Russia. What facilitates the reader's entry into this convoluted time-space is the copiously recorded "social melancholy" of early twentieth-century Russia, readable in an assortment of melancholic dynamics with which Bely furnishes his characters. But the translation of this social mood into a linguistic form seems to have been Bely's greater concern. Noticeably organized around a search for an uncorrupt verbal expression, Bely's novel enacts the foundational obsession of literary modernism that, in the wake of Nietzsche's and Mallarmé's interventions, shattered epistemology, ethics, language-science, and language-art; namely, the simultaneous mistrust in and exaltation of language. My interpretation of *Petersburg* accentuates the hitherto unattended melancholic structuring of the symbolist project and reads Bely's performative engagement with the melancholic symptom as a means not only to reinvigorate the genre of the novel but also paradoxically to challenge "social melancholy" itself.

Chapter 3 traces the more ominous nuances of the same performative concern in Kafka's *The Castle*. Committed to paper in an outpour of creative energy in 1922 but conceived, planned, and drafted in a period of at least five years, Kafka's novel came into being against the backdrop of tremendous changes in Czech society: the First World War and the disintegration of Austro-Hungarian monarchy, the establishment of the shared state of Czechs and Slovaks, and the rise and fall of anti-Semitism in this new multiethnic context. Coupled with Kafka's intimate interest in the issues of Jewish assimilation and the conceptual framework of melancholia, this social climate found its circuitous way into *The Castle*. It shaped the novel into an investigation of the relationships between the margin and the center, authority and subalterity, and belonging and non-participation; and it introduced in Kafka's text the characteristically modernist concern with home as absence. All these issues are probed in chapter 3, where the text's innovative chronotope is reinterpreted as a symbolic time-space "in between the two deaths." Such organization of the time-space of the novel suspends mourning in a manner that resonates with the historical and intertextual vicissitudes of the text's production. Kafka's transcription of the melancholic speech in its grave, desentimentalized modus (characteristic of the more severe forms of the condition) operates in a comparable fashion, I further argue. While it installs the much discussed sense of epistemological instability, its primary function is to emplace historical melancholia in the text, confirming it as a privileged affective container for undecided identities. In particular, the "melancholic" instability of Kafka's sentences is instrumental in his effort to capture the simultaneity of historical presence and absence on the page. Indeed, the link between (imagined, fugitive) space-time and (imagined, fugitive) language is nowhere more consistently investigated than in Kafka's unfinished novel.

The attempt to speak simultaneously the language of presence and the language of absence, and thereby to illuminate the issue of participation or non-participation in history, also informs Woolf's *Between the Acts*, I argue in chapter 4. Written at the beginning of the Second World War and set in rural England during the *Sitzkrieg*, Woolf's novel narrates a moment of extended stasis, *in between the acts*. Structured around an imperative to restore meaning under conditions of (historical) unintelligibility, Woolf's text responds to a directive of social engagement the writer imposed on herself in the late 1930s—with both

humor and despair. Notably, Woolf's novelistic interrogation of the issues of historical engagement, the inadequacy of the operative models of recording past,
and the relationship between art and the material world is oriented by what Freud
called "mourning in advance." Similarly to Bely and Kafka, Woolf utilizes some
distinct features of the melancholic speech not only to relay the complexities of
past and present history but also to forebode a future cataclysm. The constant
interaction between these different temporal planes eventually transforms the
novel from a story about a nation in crisis into a more general investigation in
the nature of communing and the possibility of mourning under conditions of
catastrophe. My reading focuses on the ambivalences of this melancholic performance: on gaps and elisions that simultaneously glorify the obscured subject and
silence it; on the novel's genre-transports that poeticize the hope of interpersonal
mournful expression as much as they mock it; on "the orts and scraps" that signal
Woolf's vision of community; and on the ethics of perdurance that her text finally
appears to propose.

The frequently self-conscious manner in which modernists like Bely, Kafka,
and Woolf deployed symptomatology of melancholia suggests their intimate
understanding of both potentials and limitations of the melancholic utterance. To
propose, as I have done here, that their artistic engagement with the melancholic
symptom might have been strategic, however, begs, in conclusion, the question of
sentience: how much aware of a symptom can its possessor be? Such awareness can
only be partial, Freud maintained, for knowledge and non-knowledge coalesce in
the symptom. I tend to perceive this issue not as a hermeneutic paradox but as
a methodological aperture. The heightened self-reflexivity—the signature trait of
the modernist enterprise—suggests the vigorous activity of meta-symptomatology,
but it does not cancel out the possibility that the modernists' use of the melancholic symptom is, simply put, a symptom; an aching, period-specific, reaction
to societal shudders and restructurings. One comes to realize that, in the majority of modernist literary works (including the three novels under scrutiny in this
book) aesthetic countermourning is keyed in this dual mode: as a symptom and a
performance of symptom. One needs not be afraid of admitting this contradiction
into our critical reflections on modernism. In fact, this is probably one of the more
profound lessons that dealing with modernism and melancholia teaches us: that
each work of art hosts not only the semantically reconcilable but also the "unappropriable" material; and that this duality of material has to inform our interpretation. Unlike either the concept of "mourning" or that of "anti-mourning," the
notion of countermourning enables us to honor this complexity, and to recognize
the convoluted relationship between the modernist text and its context not as an

aberration to be logically straightened by critics but as a working contradiction that will productively curve our own reading.

It is precisely this melancholic awareness of inconclusiveness and frailty of text in history that agitates Bely, Kafka, and Woolf, as they write and rewrite (and leave unfinished) the three novels under consideration here. Hence it is apposite to open this book with an acknowledgment of the most significant attribute that modernist art and melancholia share: they both voraciously feed on the lack of closure.

1 Modernism

The Rise of Countermourning

Preamble: Mourning and Countermourning

Rarely do we investigate mourning. Precisely because it has been with us since the dawn of time and because it is grounded in one of the existentially most common human experiences, that of separation, mourning does not lay claims to exceptionality. The topic grows to be alluring only when mourning itself becomes problematic: significantly, it is the twentieth century thinkers who undertook the work of articulating the diverse aspects of mourning—its symptomatology, ethics, erotics, and, most importantly for my present purposes, its waning as a cultural practice.[1] This multiplicity of approaches is subtended by one major distinction that is also of substantial importance for our understanding of modernist art. On the one hand, mourning may be viewed as an intimate *experience*, and, thus, in psychoanalytic parlance, a counterpart to another intimate experience, that of melancholia. At the same time, mourning may be defined—perhaps more accurately—as a specific *culturally constructed type of behavior*. While most contemporary discussions of mourning either conflate the experience of loss with the ritual triggered by that experience, or substitute one for the other, it is wise to distinguish between grieving and a social symbolic articulation of grief. For example, psychoanalysis, contrary to common perception, does not actually concern itself with mourning (practice): it focuses on grieving (experience) and pays little or no attention to mourning rites (Homans, "Introduction," 7). Still, it is precisely an exploration of the *relationship* between the two that is vital for our understanding of the cluster of issues related to the experience of loss, since such inquiry connects the individual affect and the operation of society and acknowledges the symbolic expression of grief as not only a significant, but also transformative aspect of the social realm. As a symbolic practice that compulsively revolves around the question of loss, modernist writing deserves an illumination in this context—that is, as both a historically identifiable experience and a certain type of cultural behavior.

Sociologically, mourning is a symbolic-performative reaction to grief, a "culturally constructed social response to the loss of an individual" (Counts and Counts 7). Anthropology understands the ultimate loss, death, as a bifurcation-force in society, one that splits the community into the spheres of those present and of the absentees. To enable the social processing of loss and the reunification of the split society, the public performance of rituals is required, anthropologists argue (cf. Turner 39). On this reading, mourning rites "enact" the loss, serving, in psychoanalyst Wilfred Bion's terms, as a group symbolic "container" for the loss in question: ritual "represents" the death/loss, and by doing so, alleviates the social tension attendant to it, transforming this shattering experience into a communal, sometimes creative, work in society. In this context, mourning rites also present the Lacanian "second death" of the object, the repaying of symbolic debt that might enable the "debtors" to begin anew: lamentations and elegies, memorials, mourning robe, and, finally, the funeral itself, all encourage the mourner to leave behind the lost object and redirect attachment toward a new object and the now changed society. Traditionally, the period in which these rites unfold has been symbolized by the metaphor of the journey, an image vigorously exploited in Kafka's *The Castle*. There is much truth in this representation, Robert Hertz and Arnold van Gennep, respectively, argued in the 1910s: it is possible to envision the relationship between the deceased, the mourners, and mourning in terms of two parallel journeys, from being part of society, through the transitional stage of unattachment to society, to the return to society (for the deceased, in a symbolic form) after a "secondary burial" (Hertz 27–86; van Gennep).

Mourning becomes more problematic proportionally as we expand the notion of loss. A group, especially a group of substantial size, is much harder to mourn than an individual. In order to be mourned, an abstract loss, like a loss of a nation or a loss of a cherished concept, has to be first recognized as such, and psychological, cultural, and political vicissitudes frequently make such recognition well-nigh impossible. Even when acknowledged, an abstract loss does not lend itself to easy expression: rites appropriate to this type of loss are conspicuously lacking in contemporary society. An awareness of this deficit informs the anthropologists' observation that mourning has undergone a profound change with modernization. The urban modernity of the late nineteenth and early twentieth century, with its accelerated pace of life, attenuation of community bonds, dissolution of traditional sources of authority, and scientific, demographic, and political changes, inserted the sense of an unspecifiable loss in a spectrum of areas linked to the symbolic-ritualistic functioning of society. This general climate found expression in the chronic waning of rituals. As Eric Santner has noticed, the crisis affected in particular the operation of those social rituals where symbolic investiture was pronounced, like acts of institution and interpellation (naming, denominating, and assigning titles) (xii, 145). But it may well be argued that the attenuation of symbolic codes impinged on all communal rites, including society's grounding ritual, that of mourning the deceased. Traditionally, the historian Philippe Ariès recounts, public rituals would "tame" the experience of death for both the dying and those left behind (*Western Attitudes toward Death* 4). Mourning used to be a matter of community rather than solely of the dying person's family; resonant and public, it started before the person's death in order to impart meaning on the final hour. However, advances in medicine, waning of traditional community, and containment of the experience of grief in privacy all brought about the phenomenon that Ariès terms the "forbidden" or "invisible death" (*la mort ensauvagée*). The latter is a private and medicalized—hence, inwardly unexpected and abstract— death, incomprehensible to, denied, and feared by both the dying person and society. The phenomenon of "invisible death" is inextricably linked to the decline in mourning rituals, and thus also to the emergence of a particularly modern kind of group affective behavior—the inability to mourn.

Whereas Ariès sees this tendency gradually developing over the course of the last few centuries, other researchers connect the modern inability to mourn specifically to the social and political context since the second half of the nineteenth century, and, in particular, to the devastating psychological impact of the two world wars (Gorer; Mitscherlich and Mitscherlich). There is a poignant, if mechanical, continuity between the "invisible death" and the advance of warfare in this period, a circumstance to which Freud himself was not blind (see his "Thoughts for the Times on War and Death," 1915). It is this latter context, however, that also provides evidence to the contrary: it is possible to argue that mourning has not entirely disappeared in the early twentieth century. Precisely in order to forestall the social catastrophe of dissolution in indifference, the negotiation of grief has sought alternative modes of public expression; for example, the literature of the First World War has been frequently cited as an unconventional commemorative practice (see, among others, Fussell; Winter). While such claims can have a wide relevance (literature as such has an inherent potential to "do" mourning), noticeably it was only with the waning of traditional mourning practices that literature became one of the most important mourning rites available to modern society. And whereas this process could be read as unique to Western societies—Ariès is concerned with these—there is now more evidence that comparable dynamics could be identified whenever and wherever modernization and the attenuation of public mourning rituals take place, and where a constellation of social factors associated with modernization necessitates an alternative expression of mourning.

Insofar as modernism is a response to modernization, it finds itself in structurally the same position as mourning in the new age: the modern "inability to mourn" operates as both a gripping topic and a formal challenge in modernist texts. What is distinct in the modernists' attempts to replace the reified forms of mourning with experimental expressions of grief is a routine questioning of the "healing" aspect of traditional mourning practices. For this reason, the alternative mourning that their texts offer is at once therapeutic and interminable, suspended in the very symptom it endeavors to overcome in presentation; modernist literature performs an impossible mourning, driven by the force of its unattainable "cure." I find this type of mourning practice resembling what Peter Homans has called "countermourning," a mourning that refuses— to mourn. The idea of "countermourning"—unfortunately not developed any further than a sentence or two—occurs to Homans as he speculates on James E. Young's treatment of the term "countermonument" (*Gegendenkmal*), itself introduced by German artists Jochen and Esther Gerz.[2] According to Young, countermonuments do not console or heal. Being "awkward" and "tormenting" monuments, they acquire their heightened social function precisely through the perpetuation of the loss they memorize: in other words, they combat societal petrification of memories. In his brief conjecture, Homans, then, engages the idea of a comparable mourning practice. This type of mourning, he says, would "ask mourning to move against itself;" it would be "a principled, deliberate, and self-conscious refusal to mourn." In effect, countermourning would counsel against attitudes such as "acceptance" or "resignation" (23). As I open this book, I propose that the concept of "countermourning" may serve as a superior framework to address modernist interventions in the socio-symbolic functioning of society. The term "countermonument," I argue further, may be applied to a good number of modernist texts.

In the same breath, let me acknowledge that this "impossible" mourning properly belongs to a better-known conceptual framework. It is the symptomatology of melancholia that provided modernist writers with templates at once to represent society in crisis and to debar attitudes such as "acceptance" and "resignation," while engaging what they viewed as historically specific affects and discursive practices. As the following pages argue, this multiplicity of roles to which melancholia could lend itself led to its swift establishment as a modernist dominant. And it provoked one of the most significant theorizations of dealing with loss in cultural history.

Freud, Modernists, Melancholia: Three Thousand Cases and More

The year 1897 may well have been a tipping point. Throughout the 1890s an unprecedented amount of writings dedicated to mood disorders was published, discussed, and made intellectual property in a variety of global settings: salons and asylums, courts and universities, cafés and bedrooms. Among scholarly publications, the accounts of melancholia predominated, ranging from elegant discussions of psychopathology such as Georges Dumas's *Intellectual States in Melancholia* (1895) to "hands-on" clinical accounts like Theodor Ziehen's "The Diagnosis and Treatment of Melancholia" (1896). Yet they all seem to have been only a preparation for the momentous scholarly output of 1897: innumerable debates by psychiatrists, philosophers, patients, ex-patients, and commentators in journals, magazines, and tabloids worldwide, and a series of significant publications like Jacques Roubinovitch and Édouard Toulouse's comprehensive discussion of history, symptoms, and institutional and legal repercussions of the condition, entitled *Melancholia*; Jules Séglas's seminal account of the Cotard Syndrome, *Delusion of Negation*; Edward Brush's assessment of one hundred cases of asylum patients suffering from "acute melancholia" and physical disease; and, most sensationally, perhaps, Silas Weir Mitchell's report on three thousand cases of melancholia, which assessed the impact of seasonal changes on the illness and viability of "rest cure" (a therapy later prescribed to Virginia Woolf).[3] More modestly recorded but perhaps with greater consequences for our understanding of the condition, an aspiring neurologist named Sigmund Freud was also pondering the topic in 1897. In a draft attached to his letter to Wilhelm Fliess, dated May 31, 1897, Freud discussed melancholia in psychoanalytic terms for the first time. Highlighting the work of a guilt-producing agency, the young doctor hypothesized that melancholic symptoms were caused by ambivalence of feelings and repression in wake of loss.[4]

"Melancholia," Julia Kristeva has observed, "establishes its archeology, generates its representations and its knowledge" (*Black Sun* 8). The overwhelming discursive presence of melancholia in the years leading to the twentieth century testifies not only to the epoch's infatuation with this mood-bending ailment, but also to certain transformations of public and scientific attitudes. As the era progressed from the economically precarious 1890s into the politically tumultuous first decades of the twentieth century, general interest in affectivity increased (Berrios 289). The scope and content of fin-de-siècle discussions indicate that the sense of "exceptionality" formerly attached to melancholia yielded the floor to an appreciation of the condition's ubiquity: no longer simply an isolated "pathology," or a "divine gift," melancholia turned into a psychological universal emblematic of and necessitated by contemporary history. Thus reactivated and universalized, melancholia gradually became a societal paradigm, a synergic point in which diverse aspects of urban modernity converged. But the new accounts also complicated the traditional image of melancholia as a sentimental withdrawal from the joys of life and a dispositional ailment. As the discursive genre of testimony gained popularity among the general public, the voices of those clinically treated for melancholia were suddenly given prominence in hospital reports and philosophical discussions. In their letters, diaries, and public statements, hospitalized melancholics frequently related their affliction to the social and intellectual tremors of the era; in particular, to their own rebellion against "abuse of power" and their habit of "chewing the cud of philosophical bitterness."[5] To respond to these claims, there was a steady rise of interest, both scientific and public, in what William James judged to be a more detrimental aspect of melancholia, namely, the state of "positive and active anguish" that expressed itself through a Nietzschean loathing to act, irritation, and various forms of interpersonal and cultural anxiety (*The Varieties of Religious Experience* 101). But, speaking in 1901, James was already late in taking the pulse of his epoch. Anxious melancholia, which he reported to be a "new century" phenomenon, had already been recognized as a group psycho-social posture at the dawn of this era: in 1845 Søren Kierkegaard suggested that there existed an intrinsic relation between the prevalence of depression and the contemporary climate of crisis, unrest, and fermentation (*Journals and Papers* V: 265, n. 5761).

Melancholia "does assert itself in times of crisis," Kristeva would confirm more than a century later (*Black Sun* 8). From the very beginning, modernism was, genuinely and through self-fashioning, a response to an "epoch of crises, real and manufactured, psychical and metaphysical, material and symbolic" (Levenson, "Introduction," 4). The coordinates of this climate of crisis have been successfully recounted in modernist studies: now their record includes a range from

dramatic public manifestations (wars, revolutions, labor struggles, suffragette ral-
lies), through transformations of everyday life, to the changes in the domains of
epistemology and ethics. The accumulation of social angst, it is said, exploded in
several historical breaking points, at least two of which, the First World War and
the October Revolution, reshaped the way humans perceive conflict, community,
and themselves.[6] Those and other historical tremors reinforced the notion of conflict as a given of our inter- and intrapsychic life, and directly contributed to the
restructuring of social space into an ethically and ontologically relativized landscape. Bereft of the comforting notions of pre-design or intention, and recognized
as only one among many objects of dubious purpose, the modern(ist) subject
experienced alternating bursts of ontological loneliness, existential constriction,
compulsive self-reflexivity, and vivacious anticipation of the new. As recorded by
Georg Simmel in his 1903 discussion of the mental outlook of city dwellers, limited
existential possibilities were open to the social subject shaped by this movement
of "melancholic" currents: the swift pace of urban society could either engulf one
within its own momentum—a situation in which constant mobility brings about
social oblivion—or cultivate composite behaviors such as blasé self-absorption
and frantic interactivity (174-76, 178-79, *et passim*). In this climate, dislocation
and fragmentation, two vectors of melancholic psychic configuration, became
modernist marker-sentiments. Both spoke out in Charles Baudelaire's, and, later,
Freud's, exaltation of the fugitive, transient, ephemeral aspects of modernity.

Charles Taylor has convincingly argued that what binds different artistic and
philosophical constructions in the epoch of modernism is an epiphanic search
for "unmediated unity" and "merging with the other" (471). This impossible quest
was glossed diversely by contemporary thinkers as a pursuit of "oceanic feeling"
(Freud), longing for the "primal unity" of the infant-mother dyad (Klein), the
homeless's search for "undivided totality" (Lukács), or approximation of Being
(Heidegger). This search replicates, almost too vividly, the dynamics of melancholia: revolving obsessively around the gap occasioned by primary separation, melancholia is both a testimony to and a symptom of an impossible (re)merger. While,
of course, the separation of the consciousness/subject and the world/object is not
a modernist discovery, to express the loss of this continuity as incorporation of the
lost other, a condition where the subject's occasional breakthroughs both hinge on
and are vitiated by vigorous functioning of the incorporated other, is an exemplary
modernist move. One should distinguish, however, this modernist affective positioning from "nostalgia," a sentiment under which (modernist) melancholia is too
easily subsumed. Melancholia, it is worth keeping in mind, is a mood disorder that
elicits symptoms such as compulsive self-reflexivity, epistemological and affective

insecurity, and problematic relation to the "logocentric" and symbolic processes (including, notably, difficulties in expressing what exactly has been lost)—none of which is distinctive of nostalgia. In contrast, nostalgia is a mental state oriented toward a recognizable time-place in past, which does not necessarily impede articulation or cognition. Precisely because modernists' affects were defined by ambivalence, and because they entailed self-reflexive responses to that ambivalence, the modernist structure of experience cannot be equated with the "nostalgic paradigm."[7] Modernist nostalgia, if such existed, was a melancholic nostalgia—a rebellious struggle with an unknowable lost object and the sometimes debilitating symptoms it has left in its trace, a combat which, as in every good psychoanalytic tale, binds the repressed trace of the past, the aberrations of the present, and the unpredictable future.

However we describe this social affect, one is certain: the arts were its beneficiaries. Attached to history, melancholia provided modernist artists and writers with a befitting "objective correlative" for both their view of subjectivity and their ambivalent response to social-political, economic, demographic, and cultural changes. The melancholic palpitation galvanized a variety of aesthetic practices, diverse products of which we cumulatively (albeit never with an easy heart) identify as modernist: Auguste Rodin's constricted sculpture forms and Umberto Boccioni's sculptures in motion; Gustav Klimt's and Pablo Picasso's large canvases; Arnold Schoenberg's expansion of tonality and Igor Stravinsky's primitivist poly-rhythms; Jorge Luis Borges's Buenos Aires poems and Georg Kaiser's expressionist plays; Germaine Dulac's surrealist cinematic meditations and Michelangelo Antonioni's high modernist films; Zora Neale Hurston's ethnographic plays and Russian futurists' *zaum* language, and thousands of pages by Robert Musil, Marcel Proust, Naoya Shiga, and many others. But those who used the melancholic symptom to respond to the times understood melancholia as not only expressive of the affective climate in which they were writing but also generative of innovative, potentially subversive, artistic strategies. Several complementary insights shaped this perception. First, melancholia was seen, traditionally and by Freud, to facilitate those sublimatory moments when despair-over-expression yields art and the continuity between the subject and the world/object is approximated. At the same time, being a condition that connotes disorder and exception, and dangerously borders death, melancholia was simultaneously seen as an apposite correlative for the state of revolt. Furthermore, the perceived proximity between the melancholic aberration and the standard social functioning validated melancholia's entry into a variety of public discourses. Sociologists Carney Landis and James D. Page spoke a common wisdom when, in 1938, they contrasted melancholia, or manic-depressive illness, to other mental disorders on the grounds of its sufferers' opportunities for normal, even outstanding, functioning in society (qtd. in Jamison 297). For all these reasons, melancholia—rather than the sentiment of nostalgia, or more overtly debilitating mental ailments such as hysteria or schizophrenia—turned into the dominant socio-symbolic emblem of "modern times."

Freud's theory of melancholia was both a product of and a major contributor to this climate. As such (and because of its intrinsic relevance for my argumentation), it deserves an overview in the context of contemporary social and cultural history. Not incidentally, Freud first publically addressed the subject of melancholia during the First World War. The twin essays of "Thoughts for the Times on War and Death" and the article "On Transience" (1915) specify three interrelated "symptoms" of the period, all bespeaking social melancholia: a changed attitude toward death, demand for immortality, and revolt against mourning. The first two symptoms indicate a transformation in social and private acceptance of death and everything death signifies—turn of generations, mortality, forgetting; they gesture what I have glossed as the specifically modern problem of "invisible death." In "On Transience," Freud's semi-fictional account of a walk with a young poet and their mutual friend in the summer before the war (perhaps a reenactment of his actual talk with Rainer Maria Rilke and Lou Andreas-Salomé at the Munich Congress in summer 1913), however, the thinker associates the yearning for immortality and inability to accept transience of beauty with "revolt against mourning" (*SE* XIV: 305-6)—a condition easily related to what I term "countermourning." The revolt against mourning is aggravated by the prospect of war and Freud's companions seem to experience it in a particularly complex form: as an urge to "foretaste mourning," a paradoxical "intention to mourn that precedes and anticipates the loss of the object," as Giorgio Agamben would later describe it (*Stanzas* 20). Deceptively, Freud models himself as the only "successful mourner" in the group, the only one who is able to embrace transience and enjoy the new in the wake of loss.[8] And so the essay closes on a lofty note, indexing the current and future history: "We shall build up again all that war has destroyed, and perhaps on firmer ground and more lastingly than before" (*SE* XIV: 307). Yet, positioned as it is after an extensive melancholic interlude describing the multifaceted losses occasioned by the war, this optimistic closure resonates emptily. As a modernist intimately, culturally, and historically marked by the dynamics of loss, Freud must have known better.

Indeed, the three texts of 1915 may also be read as Freud's first public pronouncement of an uncomfortable insight that would thereafter mark his theory: that the loss of symbolic meta-guarantees, interacts, disturbingly, with the factual landscape of "dead bodies" and "ruined houses."[9] It is therefore reasonable to interpret Freud's 1915 texts in the context of specific historical and personal anxieties that accompanied them: the First World War, the breakup with Jung, Freud's fatalistic projections about his own death.[10] By 1919, however, Freud was ready to declare that such a mental outlook was more universal. In a letter to Ernest Jones he described war neurosis as a "case of internal narcissistic conflict within the ego, somewhat analogous to the mechanism of Melancholy, exposed in the 4th volume of *Schriften*."[11] Here Freud refers Jones specifically to an exemplary modernist document: his hitherto most extensive discussion of melancholia, "Mourning and Melancholia" (1915-17).

Acting out the role of exemplary mourner, Freud had but one topic and one discursive strategy opened to him in the war years: the juxtaposition of normative and pathological reactions to loss. Taking a cue from Shakespeare's elaboration of the competing ways to deal with the loss of the loved object in *Hamlet*, but characteristically transferring mourning from the realm of political symbolic rites to that of inner experience, he pursued this strategy of contrast in "Mourning and Melancholia." According to Freud's 1917 essay, mourning and melancholia have the same causes (loss of a cherished person, object, or concept) and they entail similar symptoms (dejection, inhibition of the capacity to love, cessation of interest in the outer world, and others), but the two responses to loss differ in the structure of the relationship established between the subject and the lost other: while melancholia "pathologically" preserves the lost object in the mourner's ego, mourning, a "normative" grief experience, dispels it. In a discourse strongly reminiscent of contemporaneous anthropology, Freud describes mourning-work (*Trauerarbeit*) as a slow, painful process of detaching oneself from the lost object through hyper-cathected reality testing.[12] Although this ritualistic activity encounters strong psychic opposition and requires time (typically, a year), the mournful flow of libido steadily diminishes until, eventually, "the ego becomes free and uninhibited again" and the mourner accepts the irreversibility of absence (*SE* XIV: 245). The optimism about the possibilities of complete mourning and the ensuing "freedom" of the ego that these conjunctures seem to project has troubled scholars and psychoanalysts ever since.[13] Freud's model of mournful "individuation" appears to leave little room for the memorial continuance of the lost object in the ego, and thus it might be seen as both inaccurate and unethical. Researchers' insistence on this interpretation is curious, however, since Freud actually never developed a proper theory of mourning, and it is likely that he used the concept solely for the purpose of discursive juxtaposition in "Mourning and Melancholia" (Homans, "Introduction," 7).

Befitting the affective climate in which it was written, the main topic of this essay is—melancholia.

To describe the symptomatology of melancholia Freud puts forward a parallel already utilized in his *Draft G: Melancholia* (1895), now enriched by historical resonance: in the wake of a loss, he writes, "the complex of melancholia behaves like an open wound, drawing to itself cathectic energies [...], and emptying the ego until it is totally impoverished" (*SE* XIV: 253). This "open wound" generates a range of symptoms among which insomnia, feeling of emptiness, refusal of nourishment, cannibalistic phantasies, difficulty in expressing oneself, and obsessive self-vilification are most common, and thereby most commonly vocalized in the case studies to which Freud and modernist writers could have had access in 1897-1917. Freud highlights the following paradox in this symptomatology: although it entails inhibition of the ability to verbalize, melancholia is characterized by "insistent communicativeness," by the melancholic's unrelenting attempts to exteriorize the affect in language (247). This mental picture, Freud's implicit gloss on pseudo-Aristotle and explicit references to Shakespeare confirm, is related to creativity. The silence of melancholia and the clamor of literary creation, Klein, Segal, and Jamison will substantiate later, are inextricably linked.

To claim that a comparable affective cluster had never been described before would be straining credibility (think, again, of Shakespeare), but there are other features that associate Freud's theorization of melancholia specifically to the modernist context. The most significant among them are the blurring of boundaries between the subject and the object, and the consequential impossibility to identify loss. In melancholia, Freud hypothesizes, libidinal cathexes to the lost object regresses to, in part, the developmental stage of narcissism and, in part, to the earlier stage of sadism, where it activates destructive energies characteristic of the condition. En route the ego is subject to a split: a part of it identifies with, or "becomes," the lost object, and, "in accordance with the oral or cannibalistic phase of libidinal development in which it is, it wants to do so by devouring [the object]" (249-50; see, also, Abraham and Freud 217).[14] This process precipitates the separation of a critical agency that henceforth compulsively "judges" the part of the ego altered by identification (249). (Here Freud's scenario intriguingly corresponds to Kierkegaard's insight that "melancholy's point of contact with insanity is [...] that one himself becomes an object;" *Journals and Papers* II: 186.) Since the subject and the object are no longer psychologically divided, the melancholic can never fully identify what he/she has lost (245); cognitive inaccessibility is the crucial trait of melancholia.

For this reason Freud's own argumentation has to rest on a procedural gap: he remains "modernistly" indecisive about what is actually lost in melancholia. Melancholia, he claims, may develop around the loss of a social abstraction such as "fatherland" and "liberty," or around the loss of an actual individual (*SE* XIV: 243; 245); it can be triggered by loss, or intimation of loss, of an idea or a whole system of symbols (243; 256); and its motivating factors, he suggests, "extend for the most part beyond the clear case of loss by death and include all those situations which can import opposed feelings of love and hate into the relationship or reinforce an already existing ambivalence" (251). Such meditations have their own historicity. Developed during the First World War, Freud's unwieldy description of the exciting causes of melancholia also relies on a specific, historically bound, referential scope and the corresponding discourse—that of the loss of "fatherland" (*Vaterland*) and "liberty" (*Freiheit*), of the loss of ideals or systems of symbols and beliefs, and of the struggles of ambivalence. Whatever values we ascribe to such discursive embeddedness in contemporary history, the following is notable: from Freud's circumvention, loss emerges as at once individual and group, physical and abstract, factual and fictive, past and present, as its meaning and status are constantly renegotiated.[15] It is precisely as such that loss also appears in modernist literature.

The ambivalence of feelings was Freud's concept that Bely, Kafka, and Woolf appreciated most. Freud himself found the struggles due to ambivalence most easily observable precisely in the melancholic's symptomatic self-accusations. This excessive activity of the super-ego, ethical vigilance of self-destructive proportions, hides reproaches to the lost object, Freud argued; melancholia proceeds from "a mental constellation of revolt" (248). When melancholia changes around into mania, a condition both opposite and complementary to "depressive" position, these ambivalent libidinal impulses are freed: the revolt becomes public, expressing itself in obsessive pursuit of new object-cathexes—until it reverts back to "passive" melancholia and to an actively practiced disgust of the world (253-54). Neither of these states should be mistaken for a behavioral posture: the French patient I quoted earlier insisted that the repugnance he felt against "abuse of power" was not mere world-weariness (Roubinovitch and Toulouse 171). This disgust—Baudelairean-Nietzschean nausea—has been rarely considered in accounts of Freud's theory of melancholia, including those that aim to use it in literary studies, and yet it is this social and personal disgust, Kristeva reminds us, that "leads subjectivity to a melancholia in the Freudian sense of the term: [...] to the subject/object, language/affect, sense/non-sense borders" (*The Sense and Non-sense of Revolt* 51-52). It is for this reason, as elaborated in my chapters on Bely's and Kafka's fiction, that the association of melancholia and nausea vitally shaped the affective map of modernism.[16]

What is significant for the present interrogation of the modernist Freud, how-ever, is the thinker's recasting of this state of covert revolt as a function of porous boundaries. To relate the structure of melancholia to the phenomenon of per-meable borders (geographical, subject/object, language/affect, subjectivity/com-munity, interior/exterior borders) means to discuss melancholia in modernist terms. Porosities, outpours, influxes, permeations, and other types of fluctuating exchange between distinct units or dimensions were the preeminent modernist concern across a vast spectrum of areas since, at least, the publication of Ernst Mach's *Contributions to the Analysis of Sensations* (1886). Artistically captured in more modernist literary works than it would be sensible to name here, the notion of permeability testified to a vividly changed world, where inventions such as electricity, the telephone, the radio, and the X-ray made some borders invisible and politics made others visible, where subjectivity was anxiously reconstituted as inter-subjectivity, and isolated objects were recast as interdependent units. Like that world itself, permeability was both saluted and feared. It is the underscoring of the function of permeability, I contend, that makes Freud's assessment of mel-ancholia a paradigmatic modernist theory.

Freud's argumentation is itself affected by conceptual porosity: the question of finalizability/curability of melancholia remains unanswered in "Mourning and Melancholia." His only hypothesis—that the melancholic fury could simply spend itself—leaves Freud unsatisfied (257). The abrupt closure of the essay implies that there is no secure means, perhaps even need, to convert melancholia into mourn-ing. I suggest a reading of this "omission" in the light of Freud's subsequent theo-rizing on loss, as it evolved, under the regime of permeability, into a theory of inevitable losses. The latter is inchoate in his final reframing of melancholia as a shattering testimony of love toward the end of "Mourning and Melancholia:" it is "by taking flight into the ego [that] love escapes extinction," Freud conclusively meditates (257).

Twelve personally and historically turbulent years separate this intimation and Freud's 1929 letter to Ludwig Binswanger, where he recapitulates the effects the loss of his daughter had upon him as follows:

> Although we know that after such a loss the acute state of mourning will subside, we also know we shall remain inconsolable and will never find a substitute. No matter what may fill the gap, even if it be filled completely, it nevertheless remains something else. And, actually, this is how it should

be. It is the only way of perpetuating that love which we do not want to relinquish. (*Letters* 386)

A reevaluation of the mourning-melancholia dynamic, such that it accommodates the persistence of the lost object as inevitability and even a welcome reframing of psychological makeup, is conspicuous in these lines. Unsurprisingly so; this testimonial note in fact reiterates what Freud proposed a couple of years earlier in *The Ego and the Id* (1923). While his account of incomplete mourning in the letter to Binswanger foregrounds the ethics of emotions, Freud of *The Ego and the Id* treats the condition in morally and emotionally neutral but universalizing terms. In his 1923 model of the psyche as divided into the ego (the I, *Ich*), the super-ego (the critical agency; *Über-Ich*), and the id (*Es*), melancholia plays a formative role. Freud abandons his original proposition that in successful mourning all libido withdraws from the lost object and is reinvested elsewhere—the hypothesis on which, incidentally, much of the literary criticism that utilizes Freud's conceptualization of melancholia and mourning relies—and proposes that the cathexes to the lost object persists in the ego in the form of internal identification. The first melancholic identifications, those with one's parents, are most influential, Freud argues. The child's relinquishment of the first object-cathexes occasions a stage of tumultuous melancholia whose consequences are a lasting narcissistic identification with the lost objects and the tripartite constellation of the psyche (*SE* XIX: 34-35). The ego, then, "comes into being on the condition of the 'trace' of the other," as Judith Butler influentially summarized this developmental scenario (196).[17]

But the melancholic trace of the first cathected object is not the only one that sculpts the ego. Freud suggests that all subsequent losses also get internalized. In this way the porous ego is constantly formed and re-formed by abandoned/lost loved objects: "The character of the ego is a precipitate of abandoned object-cathexes and [...] it contains the history of those object-choices," Freud writes (*SE* XIX: 29). This continuous melancholic processing, Tammy Clewell has shrewdly noticed, makes the ego an "elegiac formation" ("Mourning beyond Melancholia," 43). The seeming contradiction that this Freudian I-as-Other is essentially a melancholic structure should not keep us from considering it the locus of not only intra-psychic but also inter-psychic/relational dynamics. Rather, we should partly modify our view of melancholia, that "unforgetting" of the otherness in the self, and acknowledge the distinct social relevance of Freud's reconceptualization of subjecthood.

The postulation of the subject's inherent heterogeneity confirms Taylor's thesis that modernism is anchored in the drive to "merge with the other" (269)—a goal that Freud would view as both impossible and always already achieved. But Freud's heterogenic turn is also representative of the post-First World War climate and it has some identifiable social referents. As a challenge to the sanctioned kind of mourning, the melancholic splitting of the self establishes—deliberately or unwittingly—a critical relation toward the community that rests on the homogenic model of subjecthood (see Bhabha 65-66; Butler 196-98). That this model of totalitarian community came increasingly under attack in the post-First World War modernist literature has been amply demonstrated by, among others, Jessica Berman and Rebecca Walkowitz, and related to writers such as James Joyce, Marcel Proust, Gertrude Stein, and Virginia Woolf (Berman; Walkowitz). The modernist texts entertaining the opposed cultural strategy of nationalism or homogenization could also be said to have responded to this heterogenic turn—if only through attempts at containment and devaluation (cf. Lewis [Pericles]). Here I would like to suggest that the modernists' (including Freud's own) interest in "melancholic representation" should also be understood in the context of this questioning of political homogeneity. The melancholic subject is an exemplary model of heterogenic subjecthood—admittedly, not the most jovial manifestation thereof—and it was used as such in all three novels I discuss in the following chapters.

Let me caution, in closure, that, even when praising it as an ethical perpetuation of love, or a formative move of the heterogenic psyche, Freud is not blind to the damaging sides of melancholia—a condition in which, he theorizes, a portion of the death drive starts operating as "an inclination to aggression and destruction" (*SE* XIX: 54-55). It is what he felt to be the hyperactivity of the death drive in contemporary history that gives both shape and content to Freud's late "cultural texts" such as *The Future of an Illusion* (1927), *Civilization and Its Discontents* (1929-30), and *Moses and Monotheism* (1939). These texts confirm Freud's 1915 insight about the interlock of destructiveness and auto-destructiveness in contemporary history, while insisting on continuity between the subject and the material world, and, more problematically, individual and group psychology. Detecting everywhere the aggressive extremes of an unbound social melancholia, Freud—by now a willful melancholic—presents this condition as ever-lasting rather than period-specific. Casting a retrospective glance on his theory of loss in *Civilization and Its Discontents*, he argues that the world is not our home, much less the primordial home in which the instinctual flows pour out unhindered. Instead, Freud comments, we build our civilization upon an "organic repression" of our drives, a circumstance that binds our individual lives and societal functioning fatally to the workings of melancholia and its key symptom, the feeling of guilt. To make this situation bearable, we generate auxiliary constructions such as religion, quest for knowledge, creation and consummation of art, and other practices that purport, illusorily, to resuscitate the feeling of oneness with the world/object (*SE* XXI: 97). While Freud depreciates sublimatory activities as delusional and not only unable to alleviate but actually fostering the unease we feel in civilization, he also deems them necessary; specifically, sublimation in art/literature and science gets a stamp of approval, even one of urgency, in Freud's late texts. Both a melancholic account of history and a reappraisal of artistic sublimation are characteristic of the intellectual climate of the 1930s. Woolf's *Between the Acts*, a novel that came into being while she was reading Freud's *Group Psychology and the Analysis of the Ego* (1921) and *Civilization and Its Discontents*, will assist me in exploring the nature of this affective response.

Unlike the topic of mourning, to which Freud never returned after the 1917 essay, melancholia, we have seen, remained a constant in his theoretical and clinical preoccupations. Over the course of years, Freud's various assessments of melancholia consolidated, cross-temporally and cross-textually, into what I argue to be not only the quintessential Freudian theory, attendant and even primary to that of the Oedipus complex, but also a paradigmatically "modernist" theory. Like the postulation of inherent heterogeneity, Freud's attributing of universality and even creative surplus to a state which is defined by negativity or lack of capacity presents the thinker's response to the changing social-symbolic landscape of his era. These revaluations reflect not only modernists' cultural and ethical concerns but also their ambiguous self-fashioning as at once exceptional (actively aberrational) and characteristic (typical of the times) subject-group. It is precisely the challenge to the socially sanctioned binary between the normative and the aberrant that subtends modernists' obsessive probing, artistic and speculative, of the borderline condition of melancholia.

When History Gives You a Back Kick: The Melancholic Symptom and Society

Not incidentally did Freud describe the destructive component that entrenches itself in the melancholic's mind in terms of culture: "What is now holding sway in the super-ego," he hypothesizes on melancholia, "is a pure culture of the death instinct" (*SE* XIX: 53). The suggestive phrase that Freud uses to illustrate the destructive potential of melancholia has been frequently evoked in later discussions of the period. But phrases, especially redolent phrases such as "the culture of the death drive," tend to petrify relations, and Freud's own tendency to apply the parameters of individual psychology to society (and vice versa) has been criticized for being founded on an unwarranted analogy. He himself was eager to describe melancholia in non-analogical terms, though: he seems to have conceived of it as a metabolic phenomenon unfolding between an individual, her/his immediate inter-psychic surroundings, and a wider community. Such is also the nature of the culture of the death instinct, or, if one wishes to pursue the analogy, that of the modernist engagement with "the nightmare of history."

The last, of course, is another redolent phrase. It comes from a declaration by Stephen Dedalus, the hero of Joyce's *Ulysses*: "History," Stephen agitatedly exclaims in an early section of the novel, "is a nightmare from which I am trying to awake" (34). Although highly overdetermined, the remark has traditionally served critics as an epitome of the modernist "despair" over, or withdrawal from, history; more specifically, a Nietzschean disgust over our obsession with recording history.[18] Less commonly invoked, however, is the context of the extrapolated phrase; and yet it is this context that naturally illuminates both Joyce's novel and modernist historical melancholia (if such indeed is readable in these lines). Stephen's assessment of history occurs in Episode Two ("Nestor") of *Ulysses*, in the course of his conversation with Mr. Deasy, an exchange that is focalized through a specific historical lens. As the young teacher receives his pay from the headmaster and is simultaneously asked to arrange the publication of Mr. Deasy's letter on foot-and-mouth disease, he is also forced to listen to his employer's anti-Semitic litany. He attempts to cut it short by polite but stern rejoinders, as befitting the episode whose technique has been described by its author as "personal Catechism" (Joyce 734). Stephen's designation of history as a nightmare presents his final attempt to close the subject by producing a general statement. To an extent, Stephen's declaration simply sums up his preceding meditation on history as a story of ambition and plunders (32-34). But the statement is not so much a genuine epiphany as an oppositional stratagem, a way to close an uncomfortable conversation while simultaneously dethroning Mr. Deasy and his "wisdom" (a mixture of chauvinism, misogyny, and vulgar theology). An amount of belligerent *jouissance* is tangible in Stephen's self-consciously depressive proclamation. It may be apposite to invoke here Slavoj Žižek's (via Lacan and Marx) description of the symptom as "a point of breakdown heterogeneous to a given ideological field," a "pathological imbalance" that lays open the falsity of the universalism of bourgeois rights and duties (21). It is precisely in this property that the discourse of historical melancholia is utilized by Joyce's hero—and to a good effect: Stephen's ostensibly symptomatic utterance successfully befuddles Mr. Deasy. Meanwhile, the pronouncement meets a markedly incongruous response from the vagrant narrator: "From the playfield the boys raised the shout. A whirring whistle: goal. What if that nightmare gave you a back kick?" (34). This cross-cutting serves to question any passivity that might be read into Stephen's assessment of history and to affiliate the protagonist's oppositional strategies with those engaged in the boys' game of hockey. The interpolated "shout" reaffirms Stephen's association with the young fighting bodies and the time of shocks and rebounds, vigorously opposed to Mr. Deasy's teleological continuum.[19] Read in its entirety, then, the scene stages historical melancholia as a ludic rebellion against both usurpation and complacence, and it productively reminds us that the symptom, as a point of breakdown, may also have a critical social function. At the same time, Joyce seems to be in earnest when describing history as a "nightmare." After all, Stephen responds to the workings of a historically recognizable, markedly *Thanatic*, ideological framework that we see operative on numerous other occasions in the novel. Thus the place where historical melancholia actually "happens" is neither Stephen's melancholic definition of history nor Mr. Deasy's tirade, but the semantic gap generated through the interaction of these two discourses.

What do we learn from this staging? To answer this question—and to probe the applicability of this reading beyond Joycean universe—let me return to the first modernist who "staged" melancholia. It has often been noted that Freud's eventual redefinition of mourning-melancholia as a universal psyche-organizing "pathology" emblematic of current history follows in the trace of the religious psychology of Søren Kierkegaard, the thinker with whose description of the modern age I opened this book. While to discuss the commensurability of Kierkegaard's and Freud's (and Joyce's) thought would be well beyond the scope of the present volume,[20] one hitherto unattended correspondence merits a spotlight. For both Kierkegaard and Freud, as well as for Joyce, melancholia is at once a paradigmatic condition and the performative of a new, modernist subjecthood. And, as a performative, melancholia is best researched *through performance*, the writing practices of Kierkegaard, Freud, and Joyce seem to suggest. In what follows I would like to introduce briefly Kierkegaard's brand of performative melancholia, for the reasons of historical precedence and intrinsic importance for modernist literature.

Kierkegaard's critique of modernity in works such as *Either/Or* (1843) and *The Sickness unto Death* (1849) has been frequently interpreted as a proto-psychoanalytic account of melancholia.[21] In Kierkegaard's psychology melancholia appears, autobiographically, as a signature-affect of the modern subject. The thinker detects melancholic symptoms—indifference, dizziness, doubt, and the sensation of being "encumbered" by history—everywhere in society. Their ubiquity points to the symptomatic disturbances in the modern subject's relation to its own "self" which Kierkegaard specifies as the despair of oblivion (being unaware that one has a "self"), the despair of not willing to be oneself, and the despair of will to be one's (imagined and fetishized) self. Not unlike psychoanalytic thinkers later, Kierkegaard explains melancholia developmentally, as an "upbuilding" stage leading to emotional, intellectual, and spiritual maturity. This maturity manifests itself as an individual's ability to make a responsible existential choice at a decisive instant in which personal history and eternity intersect (*KW* XIX: 78, 110 *et passim*; *KW* VIII). Yet this decision has to be constantly remade and thus repetition continuously reshapes the subject in his/her relation to God, an eternally inaccessible love object.[22] Linked to the necessity of repetition, melancholic battles then appear to be both a developmental stage and a constant in life. Furthermore, since without the melancholic anxiousness this responsible choice cannot be (re)made, melancholia emerges as not only a symptom of modernity but also the very "cure" for that symptom.

Kierkegaard resolves these contradictions with a paradigmatically modernist gesture: he inflects the form of inquiry. Binding psycho-philosophical speculation and literary fantasy (Nordentoft 389, n. 11), Kierkegaard's texts were the first artistically to *perform* melancholia. The melancholic experience of the fragmented self gets reflected in Kierkegaard's writings in the obsessive partitioning of the text into forewords, interludes, postscripts, appendices, and the thinker's occasionally overenthusiastic use of ironic distancing. The most surprising feature of Kierkegaard's melancholic textual performance, however, is his use of strategies of split embodiment—pseudonyms, personas, contrasting arguments in simultaneously published books—to undermine the inherited form of argumentation and authorial/existential position that sustains it. Each of Kierkegaard's ludic "embodiments" gives a melancholic testimony of his time (the seducer's indifference, the poet's oblivion, the judge's ethical doubts, Climacus's *acedia* and so forth) while serving as the thematic expression of Kierkegaard's typology of existence (aesthetic, ethic, and religious being, governed by desire, reflection, spirit, respectively).[23] More importantly, Kierkegaard's activation of different names, "masks" and stances articulates performatively the modern subject's uprootedness and sensation of void—the "melancholic sin" to which Kierkegaard dedicates the pages in question. Rather than being expressed through emblems and typologies (strategies typical of the aesthetic and philosophical works of the Renaissance or Romanticism), historical melancholia is articulated here as a symptom-ridden challenge to the inherited structures, one that relies on a compulsive play with absence. This bending of form to express social melancholia, Kierkegaard confirmed in his posthumously published autobiography, *The Point of View for My Work as an Author*

(1848; see, esp. XXII: 101-03, and 125-28), was self-conscious. With Kierkegaard, for the first time in the history of representational arts, melancholia is *not* (or not only) depicted, but purposefully *aesthetically enacted*.

This property of modernist melancholia to be at once a universal yet historically contingent experience *and* the aesthetic realization for that very experience was extensively researched by another modernist thinker, Walter Benjamin. It was Benjamin—who professedly had little sympathy for Kierkegaard's melancholic loopholes—that completed the Danish thinker's project of reconceptualizing melancholia as the very structure of contemporary experience of history.[24] Tracing the emergence of aesthetic modernism to the rapid installation of market society in the mid-nineteenth century, Benjamin has singled out Charles Baudelaire— Kierkegaard's contemporary and a figure usually associated with the onset of modernism—as the first "modernist melancholic." Like Kierkegaard's philosophical texts, Baudelaire's artistic opus offers a contradictory representation of the modern experience as at once base and noble, fragmentary and holistic, and provocatively palimpsestic. Benjamin pays visit to these contradictions in his lengthy essay "The Paris of the Second Empire in Baudelaire" (1938), where he likens Baudelaire's melancholic historical vision and his art to the specific transformations in lived experience in the Second-Empire France. In Benjamin's reading, Baudelaire is a paradigmatic figure of his time-and-space—an "urban melancholic" who has identified himself with the melancholic state of a commodity in search of buyers on the open market (134ff). History shapes the form and content of Baudelaire's writing, Benjamin suggests. The poet defended himself against the shocks of modern city life by incorporating, as a thematic and formal resource for his poetry, the very urban experience he unconsciously feared: he resourced the realm of personal memory, now transfigured by the influence of isolating urbanity into a "split structure of experience" (110).[25] Far from being Baudelaire's idiosyncrasy, Benjamin argues, the "split structure of experience" represents the distinctive "melancholic scar" that high capitalist modernity imprints on the psyche of those who traverse it.

A Marxist reading should have no problem with assigning a negative value to Baudelaire's melancholic identification with the lost (unpossessible) object. Curiously, though, Benjamin does not mourn the effects of this reification; rather, he treats this experience of loss as an *active* principle that reformulates the subject's relation to history. The chief motivational force behind this unorthodox interpretation is Benjamin's interest in his own "modernist historical melancholia"—a condition which he strategically probes in texts such as "The Story-teller" (1936) and "The Work of Art in the Age of Its Mechanical Reproducibility" (1937-1939). But this appraisal of melancholia also follows the inner logic of Benjamin's argumentation on history in a variety of texts produced in the 1930s (see Proust, "Melancolia illa heroica"). From the Baudelaire-Benjamin alliance, then, modernist melancholia emerges as a contradictory affect conjoining historical disenchantment and vigorous working-through, an inquisitive "mode," and a "structure" that corresponds to contemporary "catastrophe in permanence" (*SW* IV: 164).

This multi-operative image of melancholia is elaborated in Benjamin's well-known interpretation of Paul Klee's watercolor/drawing *Angelus Novus*. Klee's 1920 drawing, the proud owner of which was Benjamin, starting in 1921, represents the enlarged face of an ambiguous entity, staring awry into an undetermined object (see Figure 1.2). In "On the Concept of History" (1940) Benjamin argues that Klee's figure should be interpreted as "the angel of history," under whose horrified look the past is disclosed not as a chain of events (as it may appear to the rest of us) but as "one single catastrophe, which keeps piling wreckage upon wreckage and hurls it at his feet" (*SW* IV: 392). The angel, Benjamin relates, would like to stay, to "awaken the dead, and make whole what has been smashed," but a violent storm blowing from Paradise—what we call "progress"—drives him irresistibly into the future and away from the "oppressed past" (392; 396). Benjamin's historical-aesthetic "snapshot" specifically indexes melancholia by invoking the medieval concept of *acedia* (391). The latter now serves Benjamin to articulate the intellectual context of the late 1930s: the sense of historical paralysis; the experience of a forward momentum depriving one of time to reflect on historical events; and an urge to acknowledge, yet impossibility to recuperate, the obscured and the broken.

Benjamin's "snapshot," one should not forget, is part of a larger whole, a text which he conceived as an urgent call to transform the way we conceptualize and record history. The new "materialistic historiography" that Benjamin proposes in this essay as an alternative to both traditional and vulgar Marxist historiography involves deployment of "constructive principle": the arrest of thinking in "a constellation saturated with tensions," by which the thinking is crystallized as a monad, or a historical object (396)—"that image of the past which unexpectedly appears to the historical subject in a moment of danger" (391). Klee's drawing could be seen as one such monad constellating the modernist epoch with the entirety of events and eras before. But the same could be said of Benjamin's reflection on Klee itself. As a doubly inflected content-made-form—an extended gloss on an artwork in a fragmentary political-philosophical treatise—Benjamin's melancholic re-imaging of history is itself a call for action, congruent with the modernist aesthetic-political strategy which the thinker particularly admired, the

Brechtian V-Effekt. And Benjamin was by no means alone in his use of a melan-cholic image of history to *battle* historical melancholia. The history of ideas lacks a proper name for this phenomenon. I propose that we understand these modern-ist performative loopholes in the context of contemporary reconceptualization of melancholia as a borderline condition.

I have mentioned earlier that the modernists' reassessment of the melancholic symptom(s) was borne out of their more general probing of the categories of normativity and aberration, and their particular appreciation of those states that defy an easy compartmentalization in either of the two. But what is the position of such states/conditions in the symbolic and real functioning of society—for Freud, for modernists, and for us, as interpreters of their writing? To approach this question, let me first outline the complexities attending the concept of the symptom itself. Angel Martínez-Hernáez has argued that the structuring paradox of symptomatology inheres in the capacity of symptoms to be both organic mani-festations and symbolic constructions (xii). As a bodily or mental manifestation, the symptom establishes an uncanny continuity between the inside and the out-side, a dynamic particularly prominent in the case of psychological symptoms. As defined by Freud in "Inhibitions, Symptoms, and Anxiety" (1926), a psychologi-cal symptom is "a sign of, and a substitute for, an instinctual satisfaction which has remained in abeyance" (*SE* XX: 77); it is a piece of the internal world—an "idea"—that has made its way to the fore, *en route* being transformed by mul-tiple vicissitudes.[26] Its eventual manifestation is supremely important because the symptom is the content-point from which and out of which the treatment (how-ever interminable) may begin: the symptom is both an indication of illness and the first attempt at healing. Helpfully, in "A Connection between a Symbol and a Symptom" (1916), Freud cautions that the meaning of the symptom-symbol can be inferred only retrospectively and should never be understood as definite (*SE* XIV: 339-40). Yet he seems to "forget" that meaning is always derived by joint activity of the sender and the receiver of message. As a symbolic construction, and a communicative sign, the symptom stems simultaneously from the subject and from the recipient and, as such, it ramifies the subject in unsettling ways, always reflecting the actual ethical, epistemological, and political configuration of soci-ety. Michel Foucault has influentially highlighted the potential for abuse in both the perception of symptoms (by a "hearing gaze") and the practice of translating "symptoms" into "signs" (by a "speaking eye"). Both activities, Foucault suggests, are based on the tactics of coercion that inform not only the eighteenth-century "clinic of symptoms," but also the general discourse of symptoms (*Birth of the Clinic*, 115).[27]

While drawing attention to these exploitative patterns is vital, Foucault himself over-emphasizes the receiver's epistemological-political activities and consequentially denies agency to the "human sender" of the symptom-message, Martínez-Hernáez has warned us (180-85). For reasons that will presently emerge, I would like to invite the reader to be mindful of the perspective of the "human sender of the message," as much as that of the "receiver," when evaluating the modernists' engagement with the melancholic symptom. For a start, such a dual perspective enables one to appreciate that the "human sender" may engage the symptom-message through a number of modalities—from unconscious to conscious to self-reflexive—and that she/he may shape the message in a variety of ways. These depend upon the sender's personal or group "symbol disposition" and the type of participation in societal rites. (For example, to paraphrase Freud's argumentation in "Creative Writers and Day-Dreaming," a gifted modernist writer would be able to mold the symptomatic message so that it elicits individual and group phantasies in an aesthetically gratifying manner, while assuaging the shame which a disclosure of these phantasies would otherwise provoke; *SE* IX: 152-53). The meaning of the symbolic-symptomatic message is, then, estimated, albeit never concluded, in the intersection of the activities of the sender, transmitters, and the receiver.

Because of all these variables, the status of the symptom is complex. At first it might seem that a symptom naturally divides society into the "ill"/"exceptional" (with symptoms) and "normal" (unexceptional, ordinary); such understanding of the melancholic symptom was particularly prominent in the periods of fixed social structuring such as the Middle Ages or the eighteenth century, and it is against such binary systematizations that Foucault's critique is aimed (*Birth of the Clinic*, 92). Yet a closer inspection reveals that symptoms both divide and *do not* divide the societal field, a contradiction that is conveniently preserved in the everyday meaning of the word "symptomatic:" to be "symptomatic" means to be both characteristic or typical, and deviant or aberrant. To preserve this ambiguity is particularly valuable when discussing the symptom in aesthetic terms, since the symptom-turned-aesthetic-sign indeed "speaks of the times" while it simultaneously presents an aberration to "the times." As a token in societal exchange, the "aesthetic symptom," then, has a compound social function: it communicates both a "cry for help" and a social corrective. Thus, if modernist poetry and visual arts "psychotically" contradict the stabilized form of composition by asymmetry or a new symmetry, their aim is not only to forge an expression which would give voice to new historical pathologies; it is also to draw our attention to an imbalance, asymmetry, at the heart of the Enlightenment balance. If Joyce's, Stein's, or Kafka's "paranoid" texts suspend meaning and non-meaning in a discursive impasse, they verily perform inner obstructions in political epistemology. And if ellipses "melancholically" saturate the narratives of Bely and Woolf, they do indicate an elliptic history.

As modernists may well have intuited, the melancholic symptom lays particular claims to vigorous social functioning. Structured as it is around the sensation of an actual or symbolic (epistemological, ontological, political) void/loss, which cannot be adequately articulated, melancholia powerfully testifies to the unappropriability of certain objects. The melancholic replacement of the object-cathexis by a narcissistic identification perpetuates the "extraneous" presence of the love object in the ego. This impossible identification permanently questions the subject's self-sufficiency, and generates much self-aggression, but it also presents the very condition of the subject's existence. I have already drawn the reader's attention to the implications of Freud's heterogenic turn for the issue of political subjecthood and, more generally, community politics. These were summed up by Judith Butler as follows: "to accept the autonomy of the ego is to forget [the melancholic trace of the lost other]; and to accept that trace is to embark upon a process of mourning that can never be complete, for no final severance could take place without dissolving the ego" (196). In Freud's paradoxical vision, then, it is that inassimilable trace that both links the subject to the outside world (the ego is a melancholic precipitate of the traces of lost others) and prevents the subject's unruffled engagement with others—precluding, also, easy identification with community and with the sanctioned concepts of political subjecthood. The latter circumstance evidently limits melancholics' social agency, yet one is tempted to argue, together with Giorgio Agamben, that this negating property of the melancholic psyche could still be preserved for liberal consideration. Examining the philosophical, social, and artistic operation of melancholia in *Stanzas: Word and Phantasm in Western Culture*, Agamben described the condition as a response to the human spirit's "impossible task of appropriating what must in every case remain unappropriable" (xviii). In accord with this claim and my unfolding argument about the modernists' use of the melancholic symptom, I suggest here that the simultaneous denial and affirmation of the object in melancholia has a powerful, if indirect, social role—precisely of the kind favored by modernists: it is a symptomatic sign of an existing "rupture" in society as well as a critical corrective to the "wholeness" of society.

To engage artistically or theoretically with this state means to respond to social melancholia by constructive reconsideration of its critical potential. Not incidentally, Agamben's "melancholic project" to enter "into relation with unreality and with the unappropriable as such" in order to "appropriate the real and the positive" could have stood as the credo of Virginia Woolf's mission to present a history of the Obscure (Agamben, *Stanzas*, xix; Woolf, *Diary*, III:37). While traditional historiography rests on the premise that everything can be semantically pinned down, the melancholic insistence upon the vacancy that cannot be contextualized or filled in appears as a subversive "unthought" in history: it voices incompletion, inconclusiveness, lack of homogeneity or consent, and thereby it acknowledges semantic and social unappropriability as the condition *sine qua non* of an honest dealing with historical occlusions. Through an audacious conceptual transfer, modernists like Woolf came to perceive history/historiography and society as simultaneously the sites of lack (which they need to represent) and the sites of forced "wholeness" (whose "gaps" they need to expose). They used the association between the "unappropriable" and the "unrecorded" fruitfully to complicate their poetic politics: to record the "unrecorded" and yet to insist that this "unrecorded" defies semantic appropriation.

Thus, although their engagement with social melancholia did occasion some sentimental proclamations (one may detect those in Kierkegaard's journals, Baudelaire's poetry, or, indeed, Joyce's and Woolf's oeuvres), modernists rarely simply bemoaned their historical condition. Rather, they performed it. This performance, as sketched above, is marked by one illuminating paradox. While the literary articulation of melancholia may be seen as necessarily aimed at "healing" the symptom, the socially critical potential of melancholia can only be activated through a performance which, rather than curing, *sustains* the melancholic symptom while articulating it. This artistic position fuses melancholia and mourning in an aesthetically resonant suspension which I have termed "countermourning." Such artistic practice questions the viability of exacting separation between mourning and melancholia—as well as the effectiveness of an interpretation of modernism based on the strict division between the two. Appreciative of this interlock, we can now revisit Stephen's aphorism and recognize in it conclusively a typical expression of modernist "countermourning." For Stephen's (language of) melancholic incorporation—a strategy to defy the discourse of the Master by deflection—could be interpreted in terms of what Homi Bhabha called the "disincorporation of the Master": the melancholic entombment of the Law at the point of its ideal authority in order to be able to contest it (66). Such critical rereading, I suspect, may illuminate not only the Joycean fissure of discourses but also various other strategies that modernists used to foreground melancholic palpitations in their texts.

History and Form

What particular set of relationships obtains between historical melancholia and modernist artistic practice and how the modernist aesthetic of melancholia differs from those engaged by artists and writers of previous epochs? My general observation holds that modernists were markedly less interested in the allegorization of "melancholy" and creation of melancholic types than in the demonstration of the continuity between the melancholic structure of experience and the melancholic structure of an artwork. (Here, as elsewhere, the terms "melancholy" and "melancholia" are used contrastively to signal the difference between a symbolized behavioral posture and a structure of experience/medical condition.) To usher us into this new type of representation, where historical melancholia is not only discursively probed, or portrayed, but also aesthetically enacted, I shall juxtapose, briefly, a modernist "historical-melancholic" artifact with which we have already acquainted ourselves, Klee's *Angelus Novus*, with another influential representation of the angel of melancholia in art history, Albrecht Dürer's drawing *Melancholia I* (1514).[28] (See figures 1.1 and 1.2).

Fig 1.1 Albrecht Dürer, *Melancolia I* (1514). Engraving plate 24 x 18.5 cm. The Metropolitan Museum of Art, Harris Brisbane Dick Fund, 1943 (43.106.1). Image © The Metropolitan Museum of Art.

Fig 1.2 Paul Klee, *Angelus Novus* (1920). India ink, color chalks, and brown wash on paper, 31.8 x 24.2 cm. Gift of Fania and Gershom Scholem, John and Paul Herring, Jo Carole and Ronald Lauder Collection, The Israel Museum, Jerusalem (B87.0994). Photo © The Israel Museum, Jerusalem, by Elie Posner.

The juxtaposition of the two angels, one embedded in the artistic practice and worldview of the German High Renaissance and the other, awash with anxieties of the post-First World War years, is illuminating. The centerpiece of Dürer's copperplate engraving is a winged female figure shrouded in the conventional emblems of melancholia (dark face, attitude of absorption) and a range of mathematical and alchemic symbols. Although the arrangement of these objects harbors some ambiguities, these do not affect the calm, analytical style in which the painting is executed: the engraving is detailed, precise, and meticulously balanced, as typical of Dürer's drawings of both physical and metaphysical objects; "melancholy" itself is anthropomorphized in a realistically represented, female gendered, human body. By contrast, Klee's 1920 work, one of Klee's numerous paintings of angels, presents us with a grotesquely enlarged and only tentatively human face in a hazy mixture of media and genres. *Angelus Novus* is an oil-transfer drawing and watercolor on paper on cardboard, wherein disconcerting shades of red dominate. Both pictures foreground a sense of metaphysical angst and the surplus of vision traditionally associated with the melancholic's world-weariness. Yet, there is a crucial difference in the nature of the Renaissance and modernist "angst": whereas Klee's watercolor appears suffused with history, the medley of symbolic objects in Dürer's drawing weighs down any "real-life" significations of this angst and makes this representation of melancholia ahistorical. In effect, the Renaissance representation of the melancholic *type* (or emblem) hides a covertly optimistic vision of human capacities and creativity—what Klibansky, Panofsky, and Saxl called "inspired melancholy" in their influential reading of Dürer's drawing (284-305). One grants that the sorrow of Dürer's angel might have also been informed by history, in detour ways in which each work of art is shaped by its historical moment, or insofar as the melancholic separation from the flow of time that one may read in the detritus accumulated under the angel's legs could be deemed a social gesture (Agamben, *The Man without Content*, 108). Yet there is nothing in Dürer's picture that would approximate the alertness and historical anxiety with which Klee's "angel of new time" simultaneously aims at and diverts his gaze from the spectator, fleeing from human history while being inextricably bound to it: Klee's angel is not an emblem of melancholy but the subject and expression of melancholia.

This comparison reveals that modernists were much more apprehensive of the symbol's sway in melancholia than their predecessors. Klee's crooked shapes, ambivalent representation, uncertain boundaries of the image, and the fusion of media, *articulate*, rather than symbolically depict, melancholia. Now melancholia is readable not (solely) in emblems, portraits, or literary types, but primarily in the very texture of artwork, in the inflections and ambiguities of form and media. This exteriorization of historical anxiety at the level of form presents the most important feature of modernist melancholia, one that distinguishes it from all preceding aesthetic engagements with the condition. Unsurprisingly, this effort to make artistic devices into strategies of "obstruction" accords well with the twentieth-century reconceptualization of clinical melancholia as readable not in symbols but precisely in the symptomatic *obstructions* to the used system of signs. A memento to the installment of these new clinical and epistemological models, the shift in representation observable in Klee's drawing profoundly affects the viewer, and does so exactly in the manner hoped for by Benjamin: it propels "distracted" consideration rather than contemplation (*SW* IV: 267-69).

Similar "melancholic" inflections could be observed in a range of modernist artifacts, but it is the modernist novel, a form which Philip M. Weinstein has recently described as "the fiction of obscurely resonant trouble" (173), that appears to have been especially amenable to affective mapping. The high productivity of historical melancholia in the modernist novel could be attributed to the very nature of the genre: the novel's intrinsic permeability, its "openness" to historical circumstance, its special receptivity to shifts in group psychology, and its voracious appropriation of extra-novelistic discourses (in particular, contemporary discourses of psychology, sociology, and historiography). While most theorists of the novel agree that the relationship between the novelistic text and the material world is never direct, a substantial number of them have also argued that the aesthetic and socio-political workings of the novel are most intriguing precisely in those texts that purport to eschew realistic representation of their era. Paul Ricoeur, for one, emphasizes that, rather than in "the novel [that] has a direct historical or sociological role [...], the true mimesis of action is to be found in the works of art least concerned with reflecting their epoch" (III: 191). Ricoeur—who, incidentally, discusses modernist fiction in this part of *Time and Narrative*—echoes Theodor Adorno's more general argument made in relation to another modernist representation of "catastrophe in permanence," Samuel Beckett's *Endgame*: that artworks get a better grip of contemporary historic-political reality the less overtly they deal with its facts, for art is categorically different from the discursive cognition of the real ("Trying to Understand *Endgame*" 127 *et passim*). Both Ricoeur and Adorno take as a premise that, whatever its author's intentions, type of representation, and scope of dissemination might be, an artwork, and a piece of novelistic fiction in particular, is always productively situated at the intersection of the public and the private realms. As such, it is the locus of vigorous distribution of knowledge, values, desires, and concrete socio-political utterances. As the most vibrant instantiation of what Jürgen Habermas called "public sphere" (*Öffentlichkeit*), the novel seductively relegates privacy and private opinions into the public realm, thereby indirectly stimulating legislative and political changes[29]—a circumstance of which modernist writers, shaping their novelistic practice in the context of the high sales of novels at the end of the nineteenth century, were acutely aware. While seemingly unconcerned with direct social impact, modernist fiction nevertheless aspires to reframe the discourses of legality, politics, and historiography through an exteriorization of the private and the subjective. With the ambition to be both transmitter and transformer in the field of human actions, the modernist novel, then, presents itself as a particularly self-conscious instance of the discursive form we call "narrative."

A narrative, Hayden White insisted, is never neutral, but it "entails ontological and epistemic choices with distinct ideological and even specifically political implications" (ix). The most important of these choices in modernist fiction is the novel's "will to self-reflexivity." Rather than being a playful display of the author's virtuosity, as was the case of self-conscious narration in previous fiction, the modernist self-reflexivity is the expression of "an internal crisis of presentation." The latter, John Fletcher and Malcolm Bradbury maintain, brings to the fore the complicated relations between the real world and the artistic imagination and the labor of *becoming a narrative* (395-96). This effort to generate a representation while being acutely aware of the inadequacy of tools and methods of representation—what one may also call the labor of countermourning—presents both the most general and most profound structural link between modernist fiction and the symptomatology of melancholia. The melancholic's compulsive examination of verbal and representational tools has been singled out as a dominant symptom in most theoretical and clinical studies of melancholia since Freud. As the melancholic probes and discards, one after another, words, phrases, modalities, and techniques of representation (none of the links between words and things appears "good enough"), a neurotic litany comes into being—an enunciation that is searching but self-indulgent, bearing witness to a stalled psychic movement between inner and outer worlds. The modernists' obsessive probing of the means of representation has something of the infinite and tragic nature of this search: the modernist writer pursues the commensurability of "words" and "things" while being fully aware of their irredeemable split. Indicatively, Julia Kristeva's sketch of "melancholic text" as a narrative whose "prosodic economy, interaction of characters, and implicit symbolism constitute a very faithful semiological representation of the subject's battle with symbolic collapse" (*Black Sun* 24) may well describe a great number of modernist novels.

This melancholic striation renders the position of the author paradoxical, even questionable, and thus the authorial persona becomes a preferential subject for interrogation in the novels of Beckett, Bely, T. S. Eliot, Joyce, Marko Ristić, Tayeb Salih, Woolf, and many others. Kristeva hypothesizes that such melancholic literary practice may eventually prove therapeutic, not only for the writer, but also for wider communities (*Black Sun* 217). I should like to take this claim seriously. Precisely because there is an effort to forge a narrative, because the paradoxes of this effort constitute a modernist topic in its own right, and because the social performance of this "asocial" symptom is so remarkably varied in modernist fiction, it would be myopic to discredit the modernists' use of the melancholic symptom as simply, or exclusively, historical escapism. It is in order to engage with the unprecedented historical matter that the modernist novel takes up the transcription of the psychological state that indexes negativity and lack; and it is out of this "impossible" task—to create something as a representation of nothing—that

modernist literary experimentation comes into being. The last has also been recognized by Esther Sánchez-Pardo, who has suggested that melancholia, as a condition associated with the symptomatic "lack of frame," influenced directly the
modernist heterogenization of forms such as the novel, biography, and autobiography (213-14). Following this insightful lead, the next pages discuss in detail what
I have identified to be the constituents of the novel that have undergone the most
substantial transformation as a result of modernists' engagement with melancholia: the character, the chronotope, and language. These correspond to the specific
focal points of my subsequent discussions of Bely's, Kafka's and Woolf's fiction.

Shivering Fragments: Modernist Character as a Twice-Dead Librarian

The concept of the "self," philosophically and performatively squared by
Kierkegaard, was the fulcrum around which various modernist inquiries flexed.
Already in 1886, Ernst Mach spoke for many when he challenged the purposefulness and centrality of the concept and defined the self as an imaginary, unan-
chored, and transient entity—a mental-economic coalescing point for sensations
(see Mach, *The Analysis of Sensations*, 14 et passim). The insight about the subject's fundamental dislocatedness informed two related transformations in group
affectivity, both influencing the invigoration of aesthetic forms in modernism: the
feelings of homelessness and fragmentariness of existence. I have already touched
upon these social-affective dispositions in my discussion of Freud's theory of melancholia, but here I would like to specify their consequences for modernist prose.

The first of these affective postures, impeccably diagnosed by Georg Lukács
(following Kierkegaard), concerns the lack of givenness or oneness with the world.
It got epitomized, Lukács argued in his 1916 *The Theory of the Novel*, in the demise
of the literary discourse that expresses "a totality of life that is rounded from
within" (namely, the epic) and the upsurge of the form that, by its episodic structure, mourns the loss of this totality (the novel).[30] Yet when he defines the novel as
a momentous artistic expression of "transcendental homelessness," Lukács—later
a vehement opponent of modernism—seems to describe most accurately *modernist fiction*. Exteriorizing the reflexive moves that Lukács finds typical of the novel
form, a great number of modernist narratives are structured as homecoming or
home-searching journeys.[31] Unlike its generic predecessors, however, the modernist novel stages an impossible search: all routes to "wholeness" or "primordial
totality" appear barred or, else, impassable, to modernist characters, dislodged in

an emphatically self-conscious performance of "transcendental homelessness." Irrespective of the ways they represented "home"—as an Italian provincial town (Luigi Pirandello's *The Late Mattia Pascal*, 1904), a bleak village in the shadow of a castle (Kafka's *The Castle*), a house in Dublin (Joyce's *Ulysses*), a "heart of darkness" (Conrad's eponymous novel, 1900), or a dot on the map of Russia (Bely's *Petersburg*)—modernists seem to have perceived in it, with anguish and humor, a site whose radical insubstantiality precludes both the possibility of return and that of establishing a new home. Unending itinerancy, then, emerges as at once the privileged mode of experiencing and projecting the world for the protagonist and the structuring principle of the novel itself in modernist fiction; as such, it both fuels and reflects the "itinerancies" of signification in the novels themselves.

While the consequences of this affective development for the structure and thematic scope of modernist fiction were paramount—and I therefore revisit them in the following chapters—it is another posture, established in interaction with this sense of homelessness, that primarily interests me here. It concerns the modernists' engagement with the fragment as a function of dislocation. In retrospect, one can describe the modernists' compulsive use of fragment to render the experience of the (dislocated) self and the (unlocatable) world-home as governed by ambivalence. On the one hand, modernists treated the fragment as a marker of the loss of "totality," or continuity between the subject and the object/world/home. At the same time, the modernist fragment was poised to liberate the subject precisely from the shackles of "totality." This twofold treatment is visible in cognitive and aesthetic practices as different as the essay (Benjamin, Simmel), painting (Malevich, Schwitters), music (Schoenberg, Stravinsky), performance (DADA, surrealists), and poetry (Apollinaire, Eliot), but its impact on the form of the novel was particularly far-reaching, as innovative uses of the fragment in the works of Bely, Döblin, Dos Passos, Joyce, and others testify.

Given these ambivalent meanings attached to the fragment, it is unsurprising, Michael Levenson has noted, that modernist novelists' pursuit of fragmentary structures was still galvanized by the drive to (re)organize these fragments into an organic and meaningful whole (*Modernism and the Fate of Individuality* xii). For one, young Virginia Woolf gave voice to this dual effort, when, in 1908, she defined her literary discourse as aiming to "achieve a symmetry by means of infinite discords, showing all the traces of the minds [*sic*] passage through the world; & achieve in the end, some kind of whole made of shivering fragments" (*A Passionate Apprentice* 393). Many years later, this project would reemerge with force in her last novel, *Between the Acts*, a text where Woolf also provides a gendered reading of Freud's theory of drives. These coincidences are telling, for we may find that the epistemological-existential conundrums attending the discussion on fragments were crucial for Freud's definition of the drives itself. In *Beyond the Pleasure* Freud assesses the entwined activity of Eros and Thanatos in terms of "fragments" and "wholes:" whereas the erotic drive "makes wholes," the death drive, preponderant in melancholia, "dissimilates" and "separates the particles" (*SE* XVII: 7-64). In Woolf's and Freud's account, then, the ego/"self"—and thus also the representation of the self in text—is continually reshaped by the simultaneous activity of forces of fragmentation and integration. This is a historically representative assessment, for it speaks to the general modernist understanding of the mind as divided against itself. This conceptualization of the mind itself bespeaks an affective-cognitive posture on whose structural similarities to the (modernistly reframed) condition/concept of melancholia I insist; a condition where the subject experiences itself as bifurcated, split, questioned from within, while comparably insecure or "open" in its outside borders.

To signal this melancholic structure of the self on the level of figuration, modernist novelists sometimes present melancholia conventionally through typology. From the protagonists of Joyce's *Ulysses* through Rainer Maria Rilke's self-reflexive narrator in *The Notebooks of Malte Laurids Brigge* (1910) to a tragicomic, perforce self-reflexive, hero of Italo Svevo's *Zeno's Conscience* (1923), modernist fiction abounds with portrayals of "melancholics." Such characters are presented as being in contradiction with the swift move of society either through their attempt to be autonomous or through their futile search for the realms of authenticity and immediacy in a mediated world, and their social isolation and personal dejection are often depicted, in line with traditional accounts of melancholia, as being married to manic intellectual activity. But the simultaneous dominance in modernist fiction of fragmented, or weakly cohering, characters suggests that the representation of melancholia gradually moved from this typology-driven characterization to the structural refashioning of narrative bodies, and thus also from a plane of emblematics to that of composition.

An early, perhaps inaugural, example of how these new strategies affected the figuration of characters could be found in Luigi Pirandello's novel *The Late Mattia Pascal* (*Il fu Mattia Pascal*, 1904). Its "shivering fragments" constellated around the themes of home and identity, the novel follows the tortuous life-paths and (even more convoluted) mental processes of a librarian named Mattia Pascal. The tragicomic "duplication" of this character, who never succeeds in returning home *as Mattia Pascal* but who manages to "die" twice for that home, reshapes the central part of the novel into an ambiguously focalized, affect-ridden interior monologue of a split self. Causes and effects, properties and their carriers, ironic and tragic modes all blend as the novel gradually transmogrifies from a traditional narrative into a modernist pseudo-metaphysical text. The reason why I am evoking Pirandello's novel here is the nature of its eponymous protagonist—a character whose only stable attributes are self-splitting and evanescence and who, as such, not only typifies a signal modification in history and group psychology, but also exemplifies the manner in which the modernists' experience of dislocation got replicated in their figurative strategies. In this novel, like in Pirandello's plays *Six Characters in Search of an Author* (*Sei personaggi in cerca d'autore*, 1921) and *Tonight We Improvise* (*Questa sera si recita a soggeto*, 1930) or his later novel *One, No One, and One Hundred Thousand* (*Uno, Nessuno e Centomila*, 1925-26), the characters' melancholic search for (unattainable) authenticity serves to signal an epistemological and ontological void underneath, a void onto which they are, paradoxically, expected to anchor their fragmented identities. Focalized through the interiorly split protagonist and foregrounded by interior monologue, it is this expectation and its reiterated failure that leads the reader to experience the void in question as not simply a given, but a (Freudian) loss of a system of symbols and beliefs.

Surely, it is a contradictory enterprise to show as fragmented, vagrant, merged, and poly- and exo-topic what we otherwise tend to perceive as discrete, self-sufficient human bodies. The effort to represent an entity that challenges all previous understanding of psychologically "correct" and "conceivable"—as Kierkegaard was wont to express the division of the subject in modern melancholia (*Journals and Papers* II: 186)—is also taxing. Enigmatically, Woolf once described this writerly chore as a never entirely successful attempt to render the "four dimensional character" (*Diary* V: 89). Whatever narrative moves and pluralizations of vision may be necessitated by this task—and what it may have meant for Woolf herself is discussed in chapter 4—this description is evocative of the special affiliation between, on the one hand, the variety of modernist figurative strategies and contemporary non-figurative art, and, on the other hand, these two modes of representation and melancholia: modernist novelists symbolically overtax characters, or render them indexical (Bely, Mikhail Bulgakov, Pirandello), merge characters and fuse them with their surroundings (Breton, William Faulkner, Woolf), and accentuate functionality of narrative bodies at the expense of their psychological plausibility (Dos Passos, Joyce, Kafka). Thus reconfigured, the modernist protagonist becomes a "shivering fragment;" or a subject-object continuum; or a discordant multitude.

The character in fiction serves as a focal point for the representation and (re)interpretation of experience. The fragmentation, multiplication and textual dispersal of characters like Mattia Pascal, then, bring visibility to a particular trans-formation in lived, imagined, and represented experience. A fictional embodi-ment of the conviction that the increasing fragmentariness and heterogeneity of our vision of the world is both an expression and a symptom of the subject's inher-ent fragmentation, Mattia Pascal is thus a very good example of the varied ways in which "the dislocation of the self within society" is recapitulated in modernists' efforts to de-center, reconfigure, even reinvent, the novelistic character (Levenson xii). Significantly, for Pirandello, like Kafka, this dislocation and inner division concern, above all, epistemology and cognition: how much we can know about our experiential and instinctual self and whether and in what form this self may exist, outside our cognition, in relation to others.

These figurative strategies have distinct social repercussions. Commentators have traditionally viewed the figurative innovations in modernist fiction as a prod-uct of unmitigated introspection, a collapsing of the exterior space into interiority that is both unfriendly to the reader and unethical in its generalization of (the white middle-class) depressive withdrawal from society. More recently, and closer to my own argument, these experiments in characterization have been associated with a "nostalgic longing for a whole self" (Levenson xiii). Both assessments con-tain more than a grain of truth. I should nevertheless like to indicate a complemen-tary way in which the modernist figurative strategies could be evaluated. In line with Freud's heterogenic turn, to recapitulate the subject's inherent heterogeneity in a character or a group (such as, evocatively, six characters in Woolf's *The Waves*) means also to question the homogenizing organization of communities and the corollary models of sovereignty. But foregrounding the inconclusive nature of the subject's interiority in such a way does not necessarily imply lament or begrudge on the part of those who reproduce it. Instead, this picture of the self could be embraced, puckishly, as both a renewed vision of the world and a jaunty aperture to a new aesthetics. This was, at least, the way Woolf perceived the matters during one of her *flâneuries* (it is only "circumstances that compel unity; for convenience sake a man must be whole," she asseverated in "Street Haunting" [24]) and Bely affirmed in some of the more ebullient pages of *Petersburg*.

Such management of characters presents scholars with interpretative problems, though. If judged by the standards of traditional criticism, modernist characters are replete with errors of consistency, perspective, coherence, and, most disquiet-ingly perhaps, errors of credibility—those "mistakes" that concern likely proper-ties of an individual. To be interpreted successfully, I suspect, modernist characters demand a revised critical approach, one that would evaluate them using the same dynamic principles according to which they are shaped; principles that make modernist characters into multifaceted entities transiting freely across the bodily borders and textual planes, through the diverse historical, epistemological, and ontological levels of narration. To place the modernist strategies of figuration in the context of their possible template-provenance—the melancholic symptom— honors the unyielding nature of the material in hand. It helps us move beyond what could be seen as the major drawback of previous studies of the self and the character in modernist fiction: namely, their restricted focus on the character *only*, understood as being a slice of, or an analogue to, reality. The latter interpretative practice simplifies what is, I believe, essentially a detour process. The character, it is worth reminding, is a textual entity whose figuration is not directly linked to the material world; instead, the character emerges out and abides in a "config- ured" world, what Mikhail Bakhtin called the novelistic chronotope. "The image of man" in literature, Bakhtin writes, "is always intrinsically chronotopic" (*Dialogic Imagination* 85). As the organizing center for narrative events, and thus also the convergent for the meanings that shape narrative, the chronotope then determines the way in which human experience is represented and interpreted in literary text. This is so because the chronotope is "always colored by emotions and val- ues" (243). Rather than repeating the tropes about the modernist fragmented self, then, one could inquire how the modernist character, as the textual embodiment of modernist experience, functions within the modernist chronotope. Characters in modernist fiction seem especially to require this type of analysis because they are not only shaped or contextualized by the chronotope, but they also extend into the narrative time-space. Such figuration confirms the subject's intrinsic embed- dedness into the fabric of temporal and spatial relations with others.

The Modernist Chronotope and Time-Space of Melancholia: Flâneuric A-Self Wandering the Cityscape

For modernists, "the queer, shifty thing that is human nature" (Madox Ford 269) unveiled its ethical and ontological relativity only when placed in/against a particular, historically shaped, space. This function was served particularly well by the big city, a place where the old collective culture was eroding and a new "fragmented collectivity" was coming into being. In the 1920s, in particular, the continually recomposed cityscape became at once the setting, protagonist, and affective content of a wide range of novels: Bely's *Petersburg* (1916/1921), Joyce's *Ulysses* (1922), John Dos Passos's *Manhattan Transfer* (1925), Woolf's *Mrs Dalloway* (1925), Louis Aragon's *Paris Peasant* (1926), André Breton's *Nadja* (1928), Alfred

Döblin's *Berlin Alexanderplatz* (1929)... The upsurge of city-novel, like the comparable rise of city-symphony in early twentieth-century film, has been commonly
interpreted as a well-timed strategy of turning a setting into a hero. It would be
more accurate to say, however, that the modernist city becomes the hero only
in relation to the modernist observing subject, just as the modernist character
derives his/her identity only through the streets he/she is meandering. It is in this
way that, from the jostle and sensation of capital cities, a new character emerged,
a transitory accumulation of impressions whose only definable characteristic is
its unique incapacity to anchor itself; an *a-self*. Baudelaire, and Benjamin after
him, found a personification of this transient self in the figure of a city stroller, the
flâneur. A number of modernist themes converged in this character: the fleeting
nature of modern experience, the preponderance of the visual, and the lure and
danger of the city. Benjamin described this figure's everyday practice—the fine art
of *flâneurie*—as "botanizing on the asphalt" (*SW* IV: 19), and rightly so: it is the
aimless strolling, immersing oneself in the crowd yet staying aloof (so as to preserve the observing position), and inhaling and capturing the kaleidoscopic vistas
of city dwellers that distinguish this new subjectivity. Its form-space of enunciation, de Certeau would argue, is walking; its sphere of activity is the fragmentation
of totalities (98, 101).

While scholars have frequently saluted this precursor of de Certeau's walkers
as an epitome of jubilant undoing of totalities, it is noticeable that Baudelaire (like
E. A. Poe and T. A. Hoffman before him) linked this errant subjectivity not so
much to the tactical transformation of space as to the state of convalescence. In
early modernist accounts of this figure the *flâneur*'s newness of vision is contingent upon the subject's status as a convalescent (someone recovering from a grave
illness or, less dramatically, being fatigued) and upon his or her isolation/loneli-
ness. These prerogatives, I notice, also form the traditional definitional scope of
melancholia, or, at least, melancholy as a typified, or fashioned, public behavior
(see Burton). But the nature of *flâneurie* as a private-public activity makes it into
an emblem of a characteristically *modernist* kind of lonesomeness: "populated"
solitude. Indeed it is the subject's embeddedness in the chronotope of populated
solitude that Baudelaire evokes in his description of *flâneurie* in *Rockets* (*Fusées*,
1867): "Lost in this ugly world, jostled by the crowds," Baudelaire writes, "I am like
a fatigued man who sees in the depths of years behind him nothing but disillusion
and bitterness, and before him only a storm that contains nothing new, neither
insight, nor pain."[32] Striking in its fusion of Romantic mode (exaltation of the melancholic's surplus of vision) and modernist subject (a city stroller, cross-temporally
questioning historical progress), Baudelaire's fragment captures the transitory life

of the hyperconscious *a-self* as it slides from the "I" into the third person singular, and on into a reluctant "we." This transient entity appears to lament history from a particular "frozen dialectical crossroads of subjectivity and its objects"—which is how Max Pensky has described Benjamin's "melancholy dialectics" (184-85). The last association is everything but random; for the excerpt confirms the Baudelairean provenance of Benjamin's imagery in the latter's description of Klee's *Angelus Novus*. Constellated, Baudelaire's weary, nauseated *a-self*, Klee's angel, and Benjamin's dialectical image unveil a more somber affiliation between melancholia, *flâneurie*, and vision of history across the modernist century.

A twofold motivation informs my interest in the relationship between the character and the chronotope in modernist fiction. It fascinates me, first, that melancholia articulates itself as a specific imagination of time-space; a coagulation of emotions and values shaped by one's troubled relationship with a lost object. At the same time I am intrigued by Bakhtin's insight that the relationship between "a literary work's artistic unity" and "an actual reality" (or, "actual historical chronotope") is defined by, and thence readable in, the work's chronotope (243). The novel's chronotope, whenever and wherever the fictional action is seen to take place, is the locus of the text's interaction with social history.[33] The distribution of the spatial and temporal indicators of the material world within the novel happens along multiple axes, some of which bear an intense relation to the affects, discourses, projections, and phantasies ("emotions and values") dominant at the time of the novel's production, Bakhtin argues. Thus, when the chronotope undergoes such a profound transformation as it did in modernist fiction, it always happens in relation to the current affective imagining of time, space, and human history. This process is bidirectional: while building a chronotope is a procedure through which an affective image of time-space is initially shaped as a narrative, the chronotope is simultaneously the narrative point from which the reader's refiguration of the novelistic material starts. As such, the chronotope is dominantly operative in providing an answer to what Ricoeur has called the "fundamental aporia of the time of history" (III: 261). It presents both a replica of and the subject's very relation with the material world at any given moment; it is at once a metaphorical and a real historical site, and, for this reason, the element of narrative amenable to serving as the symbolic container for affects.

The chronotope in modernist fiction constitutes one such container. To relay the new experience of the material world as scattered and perspectival, the modernist chronotope melancholically fragments, polarizes, displaces, superimposes, and juxtaposes the constituents of (most often) urban space, questioning their shape, epistemological value, and ontological status.[34] It is the activities of the vagrant *a-self*—its transient views, its location and dislocation, its flight, vanishing, and reappearance—that temporarily assemble the image of this space. The novelistic space then both inspires and is inspired by the fleeting self of its protagonist. "To inspire" and "to be inspired"—this is how André Breton was wont to describe the eponymous heroine of his 1928 novel *Nadja*. Simultaneously the object, the driving motif, and the setting of Breton's novel, Nadja is a remarkable guide for my further inquiry. Like many other protagonists in surrealist prose (most notably, Marko Ristić's character Roman in his *Without a Measure [Bez mere*, 1928]), Nadja is, we are told, both "inspired and inspiring" ("*inspirée et inspirante*"). This is so because the activity she likes most is simply "being in the street" (I: 716). The represented city street is, then, as much constitutive of Nadja as it is constituted by her. The permeation of the subject, object, and setting in characters like Nadja not only recomposes the novelistic chronotope so that the street is authenticated as "the only valid field of experience," but it also gives expression to an ongoing reconfiguration of the private and public time-and-space (I: 716; see, also, Sheringham 72-75). Indeed, it is to the modernist discovery of the continuity between the private space and the public space—what I have associated with the melancholic function of porosity—that we may thank for the innovative reframing of the novelistic chronotope in modernist fiction. I would like to go a step further here and claim that the modernist chronotope is shaped by examination of the porous borders between, on the one hand, the internal and the external and, on the other hand, the past and the present, in the exact fashion in which these boundaries are challenged in the melancholic symptom.

Let me attend now to the first of these boundary crossings. In contradistinction to the organization of space and time in realist fiction, the modernist chronotope is characterized by indeterminacy and postponed consolidation of spatial and temporal indicators. Even when the spatial and temporal indices are deceptively clear—Petersburg in the autumn of 1905 or London on a June morning after the war—the reader of a modernist novel is bound to experience a vertiginous reframing of narrative space and time in the very first pages (as it indeed happens in Bely's *Petersburg* and Woolf's *Mrs. Dalloway* invoked here). This is due to the modernist novelist's proclivity to extend the inner space of characters to such a point that the "outer" landscape seems to be invaded by the subject and its purported reality and coherence threatened. Such gushing forth of interiority eventuates in an estranged spatial-temporal configuration that can be compared to the perception of time-space in melancholia—a condition where the concern with interior space takes symptomatic precedence over that with outer ("chronological") time.

Indeed the notion of ambiguous, accentuated space permeates both the clinical realities of melancholia and the discourse with which these realities have been described in psychoanalytic literature. In one of his earliest assessments of melancholia Freud assigns to the condition a mental spatiality unthinkable heretofore: he argues that melancholia institutes a "hole" in the psyche, a "hole" which behaves like a gaping wound, cathecting interior and exterior energies (*Freud to Fliess* 104). Psychoanalysts of various affiliations—as well as later theorists and cultural critics such as Butler or Baucom—have found this spatial discourse illuminating. They have continued relating the melancholic foreclosure specifically to the creation of a psychic "site" of the object's absence. Nicolas Abraham and Maria Torok, for example, have suggested that this "hole" hides a secretively established chronotope, an intrapsychic immurement where the melancholic buries not only the lost object, but everything that pertains to the object, thereby creating an "objectal correlative of the loss" comprised of the memories of words, scenes, affects, and actual or imaginary traumas cross-temporally associated with the object (*The Shell and the Kernel* 132). Like a black hole, this cryptic topography can be cognized only by its effect, that is, the melancholic's identification with this space, experienced as a "feeling of emptiness." Lacanian Marie-Claude Lambotte comments on the scopic-spatial character of this impression, describing it as an experience of both "being inhabited by emptiness" and "transmitting emptiness," in such a way that "the body becomes transparent" and "the limits of the outside and the inside" are experienced as blurred (*Le discours mélancolique* 261). Following Klein and Segal, Ronald Britton highlights that the melancholic "hole" could be felt as either a space that promises the return of the object or a space that precludes the object's reappearance (111-12). The latter, he clarifies, is the case of agitated melancholia, where the space itself is presumed to be the cause of the object's disappearance, a phantasy which "leads to obsessive manipulation of space and time" and a "compulsive space-filling mental activity" (91). But such mental activity could also be described more generally as an impulse to (re)compose and (re)structure the melancholic's surroundings, an activity that Lambotte has more recently linked to the melancholic's urge to create aesthetic objects ("L'objet du mélancolique"). The last line of thought could shed some additional light on the frequently glossed experimentation with the presentation of space in modernist fiction and non-figurative art; I shall discuss this topic in detail in chapter 2, since the melancholic "terror of space" and the ensuing space-filling activity are mounted on the level of aesthetic principle in Bely's *Petersburg*.

Meanwhile, let me note that, in most of the above descriptions, melancholia is distinguished by one activity: the transferring of the object from the external to the internal world, or "incorporation." But, observed retrospectively, from the position of symptomatology—which is the only position from which a psychoanalyst, or an artist, can scrutinize the condition—the melancholic spatial metabolism is more complex. While melancholia as a condition collapses the exterior space into an interior site of secretive identifications and foreclosed desires, symptoms in general, as detailed earlier, presuppose a move from the interior to the exterior. When one attempts to articulate the condition—an activity that is frequently perceived as necessity by melancholics themselves—the doubly folded space of melancholia is once again projected outward. Thus, inasmuch as melancholia is made visible only when it is symptomatically expressed, we can grasp its spatiality only as a double motion, from the outside into the inside and then from the inside back into the outside. Since such projection carries with itself the contradiction of non-communicability (it is in the nature of melancholia to obstruct communication), the aesthetic objects conjured up in this fashion bear the traces of symptomatic reframing of the experience of space and time suffered by the articulating/writing subject. These representational effects are visible in the structure of the modernist literary chronotope, striated as it is by the outward-inward movement that it attempts to render. In modernist texts the boundaries between the outer and the inner spaces and their sediment temporalities—and thus also the borders between the subject and the socium—are experienced as, rewardingly and dangerously, permeable. The chronotope of a novel based on the interior monologue, such as Woolf's *Mrs. Dalloway*, shuttles between the outer and the inner so as to integrate all the impressions and movements of the configured historical-social space (here, a post-First World War reconstellation of urban life) *as* it interacts with, and is transformed by, the subject's troubled interiority (here, Clarissa's, or Septimus's). More daringly, perhaps, the permeability of the inside-outside border allows for an unprecedented extension of this space into other "inner-outer spaces" (Peter's colonial India, Rezia's war-torn Italy, and on), and the presentation of this melancholic metamorphizing as neither final nor finalizable. The form of the thus created fictional world is variable, its content extendable and its boundaries impossible to fixate; for the space of melancholia is "uncertain" space (Sánchez-Pardo 213).

The modernist chronotope is vitally shaped by the interplay of two basic aspects of space—presence and absence. While any perception of reality, as well as its representation in fiction, naturally relies upon a move across these two manifestations of space, it is the condition of melancholia—premised as it is on the absence of an object that is symptomatically felt as present—that foregrounds their relationship and problems attendant to their perception. Unsurprisingly, one of the most evocative depictions of the exteriorization of inner landscape in modernism revolves around just such play. In a footnote to *Beyond the Pleasure Principle*, the book that owes much to his cogitation on personal and historical melancholia, Freud describes a game compulsively played by his grandson: the child makes his favorite toy—the reel on the string—disappear and reappear, by repeatedly throwing it over the edge of his cot and then pulling it back, accompanying this activity by alternating exclamations "*Fort*" (gone) and "*Da*" (here). Freud hypothesizes that the game, appearing in the wake of primary separation/melancholia, aids the child in mastering the unpleasant situation of the mother's absence; this insight paves the way, contrastively, for his later argument that repetition signals the hyperactivity of the death-drive in melancholia (*SE* XVIII: 14-17). But another aspect of the *Fort-Da* game interests me here: the child's melancholic concern with presence and absence incites ludic manipulation—and, eventually, mastery—of signs. In Freud's account, human speech and creativity paradoxically depend on the preclusion of direct access to the world and meanings of the object while their very purpose is to make the absent object present (following his lead, another modernist, Melanie Klein, would later affirm a direct correlation between the melancholic framing and symbol-formation, or coming into language). To the extent that I know, then, Freud's is the first theorization of an ubiquitous modernist artistic technique: the foregrounding of absence as a formative component of representation.

The inclusion of absence as a not only legitimate but also foundational—if perpetually troubling—element of the work of art effectively transforms the setting in modernist fiction into a labyrinthine, flexible, and seemingly random space. Like in Freud's footnoted case history, this representation of absence/vacancy commonly signals a latent, "repressed" presence. The underwriting of this uncertain space may be political, argued the surrealists and other lovers of melancholic allegory. Perhaps "scenes of crime," perhaps "lodgings waiting for a new tenant," the representations of the present absent, Benjamin proposed, operate as indices to the social content that has just disappeared or has not as yet come into being. They transform the complacent spectator into a bewildered interpreter of the traces of the "unremarked forgotten" (*SW* IV: 258). Guiding us into the interior space through a kind of Proustian *mémoire involontaire*, this heuristic activity, Benjamin suggests, can also recover the images of cultural and historical losses of which we have not been aware (*SW* II: 518-19). This representational strategy brings us back to Breton's Nadja—inspired and inspiring, at once compellingly present and irretrievably absent, because it is on the very pursuit of her that the narrative hinges. The desiring search for Nadja is premised on its own impossibility, as is that of the child playing the *Fort-Da* game, or that of the disquieted reader of Eugène Atget's photographs of deserted Parisian streets. And correctly so; for one of the more sinister secrets of the peek-a-boo is that the desired object (Nadja, the mother, the human subject) has already vanished, indeed, that it becomes ever more inaccessible as we try to reach it or represent it.

The modernist chronotope is furthermore continuously redrawn as it mimics and interrelates with the inner time of characters and the outer time of social processes. Time, of course, is much more than a structuring element in modernist fiction: it operates as a compulsively pursued topic, a textual analogy to history, and a model for comprehending interiority. I have suggested earlier that the modernist novel reexamines the boundaries between the past, the present, and the future precisely in the fashion these temporal categories are challenged in melancholia; that the modernist chronotope insouciantly fuses what, under conditions of normative physic reflection and linear narration, we strive to dissociate. In a 1924 letter to Nora Purtscher-Wydenbruck, Rainer Maria Rilke confided that he had just such ambition while he was writing *The Notebooks of Malte Laurids Brigge* (1910): to find a form "which would be capable of comprehending the past and the not-yet-occurring simply as presence to the ultimate degree" (Rilke V: 29; Garber 324). That Rilke, a poet, found such form in the genre of the novel is remarkable in itself. In her suggestive reading of time in modernist fiction, Ann Banfield has argued that the novel was particularly amenable to modernist explorations in cross-temporality, since it allowed the writer to play with cotemporality of personal and objective time in ways that were unavailable to non-narrative genres (48). But Rilke's reflection on this new form is also emblematic of the modernists' more general effort to articulate the temporal categories as fused or interpenetrating.[35] This undertaking was driven by a distinct need to address the "aporia of the time of history"—namely, the paradox of understanding time as a collective singular while simultaneously dissociating the past, the present, and the future (Ricoeur III: 261).

On the broadest level of the organization of the chronotope, this need expressed itself in the containment of narrative time in circularity, a structure that has ostensible filiations with the way in which temporality is experienced in melancholia. But modernists rarely pursued this strategy to its radical end. The time-structure in modernist fiction is more often based on the traditional stringing together of events, subsequently anachronized and rearranged through repetition; only in the final configuration is this structure metaphorically and formally "encircled" in terms of setting and, sometimes, time: novels end where they begin. This novelistic time-space is, however, populated by a plethora of minute narrative stratagems that question our perception of time as a collective singular that unfolds linearly: unannounced analepses and prolepses, ellipses, compressions and expansions, and non-diegetic asides which in writers such as Faulkner, Mann, and Proust entail reflections on time itself. These are presided by a garden-variety of textual counter-posing of the private, subjective time (after Bergson sometimes equalized with duration, or an interpenetrating flow of moments; oftentimes imagined as circular) and the public, objective time (sequential, "spatialized" time of discrete units; often represented as linear), and the contrasting of an embodied heterogeneous temporality and an abstract homogeneous time of system. The hope of these interventions is that the reader will experience the novelistic time—and, by extension, time as such—as at once compressed and expansive, and intermittently arrested in a synthesis of the past, the present, and the not-yet; in short, as an entity altogether different from what physics, or those whose job is to plot out the modern workday, would like us to believe.

To interpret and give social value to this treatment of time has been a major challenge for modernist studies. Scholars such as Charles Taylor, Stephen Kern, and Ronald Schleifer have argued that the modernist play with time mounts an agile critique of the Enlightenment progressivism and the idea of universal, teleological history; but they have also been confounded by the implications of this critique, most of which would appear to connote a passivist withdrawal from history (Taylor 463-68; Kern; Schleifer). The modernists' privileging of the subjective time (identified with free creation) over the objective, linear time (identified with history and imposed constriction) is a case in point. In the mature Lukács's charge, this move separated the subject's "abstract particularity" from the "outer world of objective reality," and, substituting the former for the latter, effectively divorced modernist fiction from history (*The Meaning of Contemporary Realism* 39). Banfield, among others, responded to these objections by highlighting the modernist novelists' effort to connect personal experience with history through multiplication of viewpoints and simultaneous activation of various temporal discourses—tactics, she says, that "[serve] less to shut out the external world of history as to underscore the difficulty of arriving at a single inconvertible account of it" (61). A similar claim could be made for a number of other modernist strategies of configuring the chronotope, all of which establish a productive continuity from the personal to the historical. Probably the most consequential of them is the narrative pursuit of remembrances. A remembrance describes a specific event but it also brings events in surprising personal and historical constellations. It imparts significance on the constellated incidents and, even more importantly, on the continuities between them (this is why, for Benjamin at least, "memoration"

[*Eingedenken*] has the potential to reform future). As a practice relevant to individuals as much as communities, the activity of rememoration concerns both personal and general history—and their record. Intimately linked to the effort to represent "the past and the not-yet-occurring simply as presence" (Rilke V: 29), the activities of remembering and recalling, and their successes and failures, present one of the major structuring principles of modernist fiction. "Modernism in fiction," Marianne DeKoven posited, "can be said to have memory [...] as one of its raisons d'être and central tropes" (28).

DeKoven suggestively highlights the modernist preponderance for the stuff of memory—and the ways to incite, explore, and use memories. Of course, the process of resurrecting the past, or coming to terms with it through a series of (voluntary or involuntary) rememberings, is also one of the raisons d'être and central tropes of psychoanalysis; and it is commonly associated with the dynamic of mourning. In Freudian thought *Trauerarbeit* is premised on rememoration: it is a gradual giving up of the lost object through a series of hyper-cathected rememberings of it (*SE* XIV: 244). Readable in a direct or metaphorical articulation of loss (what anthropologists call "mourning"), the success of this process depends upon an awareness of time and its markers.[36] The experience of mourning as a time-bending process that animates visual, auditory, and olfactory memories is compellingly explored in some of the most significant works of modernist fiction. Memory-work as mourning-work is a formative principle in Proust's and Beckett's oeuvres, and a vital preoccupation in Woolf's or Mann's novels; it is the textual substance of Ford Madox Ford's *The Good Soldier: A Tale of Passion* (1915), and the incentive for narration in Zora Neale Hurston's *Their Eyes Were Watching God* (1937); it envelops the thinking and acting of the two protagonists, each dressed in mourning robe, in Joyce's *Ulysses*, and it provides the haunting structure for Salih's later modernist masterpiece, *The Season of Migration to the North* (1966). The list is long. All these writings would seem to enact what Abraham and Torok define as the primary activity of mourning—"filling the emptiness of the mouth with words," that is, making loss intelligible and thereby resolvable, and reconciling the mourner with society (*The Shell and the Kernel* 128).

Yet, as the proliferation of ghosts and ghosting in these texts suggests, there are problems with this uncomplicated reading. Ford's *The Good Soldier*, a novel consisting entirely of its protagonist-narrator's remembrances, offers a good illustration of these difficulties. The narrator's rememberings are accentuated by phrases of epistemological instability—"I don't know," "I cannot well make out," and "I am not certain"—that consistently remind the reader of the compromised nature of our memories. The latter is revealed to the narrator himself as he ponders his

marriage and his own narrative account of it halfway through the novel: "But look-
ing over what I have written, I see that I have unintentionally misled you when
I said that Florence was never out of my sight [...] When I come to think of it she
was out of my sight most of the time" (88). Such flawed rememberings are characteristic of all the works of fiction mentioned above; it is precisely the *fallibility*
of memory that, as a theme-made-form, distinguishes the modernist novel from
much other fiction. Like in a psychoanalytic treatment (the procedure of which
Ford mimics in this novel), the accuracy and even cognoscibility of embodied
memories seem to be of less importance here than the dynamic of remembering
itself. This pursuit of memories in *The Good Soldier* discloses itself as decidedly
imperfect: rather than enacting a triumphant work of mourning, the narrator's
unstable rememberings verbally and contentually exemplify what Abraham and
Torok consider a failure to mourn, namely, the subject's inability successfully to
bond articulation, cognizance, and sense-giving. These obstructions of (memorial) meaning, so dear to the modernist heart, signal that a melancholic incorporation has taken place. What this symptomatic performance foregrounds is a refusal
to impart unequivocal meaning to the lacunae in personal (and, as we shall see in
the chapter on Woolf, collective) memory; a rejection to contain memory gaps,
to immobilize them, and thus consign them to the realm of the irrevocable. Such
paradoxical narrative practice can only unfold through analepses of imperfect
epistemological value, rendered through a correspondingly "faltering" language—
one that keeps repeating, "I don't know." The representation of rememoration as
an activity *in between* mourning and melancholia may be one way to describe this
type of fiction-writing. I also name it "countermourning;" a strategy of articulating
loss that relies on the symptomatology of melancholia; one that preserves the lost
object, in all its cognitive obscurity and semantic instability, as a vital part of the
fictional subject's world.

Mourning, Freud says, is a process of concrete temporality; and so is narration. The modernist novelist's decision how and when to end the string of memories in a situation in which there is no memory that is more accurate or final, is,
of course, individual. Yet, a pattern should be noted: memories cease only after
they have performed their function in enthroning the act of writing—and thus
also the experience of reading—as a superior method of relating to personal and
general history, and to time itself. When Ford's narrator acknowledges that he
"inadvertently misled" the reader, something else is also put into play: the circumstance that these "unreliable" memories are, in fact, to be thanked for the narrative itself. Modernist countermourning does seem to effect a distinct personal
and social therapy—the act of writing itself. This is why the real value of imperfect

rememberings is regularly disclosed only at the end of modernist novels, when the urge to rememorate-narrate and awareness of insufficiency of such activity are simultaneously summoned: for example, in the form of an inner compulsion felt by the protagonist interiorly undivided from its lost others (this is how Bernard contemplates the condition at the end of Woolf's *The Waves* [222]) or as an acknowledgment of "posthumous infidelity" (this is how Marcel describes it in the concluding part of *In Search of Lost Time* [VI: 309]).

Not surprisingly, such texts take lengths, and close on an open note, for their simultaneous urge is precisely to call attention to the impossibility of ever completing mourning-writing. Proust, for one, concludes the series of rememberings in his *In Search of Lost Time* with a narrative aperture, the discovery of writing itself:

> So, if I were given long enough to accomplish my work, I should not fail, even if the effect were to make them resemble monsters, to describe men as occupying so considerable a place, compared with the restricted place which is reserved for them in space, a place on the contrary prolonged past measure, for simultaneously, like giants plunged into the years, they touch the distant epochs through which they have lived, between which so many days have come to range themselves—in Time. (VI: 531-32)

Proust's closure, a luminous reassessment of the novel's chronotope, is emblematic of the changed status of time in modernist fiction: time here functions, conceptually and structurally, as a psychological-experiential container for "lost objects," to be filled in the act of narrating. It is the narration itself, fuelled by involuntary memory, that allows the loss to be identified, however provisionally and deceptively, and articulated as the work of (counter)mourning. And it is in and through writing that memories transform into distinct spaces, and time and human agency in these spaces are articulated. Yet, even more remarkable than this topical endorsement of the recuperative capacities of writing is the relation Proust establishes in these lines between the limited spatial inscription and excessively prolonged temporal extension of the human subject, a relation that ostensibly affirms the act of writing as mourning but also discloses that aesthetic fulfillment may be only an integrative phantasy. For Proust's relay of memories seems to be the kind of mourning that could extent infinitely if only there were no end to narration (and human life). Such mourning-memorial practice retrieves objects but it does not recuperate them; as Paul de Man has commented, it is precisely the flight of meaning, "truth's inability to coincide with itself," that Proust's temporal-spatial games install (78). In Proust's text—like in Woolf's fiction, as I shall discuss later—memories do not function as integrative symbolic units which give sense to the character's present activities and enable his/her safe and meaningful individuation; if anything, they implicate the character ever more in a network of undecided relations and searches.

Thus configured, the chronotope made up of memories installs a narrative cross-temporality resonant with the time-space of melancholia, and markedly opposed to the normative contemporary historiographical discourses. Not without a reason did Benjamin link Proust's involuntary memory to a social project—that of recovering hidden histories and questioning the hegemony of historical record. I have discussed the links between modernist fiction and what Benjamin claims to be history's original role as *memoration* in more detail elsewhere, so here I would like only to highlight the most important consequence that this dynamic activity has for modernist fiction: involuntary *memoration* such as we may find in Proust's epic novel resignifies the notion of remembrance from the "past-made-present" into the "past-that-implicates-the-present." This reframing makes it possible for the past actions to be not only traumatically restaged but also extended and revalued in the modernist commentary.[37] Habermas describes this insistence on radical incompleteness of the past as challenging "the power of the past over the present [...] through future-oriented memory" ("Moral Development and Ego Identity" 69). Viewed from this perspective, modernist experimentation with the countermourning chronotope emerges as a potentially revolutionary narrative practice that necessitates, above all, engagement with gaps and absences in received history. But obsessive ethic vigilance—to which, thinkers from Freud to Butler assure us, melancholics are prone—is to be blamed for a further inflection of this writing practice: a countermourning text postulates, performatively, that we can (and should) aspire to resurrect what has been obscured in cultural memory but that we can never (and should not) "write in" those gaps, subject them to unproblematic cognition and articulation. This is, I suggest, the narrative and ethical conundrum which Bely, Kafka, and Woolf faced when constructing the chronotope in their novels.

The Being/Void of Language, the Language of Void/Being

In a work of fiction, it is language, "a treasure-house of images," that is "fundamentally chronotopic," hypothesized Bakhtin (*Dialogic Imagination* 251).[38] The experience of the material world is rendered, and the fictional world is formed, in language. Thus if one wishes to understand the modernist literary chronotope—a site at which a modernist literary work's "artistic unity" and "actual historical chronotope" of the period tie up with each other—one needs to explore the specific linguistic choices and verbal tremors subtending this new, experimental language of fiction. Much could be gained from one such practice. Following Bakhtin's insightful lead, Banfield, for instance, identified in the modernist text an interaction between two verbal tenses that deal with the past—one designating the historical past (signaling an objective viewpoint) and the other denoting the now-in-the past experience of represented subjectivity—and argued that this activation of two tenses indicated the modernists' commitment to representing both the external world and the subjective experience, in a kind of clashing continuum (50-51, 60-62). I take up here a complementary inquiry in some other linguistic strategies that articulate modernist engagement with (dis)continuities between personal and historical experience, those that are intimately associated with the symptomatology of melancholia.

Melancholia, various medical and theoretical accounts agree, presents itself as a disturbance, or crisis, in the Symbolic register. The aspect of this register that bears the material traces of the affliction is language. Bringing to the fore the ambivalence of the relationship between the subject and the (lost) love-object, melancholia instates a sense that iconic verbal representation is "malfunctioning," "empty," or incommensurate to the experienced affective imprints. Yet, whereas dearth of speech and paucity of associations are indeed characteristic of severe melancholic conditions, the melancholic's sign-circumspection is more often accompanied by its exact opposite, the patient's insistent communicativeness (Parker et al. 815-23; Freud, SE XIV: 247; Kristeva, Black Sun 77). This hyperactivity with signifiers is related to the melancholic's accelerated cognitive-affective processing, ascertained in clinical studies concerning the swift turn of synonyms and the creative associations made by melancholics when presented with random word lists (Pons et al. 315-22). In such situations of verbal effusion and real or seeming creativity, Abraham and Torok comment, the "insufficient" indexical relation between the subject and the lost object is disclosed in smaller or greater disarray in the expressive forces of language, audible in the suppression of overvalued "taboo-words" (The Wolf-Man's Magic Word 20).

At the heart of modernist inquiries is a comparable crisis in the Symbolic register. Like in melancholia, mistrust in language as a symbolic formation supposedly referential to "reality" dominates the modernist posture. Michel Foucault was correct to attribute the value of an "episteme" to the set of questions raised when, with Friedrich Nietzsche and Stéphane Mallarmé, "thought was brought back, and violently so, towards language itself, towards its unique and difficult being" (Order *of Things* 300): it was the issue of verbal language and the fragility of its codes that particularly animated modernists and their co-travelers. Yet, (the belief in) human language as a system of efficaciously coordinated symbols "vastly increases our capacity to represent and to anticipate, if not always to forestall, catastrophe, including the ultimate catastrophe of death," John P. Muller rightly warned (57). Without aiming to overgeneralize, let me note that the questioning of language and its tools bears relation to the heightened activity of the death drive, as well as the impossibility to *come to terms* with the notion of death, such as we may find in manic-depressive states. With the knowledge of the discursive prominence of melancholia in the late nineteenth century, then, one can identify melancholic undertones in epochal declarations about the arbitrariness of signs such as Nietzsche's definition of truth as "a mobile army of metaphors, metonyms, anthropomorphisms [...] a sum of human relations which were poetically and rhetorically heightened, transferred, and adorned, and after long use seem solid, canonical, and binding to a nation" ("On Truth and Lying..." 250) or Mallarmé's lamenting of the fallacies of the "official" language/"language of commerce," whose mimetic relation with things is taken for granted and oppressively reinforced (360-68). That we can hear such undertones in these revolt-ridden proclamations is due to the continuities between the intellectual nausea, the "state of covert revolt" (melancholia), and what I argue to be the modernists' symptomatic reassessment of language.

Mallarmé's position is of special interest for surveyors of modernist melancholia. When he criticizes the "language of commerce" Mallarmé allows for a possibility of inventing, or disclosing, an uncorrupted, motivated language—a non-hegemonic and non-commodifying poetic discourse that, while it may be intuited in the speech of the people, is nevertheless available only *in potentio.* (Fredric Jameson has astutely noted that a modernist poetic vocation need not "posit the actual achievement of such Utopian language," but "it must affirm it as a coordinate and a frame of reference."[39]) It is here that Mallarmé presents himself as a paradigmatic modernist and a model melancholic: a disenchanted yet painstakingly committed seeker of an uncorrupted language, all the way to its radical end—muteness or chance-semiotics of "A Throw of the Dice Will Never Annul Chance," a poem composed in 1897, the tipping point year for the early modernist discourse of melancholia. Most clinical and psychoanalytic studies since the late 1890s have given a comparable picture of melancholics' engagement with language: because their ability to choose has been affected, melancholics are skeptical readers of signs, hyperattentive to the arbitrariness of language. More usefully, Kristeva distinguishes between the majority of us who acknowledge the fundamental arbitrariness of language and those who approach this issue melan-cholically. The first group, she says, has no significant problems with the unmoti-vated nature of language because they recognize that the emergence of language is contingent upon negation (*Verneinung*) of an initial loss/separation between the subject and the object; language comes into being as this "emptiness of mouth" is negated and filled with words. In contrast, melancholics deny or disavow (*Verleugnung*) this very negation: they set up a sphere of referential nothingness, but also a possibility of existence, within that nothingness, of an "unbelievable lan-guage, cut out of the painful background that is not accessible to any signifier and that intonation alone, intermittently, succeeds in inflecting".[40] If one conditionally brackets its psychopathological basis, the latter line of reasoning corresponds par-ticularly well to the symbolist project, but it also speaks to a wider variety of mod-ernist expression, where, routinely, syntactic strategies signal at once inadequacy and necessity of language.

In this context, modernist novelists were presented with a task even more com-plex than that of fellow writers. Their mission was compounded by the mimetic specifier of their chosen genre. The modernist novel had to invent its own lan-guage, which would be simultaneously adequate and inadequate, at once mimeti-cally representing the material world and undoing mimesis. My attention is drawn to one feature of this language that bears overt resemblance to the symptomatol-ogy of melancholia: the exploitation of textual markers of absence to mimic the "psychic hole" carved by the loss of the object. Both the property of language to be chronotopic and modernists' aspiration to indicate (social, personal) gaps with-out appropriating them are made visible in the modernist novelists' use of blank areas, unwarranted gaps, and surprising ellipses. Inherited from or developed in conjunction with the avant-garde experiments in typography, and associat-ing modernist texts as different as those two great novels of 1929, Döblin's *Berlin Alexanderplatz* and Faulkner's *The Sound and the Fury*, these contrivances operate as both pointers to a lapse in time-space and performance of absence or occlusion in print. This textual foregrounding of absence finds a further expression in the tendency to omit, specifically, semantic connectives. Modernist language, like that of the melancholic, has a particular penchant for parataxis, that is, the juxtaposi-tion of words/things without providing relational connectives. (Gertrude Stein's euphoric verbal series provide a good example of such disruption of accustomed sequencing.) Abraham and Torok have described such syntactic rearrangements as symptomatic of the activity of the melancholic "crypt" that hides the "forbid-den word" (1986: 16-22). At the same time, I am reminded that each such perfor-mance could also be seen as a political gesture. De Certeau, for one, insists that

the relationship between history and story is particularly intimate in the asynd-
etonic configurations of verbal space, those practices that fragment totalities by
eliminating the logically and linguistically conjunctive or the consecutive (101-2).
Susan Stanford Friedman has comparably argued that modernist novelists deploy
parataxis—"the opposite of *hypotaxis* in linguistics, the opposite of hierarchical
relationships of syntactic units"—to challenge the hierarchies in society (494-95).
Bely's and Woolf's paratactic constructions in the two novels under discussion in
this book indicate that language *could* be used to offer narrative and real-world
alternatives. More pointedly, perhaps, such linguistic performances suggest the
writers' awareness that each amendment to historical representation, or reconstitution of fissures in history, must pass through a melancholic writerly self, "the self
of the witness who remains and holds a stubborn attachment to the reference," as
Sánchez-Pardo described it (393). This self digests historical gaps and fractures by
holding onto their unexpressed references in obstinate and sometimes literal ways.

The suppression of nouns, connectives, consecutives, and other epistemologically indispensable elements of written language serves modernists not only to
indicate a caesura in the narrating character's thought processes, but also symbolically to mark a void at the spatial site and narrative climactic point where the affirmation of totality (or hierarchy) and the corroboration of the character's personal
and historical identity should occur. This double signification yields an intractable
homology: whereas ellipses stage the modern individual's feeling of existential
and linguistic "emptiness," they also critically concretize some actual gaps in the
historical record. Consequently, the socio-aesthetic value of "void-sites" in the
modernist chronotope and modernist language should be understood as ambivalently distributed between the extremes of being a melancholic sign for a lost or
inaccessible object—embodied in a forbidden word—and a marker of the critical
potential of the incomplete. Within this range, then, the gaps and ellipses in modernist text operate similarly to the melancholic "hole in the psychic sphere:" they
simultaneously signal the site of irretrievable absence and the site of potential (the
Utopia of the return of the object, or that of conquering the object-destructive
space, to use Britton's terms). This spectrum warns the critic against the danger
of ascribing a single value or meaning to this chronotopic-linguistic practice—for
instance, the meaning of a catatonic emphasis on a void beneath all human activities, or that of understanding gaps as constitutive of subjectivation and desire, or
that of deploying lacunae as a political gesture. Like in melancholia, the epistemology of these "holes" is dominated by ambivalence.

Parading with ellipses and traumatized concatenation, the modernist fictional
language finally engages in yet another property that researchers customarily

ally with the melancholic speech: it absorbs clashing semantic fields in an effort to question the inherited models of meaning-giving and history-recording. As chapter 3 will expound, the ghostlike feeling generated by Kafka's fiction is not so much the effect of its content (which has been variably described as "paranoid," "schizophrenic," and "melancholic") as that of the language deployed to render that content, a language whose accretion of seemingly logical, "exact," yet in actual fact divergent, even opposing, assertions eventuates in referential desubstantification of the represented world—so that its intimated "holes" can be seamlessly populated by "insufficient," undecidable, uncannily painful objects with overdetermined names like Odradek ("The Cares of a Family Man"). More pointedly, the case of Kafka's language reminds one that, despite the sometimes profound disruption in the capacity to string together signifiers, the melancholic foreclosure of the critical signifier does not absolutely prohibit the access to the Symbolic register in *a literary work*, that is to say, it does not prevent language; otherwise, of course, there would be no literary text. The circumstance that melancholia and mourning can never be fully distinguished in an actual literary text as it comes to us necessitates refinement of our understanding of the use of melancholic language in modernist fiction. The clinical description is again a good guide here. It is true that in severe, or psychotic, cases of melancholia, language is annihilated and intonation and melody are flattened (Hardy et al. 57-79). However, in milder forms of neurotic melancholia (those that are clinically untreated, but psychoanalytically assessed and available in wider discourses, hence those upon which a literary language could be modeled), patients are saved from total asymbolia by their compensatory concentration on the supra-segmental register of language— rhythms and sounds, their frequencies, intensities, and vocal values. A range of studies have verified that, in the phase of hypomania, melancholics tend to rhyme, alliterate, assonate, probe synonyms, and invent neologisms far more often than people unaffected by the condition (Jamison 101-47). In these situations one can detect a specific urge to explore intensities of sounds and to endow some sound fragments (syllables or syllabic groups) with emotive meanings (Kristeva, *Black Sun*, 267). This description is close to what the artistic melancholic language, or the impersonation of the melancholic speech for literary purposes, may look like.

One can relate this impulse also to the proliferation and affective enthronement in the modernist text of different environmental or marginal sounds—"Roars, Thunders, Explosions, Bursts, Crashes, Booms; Whistles, Hisses, Puffs; Whispers, Murmurs, Grumbles, Buzzes, Bubblings; Screeches, Creaks, Rustles, Hums, Crackles, Rubs;...," as Luigi Russolo surveyed them (172). It was Andrei Bely, however, who first attached this affective overvaluation of vocal values, including that of onomatopoeically elevated environmental sounds, to the representation of history. In an evocative section of *Petersburg*, Bely incorporates a disruptive sound "Oooo-oooo-ooo" into his sudden address to the reader:

> Have you ever slipped off at night into the vacant plots of city outskirts to hear the same importunate note "oo?" Oooo-oooo-ooo: such was the sound in that space. But was it a sound? It was a sound of some other world. And it attained a rare strength and clarity. "Oooo-oooo-ooo" sounded softly in the suburban fields of Moscow, Petersburg, Saratov. But no factory whistle blew; there was no wind, and the dogs remained silent.
>
> Have you ever heard this October song: of the year nineteen hundred and five?[41]

The emotive iteration of the sound "Oooo-oooo-ooo" renders the subdued intensity and intonation of the historical state in which a revolution is brewing. Thus affect-ridden, this harassing sound bestows ambivalent value on the events of recent history that Bely relates (the turmoil about to happen is the failed mutiny of 1905, a historical precursor of, and a mytheme that galvanized, the revolutionary events of 1917). In a unique exterior-interior-exterior move that I term "affective digestion," this foregrounding of sound fragments and their affective processing becomes the way to address history from a position that conjoins the external world (historical processes) and the subjective experience (sensorial apperception of a melancholically amplified sound). Its product is an embodied litany of history.

This and other instances in which the supra-segmental register of language is activated in modernist fiction suggest that, while the death drive is topically prevalent in modernism (with authors as different as Céline, Proust, Joyce, Kafka, and Woolf) and the melancholic disarraying of semantics permeates modernist fictional language, the modernist text simultaneously instantiates what Kristeva regards as the melancholic's major way to avoid succumbing to the death drive: a resexualization of sublimatory activity. The latter, Kristeva comments, happens either through sexualizing words, colors, and sounds (a range that could include Kafka's plastic-impassive depiction of erotic fantasies, Woolf's synesthesias, and Bely's over-valuation of the affective properties of sound), or a self-reflexive concentration on the sublimatory act itself (a constant in modernist fiction).[42] So I might have been imprecise, or too harsh, when defining the symbolist—and more generally modernist—attitude toward language as melancholically relating meaning to historical negativity. It is more appropriate to describe language in modernist fiction as an effort at once to perform the hyperactivity of the death drive and to battle symbolic collapse. The modernist language is a material memento to the ordeals of countermourning.

This invocation of Bely's sounding also announces the next stage of my investigation. The following chapters examine the manifestations of countermourning in three texts of international modernism, informed by different literary traditions, writerly contexts, and positions in history-as-experience. Rarely compared, Bely's *Petersburg*, Kafka's *The Castle*, and Woolf's *Between the Acts* are potent subjects for an inquiry into melancholia and history. Their common "melancholic" denominator is—resistance to interpretation.

2 Andrei Bely and the Spaces of Historical Melancholia

On Petersburg

In his 1920 book *Crisis of Culture*, Russian symbolist Andrei Bely (1880-1934) contrasts two types of writers: those who face their epoch and those who shun it.[1] The writer who turns away from rendering the "life" of his epoch will find no "salvation" and will be destined for oblivion, Bely comments. He himself avows to do the exact opposite—to present the contradictions of modern experience by means of an aesthetic practice that he calls the "spiral of symbolism." This practice, he claims, derives its effectiveness from a "tangential" association with both the subject's experience of material history and the Nietzschean realm of the supra-historical (77-81). Professed by one of the allegedly most esoteric among Russian modernists, this espousal of social engagement may strike one as a reinforced palinode. However, Bely's commitment to the representation of his epoch, or "life" (which he understood as psycho-physical inhabiting of, simultaneously, history and a spiritual realm), should be neither doubted nor underestimated. As early as 1902, the writer theorized the transcription of cultural and historical specificities of the material world into the "*noumena*-intimating" language of art in terms of reflective reshaping in an essay entitled "Forms of Art" ("Formy iskusstva"). "Art depends upon reality," notes Bely in this text, and therefore "the goal of art, or its point of departure, is often the reproduction of reality." Adumbrating many later assessments of artistic metabolism, Bely argues that this translation of reality into art is accomplished by a kind of "synthetic" reshaping that "leads to an analysis of surrounding reality" (343).

This effort to articulate the interdependence of life and art and the writing subject's metabolic processing of reality is embodied well in a curious artifact housed in Andrei Bely's apartment, now museum, in Moscow: a three-wall-wide sheet of cardboard on which Bely attempted to present his own intellectual, historical, and affective life-trajectory in pictorial form.[2] As if to testify to its author's unbound affectivity and intellectual eclecticism, the roadmap called "The Line of Life" resembles a dynamic whirlpool rather than a comprehensible bio-graph. Whatever Bely aimed to achieve with this self-reflexive artifact, it failed gloriously: the multicolored graph neither maps coherently the turbulent life and work of the novelist, poet, essayist, critic, and memoirist Boris Nikolaevich Bugaev (Andrei Bely), nor provides a legible picture of Bely's evaluation of his own accomplishments. The crisscrossed lines indicating Bely's intellectual attachments to doctrines such as Nietzscheanism, neokantianism, phenomenology, theosophy, anthroposophy, and Marxism, defy patterning, and the color scheme tells very little about Bely's shifting emotive positions vis-à-vis the material reality of late monarchical Russia and the early Soviet Union. And, while much in this artifact suggests the modernist impulse aesthetically to reintegrate the subject and the object/world/absolute, the unfinished nature and indecipherability of the chart foregrounds, if anything, the hopelessness of such endeavor.

If understood as a work of art in its own right, however, the chart might be more illuminating. It might tell us something about Bely's attempts to find a "form" adequate to the impossible task glossed above; about the remarkable fusion of sounds and colors that Bely achieved on the page; about the challenge he posed, repeatedly, to the inherited models of space (both those concerning the material space occupied by an artwork and those relating to the spatial figuration of the diegetic world); his attempts to make text intervene "haptically" in the reality of the reading act; his aptitude for the intertextual play of density and superficiality; his belief that the text results from an interplay between espousal of an idea and ironic distancing from it; and, perhaps most vividly, about his figuration of text-of-art/text-of-history as an abysmal whirlpool, anchored in material reality and tangential to the ideational world, and, due to its own momentum, always threatening to disappear in a void. It is these and other attributes of Bely's prose that earned him the label of "the most remarkable" writer of the modernist epoch.[3]

Characteristically, though, the protracted period associated with the production of Bely's most significant text, the novel *Petersburg* (1911-1922), is almost unmarked in the writer's bio-graph: it is squeezed in the bottom corner of the central graph, amidst the layers of yellow and grey (Bely once described *Petersburg* as "the tragicomedy (black-yellow) of obfuscation (grey)"; *Masterstvo Gogolia* 308). One may suggest circumstantial reasons for this provocative indistinctness: for example, that Bely—prone, like Kafka and Woolf, to conceive of his work as unfinalizable—kept revising the novel throughout his life, and that the published versions, including a film script and a drama play, all substantially differ from one another.[4] This very haziness, however, is also an appropriate visualization for the text whose affective position is singularly difficult to pin down. While superimposing harrowing apocalyptic imagery upon the picture of contemporary history, Bely's *Petersburg* nevertheless appears to promulgate a sense of aesthetic and social renewal that might emerge out of this Apocalypse—a stance not unfamiliar to researchers in the history of affects in early twentieth-century Russia (cf. Cioran, *The Apocalyptic Symbolism of Andrei Belyj*). The text's constant variation of modes (the novel is in turns comic, lyric, didactic, and tragic), generic transfers (novel-essay-poem-play), and inconsistent tone (pathetic, vivacious, meditative) serve to picture a world that is both "doomed" and "resurrected" in urban modernity. Like Woolf's *Between the Acts*, Bely's *Petersburg* delicately oscillates between despair and moderate optimism, an affective positioning that I have found characteristic of modernist "countermourning."

The following pages will address this affective oscillation and the undecided space in the bottom corner of Bely's bio-graph: how the strategy of "melancholic" representation symptomatically reshaped the material world into what is now recognized as a highly innovative, exciting piece of prose. We shall have two major stops on this journey. The first of these is a consideration of Bely's activation of traditional representational strategies to relay the copiously glossed "social melancholy" of early twentieth-century Russia; this public mood becomes readable in the text in an assortment of melancholic statements and dynamics with which Bely furnishes his characters. The second part of the present chapter is dedicated to Bely's counter-move: his utilization, or imitation, of the melancholic symptom to reshape the novelistic language and chronotope. This part will challenge the passivist implications that could be drawn from reading Bely's novel solely on the grounds of the symptomatic representation of characters. Bely, I argue, demands a lot from his reader—above all, a capacity to distinguish between social *melancholy*, deceptively thematized at the level of the figuration of characters and their actions, and artistic *melancholia*, a deliberate use of the melancholic symptom paradoxically to challenge the attitude and discourse of "melancholy." This complex representational strategy is motivated by Bely's wish to move away from an "analysis of reality" through the psychology of characters, typical of the nineteenth-century Russian novel (while intertextually glossing it), and instead to inaugurate a practice of reproducing the material world through a "synthetic reshaping" of language and the time-space of the novel ("Formy iskusstva" 343). Because this reinvigoration of the genre of the novel is inextricably linked to Bely's effort to both represent and battle social melancholy, the aesthetic and intellectual vicissitudes of the writer's melancholic performance will be our point of entry.

Melancholia and Symbol

Bely's novel has been repeatedly hailed as a major symbolist novel, and the writer's theory of the symbol and its literary manifestation in *Petersburg* have been successfully addressed by many scholars. It is not my ambition here to expound on these suggestive readings, or to engage in the ever-stimulating activity of deciphering Bely's symbols, but to take up the complementary question of the affective basis of the symbolist project as it may have informed Bely's textual performance. Such critical engagement is promising, since it was symbolism that instated the grounding principles of modernist melancholic performance, a performance animated by a sense of the simultaneous inadequacy and necessity of language. In chapter 1 I have identified the melancholic imprint in the symbolists' explicit and immanent poetics, and provided an overview of psychoanalytic grounding for this hypothesis. This is a good place to reiterate and elaborate on these claims.

The symbolist project paradoxically couples the mistrust of language with an ardent wish to recuperate language through poetry, a psychic constellation that is not unlike the melancholic patient's attitude toward language. To melancholics, Kristeva has pointed out, "a signifying sequence [appears] as heavily, violently arbitrary" (*Black Sun* 51). As remarked earlier, what is symptomatic here is not the realization of the arbitrary nature of language as such, but the melancholic's perception of this arbitrariness as an alarming imposition that he or she is compelled to address in order to revitalize the links between signifiers and the signified, links that are "felt" as existent but occluded. What Genette termed the "semi-Cratylist" drive in symbolism transformed into a symptomatic aesthetic when, with Mallarmé, language became experienced as split into an ossified "ordinary" language, whose mimetic relation with things is taken for granted but is in fact arbitrary, and a (possibility of) unmediated, uncorrupted, poetic language. In melancholia the unbelieving belief in language comparably engenders an agitated exploration of alternative verbal means to convey meaning. This zealous melancholic investigation manifests itself in the manic phase as the "pressure of speech" overriding the dominant stupor—that is, an impulse to speak much and fast, tirelessly probing synonyms, homonyms, and sound-values that might express what cannot be expressed in the "language of commerce." Out of this attempt to name the unnamable, there comes into being an (interminable) project to reinvent language, a project commensurate to the symbolist enterprise. In turn, the symbolist project itself may be described as an effect of a melancholic struggle; an effort to come to terms with the loss of belief in language on the part of those who have no other tool for their work but language itself.

The Russian Symbolists shared the melancholic linguistic concerns of their French peers, but, as Cassedy notes, the distinction between quotidian and poetic language also had its indigenous source in Russian thought. The late nineteenth-century philologist Aleksandr Afanas´evich Potebnia similarly split language into conventional/ossified and rejuvenating discourse. Everyday language, Potebnia contended, has become alienated from its "inner form" that keeps alive the archaic motivated link between the signifier and the signified; by contrast, artistic language derives its capacity to reinvent itself precisely from the vivacity of its inner form (123 et passim; also quoted and discussed insightfully in Cassedy 292). Bely was to repeat this distinction almost verbatim in his 1909 essay "Magic of Words," recasting Potebnia's "inner form" as a theurgic continuity between "living," creative words—"symbols"—and their referents (93-110; see, also, Bely's contemporaneously published account of Potebnia's thought, "Mysl´ i iazyk"). This championing of the poetic word is not unrelated to the distinctive cultural and affective climate of the fin-de-siècle Russia in which the activities of Russian symbolists such as Valeriy Briusov, Viacheslav Ivanov, Zinaida Gippius, Aleksandr Blok, and Bely himself took place. This context included the renaissance of apophatic theology, the rise of anthroposophy, sophiology, onomatodoxy ("imiaslavie") and various beliefs concerning the embodiment of essences.[5] Whereas all these doctrines had a marked resonance for Bely, it was onomatodoxy, the (re)claiming of the special status of the Word, that had immediate consequences for his and his fellows' art. Due to a deep-seated belief that there exists a "magic of words"—an aptitude of poetic language to conjure up life forms— the Russian symbolists focused rather on the materiality of discourse than on the combinatory logic of symbolic correspondences favored by their French peers. What distinguishes Bely's theoretical and artistic explorations from other accounts and manifestations of symbolism is precisely his intense focus on morphological, phonological, and syntactic behavior of linguistic units. Bely's symbolic semantics, Yuri Lotman was first to notice, can spread from a single word to the work as a whole, and shrink to elemental fragments such as morphemes and phonemes. The writer's interest, Lotman argues, lies "not only in new words or even just new meanings for old words" but in "a *new language*;" for Bely "the word ceases [...] to be the sole bearer of linguistic meaning" ("Poeticheskoe kosnoiazychie Andreia Belogo" 439; cf. Erlich 33-50). It is for this reason that Bely's own symbols take on unorthodox form: most frequently that of a sound or a combination of sounds (*"slovesnaia instrumentovka*," or sound symbolism), or of a crystallized moment of dramatic action, or even a style or mode of expression.

Equally distinctive is Bely's belief that the symbol is not a correspondence unraveled by the author in the forest of symbols, but "an image from reality," a constellation of sensations and meanings that imposes itself upon the author while he or she is engaged in creative work. As such, the symbol serves "as a model of an experienced content of consciousness," Bely writes ("Ob itogakh razvitiia novogo russkogo iskusstva" 258; cf. Keys 177). In this "model"—both a result and substance of psychic gurgitation of reality—mystic meaning, auto-perception, material world, and cognitive play coalesce. Together, they point to the Symbol beyond particular symbols. Bely repeatedly claimed that he "could not help believing" in "the existence of some reality whose symbol, or representation, is the metaphorical image [he] created" ("The Magic of Words" 110). The status and the syncretic nature of this "reality" (transcendent and immanent, universal and particular, cerebral and intuitive, embodied and beyond embodiment) has been addressed, with enthusiasm, dismay, or perplexity, by almost all Bely scholars. What primarily interests me here, however, is not the absolute Bely believed in; nor is it the conceptual or textual provenance of Bely's belief in transports between the spiritual and material worlds; nor is it even the melancholic paradox of Bely's thought—the fact that his thought "requires both immanence and transcendence and requires them to be incompatible" (Langen 22). Rather, I am intrigued by that implied process of experiential-psychological metabolism that establishes continuity between matter and psyche, or, more precisely, between the particulars of the material world, a work of art, and the absolute; in brief, I am interested in symbol-formation.

Similarly to psychoanalytic thinkers, Bely perceives symbol-formation as an innate, *inwardly imposed* activity, fundamental for the establishment and fortification of the links between the inner world of the subject ("the speechless, invisible world swarming in the subconscious depths of my individual consciousness," as he puts it) and the external world ("the speechless, senseless world swarming outside my individual ego") ("The Magic of Words" 93-94). Yet, however hopeful of its potential, Bely does not view this process and its resultants as simple, but knotted and contorted; and, for that very reason, perhaps, cognate with melancholia.

Unsurprisingly, then, Bely describes symbolization in terms of psychological metabolism. When an inward urge makes itself unbearably present (Bely uses the child's experience of fear), an object that might embody this experience is found in the external world, he writes; then, a "form of expression" is devised, and this form "reshapes" the object into a symbol. The symbol, a result of interaction between the internal and external worlds, now belongs to what Bely terms a "third world," *the reality (Pochemu ia stal simvolistom i pochemu ia ne perestal im byt´ vo vsekh fazakh moego ideinogo i khudozhestvennogo razvitiia 7-8)*. The theological-theurgic overtones of Bely's theory aside, the proximity of this model to the psychoanalytic view of the child's acquisition of language occasioned by primary melancholia should not be overlooked.[6] Analogously to Freud's account of the *Fort-Da* game, which has served as a template for all subsequent psychoanalytic discussion of symbol-formation, Bely posits at the center of his theory a young observing subject who tries to find a way to externalize a painful interior experience (separation from the mother, fear). In this effort, the subject spots an external object (say, a reel), but the object itself neither alleviates the interior experience nor satisfies the need for the contextualization of that experience in the material world. Only when a "form of expression" has been devised (e.g., a game of pulling the reel back and forth) and the sound symbols are found ("Fort" and "Da") is the painful experience negotiated and the meaning of both the internal and external worlds produced (Bely, *Na rubezhe dvukh stoletii*, 115; cf. Freud, *SE* XVIII: 14-17). This reshaped object, then, serves as what the object relation analyst Wilfred Bion would later call a "symbolic container"—a psychological stand-in that symbolically "transforms," and gives meaning to, the sometimes terrifying events and objects in the material world; that is, a symbolic-experiential bound between the psyche and external matter (31-32). That this language-activity is formative of the subject seems to be no greater mystery to Bely than to Freud, or Bion, Klein, Lacan, Segal, and many other psychoanalysts: "In the word and only in the word do I recreate for myself what surrounds me from within and from without, for I *am* the word and only the word," Bely asseverates ("The Magic of Words" 94; emphasis in original).

It is not difficult to recognize in Bely's symbolization—as in that other *selbstgeschaffene* game, Freud's *Fort-Da*—the quintessentially modernist "melancholic" concerns addressed in the previous chapter: the rift between the subject and the world, the withdrawal of absolutes, negotiation of absence, and the intimation of an (always tentative) sound-form that might bridge the felt gulfs. In particular, symbolization, as understood by Bely, testifies to both separateness and inseparability of the subject and the world, much like the activity of "countermourning" that I have proposed as a conceptual description of modernists' artistic dealing with history. The notoriously problematic finale of Bely's "Magic of Words" gives a radical form to these concerns: "'I' and 'the world' arise only in the process of their union in sound [...] If words did not exist, then neither would the world itself" (94). One can interpret this assertion of the preeminence of "union in sound" over any other meaning-giving systems in twofold fashion. We could ask whether, if Bely's "third world" is the only "real" world, both the subject (as an active agent in history) and the object (the world with historical processes) are doomed to vanish in this inclusion under an overtly ontologized entity. Or we can heed what is apparently Bely's main concern here: the glorification of creative writing as an activity of manipulating what contemporary psycholinguistics calls "phonetic symbolism"—that is, the capacity of language sounds to evoke affective associations in social communicants. It is this creative manipulation that establishes the clashing continuum between the external world and the subjective experience I referred to previously, while attempting to relay whatever spiritual content might preside over these realms. As a true "countermourner," Bely acknowledges the melancholic nature of language, history, and existence, but boldly seeks a "form of expression" to "mourn" these epistemological and emotional drifts. He posits the exploration of sound as both meaningful and meaning-giving (indeed, world-shaping) activity that enables us not only to represent the thorny continuities between the inner experience and material history, but also to produce them: to participate in a relay of meanings that both subtend those continuums and are created by them. It is through and because of such activity, Bely suggests, that the creative writer is an ethical agent in history.[7] Bely's own performative exploration of sound, we shall see later, takes the form of mimicry of the melancholic symptom. My present concern, however, is the more general question of how this poetics impacts Bely's views on representing the material world in *Petersburg*.

Representing the *Stikhiinost'* of History and Other Cerebral Games

Famously, Andrei Bely once commented that the Revolution of 1905 and everyday life of the period entered the fabula of his novel *Petersburg* accidentally (*Peterburg* 516). Yet the history and "tenor" of the era have become such an integral part of the text that Bely's novel is unimaginable, thematically and structurally, without them. Rather than providing a background, historical events shape the novel as we know it today—as a tale about the city of Petersburg at a particularly charged moment in its history, the autumn of the 1905 revolution. The first ten days of the General Strike, a period covered by the novel, is a stage in which historical anxiety peaked, coming in the wake of mass protests and riots in winter, spring, and summer 1905; the General Strike itself was to trigger the presentation and signing of the Manifesto pledging a constitution and extended franchise to the parliament in October 1905.[8] This historical setting is both replicated and extended in the plot of the novel that revolves around a conspiracy to assassinate the reactionary senator Apollon Apollonovich Ableukhov, the deed that the senator's own son, an impressionable student named Nikolai, is entrusted to perform. Dudkin, a member of the illicit society organizing the assassination, equips Nikolai with the weapon (a can of sardines containing a time-bomb) very early in the narrative but the assassin-to-be finds out whom he has to execute only at the mid-point in the book, when the political thriller intertwines with the masquerade/love affair subplot. The narrative climax sees Ableukhov's estranged wife suddenly returning home, and the bomb exploding, but without physically injuring anyone; in a parallel plot, however, Dudkin goes insane and kills Lippanchenko, the alleged mastermind of the assassination. The brief Epilogue tells the post-festum: Nikolai returns to Russia after years of globe-trotting and spends days roaming the fields in an attempt to recover his Slavic roots. This closure effectively blends the anti-climatic endings of personal and historical rebellions against the "father:" in the wake of October 1905 Russia is given a constitution and Nikolai is granted a passport; both documents appease their receivers yet produce few actual changes. Built on those analogies, and galvanized by questions of national identity, decline of the West, and potential for historical transformation, the novel presents itself as a snapshot of the moment in which the Benjaminean "continuum of history" failed to "explode." What does "explode," however, is the narrative form itself: studiedly fragmented and insouciantly heterogeneous, Bely's text challenges all inherited models of novelistic figuration. If the aborted patricides in the novel promise any social change, then, this transformation is cognizable only in the protean nature of the text itself.

As repeatedly noted in Bely scholarship, the Petersburg of 1905, the chronotope and the protagonist of Bely's novel, is at once intelligible and indecipherable in historical terms. Bely portrays the imperial capital with deceptive exactitude: his pedantic regurgitation of the Petersburg architecture and the social events and intellectual fads of the autumn of 1905 hides more than it discloses, and consulting the Baedeker or reading the daily press of the period (both of which have been attempted by Bely scholars) proves to be of limited usefulness. I suggest that, rather than providing an accurate picture of the 1905 Petersburg, Bely furnishes

the reader with the *affective map* of a capital caught between its past imperial gran-
deur, its present economic decline, and an accelerated flight into its future. This
ambition to represent not so much the material reality as the affects correlative
to that reality is evident in the prevalent textual strategy of merging the pictures
of the external world with the images drawn from the characters' internal world.
These merged images are then symptomatically transformed: shapes elongate,
shades intensify, spaces contract and expand, in mimicry of the affect the writer
has set out to record. To complicate matters further, both the affective condition of
the epoch and this very process of artistic transmutation are meta-textually examined in the novel. It is Bely's ambitious organization of the novel as both an affective processing of reality and contemplation on that very procedure that makes
this multifaceted historical commentary so difficult to interpret.

There are various ways to enter the realm of this complex performance. I opt
for consulting Bely's early reflections on the novel in his letter to Ivanov-Razumnik
of December 12/25, 1913. Bely scholars have often debated the second part of this
statement, yet the writer's self-assessment has been rarely quoted in its entirety. It
is beneficial to do so here.

> My *Petersburg* is, in fact, a captured image of the unconscious life of people
> consciously [*soznatel'no*] distanced from their own elementalness [*stikhi-
> inost'*: natural, spontaneous force, impulse, chaos]; the mind of the one who
> consciously denies the experience of this elementalness [*stikhiinost'*] will
> be destroyed by this very force when, for some reason or other, it becomes
> unbound [*vystupivshem iz beregov soznatel'nosti*]; the real action-place of
> the novel [is] the soul of some character not given in the novel, a char-
> acter over-exhausted by the workings of his brain; and the acting charac-
> ters are pre-conscious forms of thought, so to speak. And the everyday, the
> "Petersburg," the provocation with the unfolding of the revolution some-
> where in the background—all this is merely a conditional "clothing" of
> those forms of thought. It might be possible to call this novel "The Cerebral
> Play" ["*mozgovaia igra*"]. (Appendices, *Peterburg* 516; my translation)

A due amount of critical attention has been paid to Bely's interpretation of the 1913
text as a mind-game of an "ahistorical" integrative subjectivity, but scholars often
find that Bely's self-assessment creates more interpretative problems than it solves.
(To name but one: later in the same letter, Bely assures his correspondent that he
will make corrections to the manuscript concerning, precisely, the treatment of
material reality and affective picture of the epoch; 517.) Nevertheless, when read
in its entirety and in the context of the letter, Bely's comments are valuable, for

they speak to the issues I have been examining in this chapter. Bely correlates the affective (Dionysian) *stikhiinost'*, a force at once psychic and historical, and the cerebral (Apollonian) activity of analyzing the effects of embracing or refuting that *stikhiinost'*. The relation between the two should be understood in light of Bely's discussion of the affective-metabolic process of symbolization. That the action-place of the novel is purported to be the *soul* of a character that does not appear in the text is telling: for it is in one's "soul" that this creative digestion is traditionally seen to take place.

But *stikhiinost'*, like that other word obsessively reiterated in Bely's account, *soznatel'nost'*, is not an innocuous word. A long-term property of Russian socialist discourse, the terms *stikhiinost'* and *soznatel'nost'* regained historical urge with V. I. Lenin's 1902 pamphlet "What Is To Be Done?", where Lenin argued that *stikhiinost'*, while useful as a spontaneous affective response of masses to injustice, was not enough: the revolution could be achieved only if the non-workers (intellectuals, the party) lead workers from spontaneity (*stikhiinost'*) to "consciousness" (*soznatel'nost'*) (73-75). In late 1905 Lenin would amend this view, intoxicated by what he then saw as the spontaneous (*stikhiinyi*) display of revolutionary spirit. In 1912-1913, the time of Bely's letter, Lenin, but also a whole host of Mensheviks and Bolsheviks, would change their views on *stikhiinost'* and *soznatel'nost'* yet again, and would reaccess the 1905 revolution through this paradigm (see Haimson 57-59, and 63-71). Bely's statement enters this debate on political pathways headlong: as a novel about the events of 1905, *Petersburg* purports to show how the elemental cannot be cancelled out by, or forcibly subsumed under, the "conscious." In this ambition, Bely writes in the letter to Ivanov-Razumnik, the novel presents the second part of a trilogy, in which the first part (*Silver Dove*) treats the purely destructive working of *stikhiinost'* and the third part concerns the productive fusion of *stikhiinost'* and *soznatel'nost'* (516). While it would be difficult to determine Bely's actual stance on the matter—not the least because the third part of the trilogy never materialized—one thing is certain: the terms are not chosen accidentally. The real provocation here is not "the unfolding of the revolution somewhere in the background" of the novel but Bely's very statement that the revolution is accidental to the novel.

A similar narrative loophole, or provocation, comes into focus if we apply Bely's comment about an all-encompassing creative subjectivity to the novel itself. As the proliferation of scholarship on the "*mozgovaia igra*" testifies, this entity is both ubiquitous and unlocatable in the text.[9] Like Cervantes's *Don Quijote*, Bely's *Petersburg* keeps generating narrators and figures of symbolic authority. Unlike its comic predecessor, however, Bely treats the instability of the authorial voice as the melancholic function of an unstable and undecided world, the world in which the symbolic power is "in transition," as Ableukhov's favorite phrase has it. Rather than identifying the brain that engenders the text, Bely's comment draws our attention to "authorial undecidedness" and the melancholic questioning of the symbolic functions and authorized social codes in the diegetic world itself. While thus toying with *"mozgovaia igra"* and unlocatable authors, Bely has finally planted an important interpretative clue for us: that one should approach the novel's melancholic performance simultaneously from two, or perhaps even three, distinct perspectives—as an image of psychic processing of contemporary history (thematization of social symptoms like the attenuation of symbolic investiture), as a performative (the actual performance of authorial instability through changes of voice, mode, etc.), and as contemplation on these activities (the distribution of meta-textual comments concerning *"mozgovaia igra"*). Jacob Emery has recently proposed that Bely's novel self-consciously oscillates between metaphors and a reflection on the nature of the metaphor (*76ff*). In a similar way, I argue, the novel engages its grounding metaphor, the "melancholy of history."[10] The text presents the "melancholy of history," contemplates it, sometimes parodies it, and then parses it into the symptomatic performance of melancholia. Such exteriorizations are, of course, a property of many works of fiction. But what is intriguing in the case of Bely's novel is that these two poles, one that presents and reflects on the "melancholy of history" and one that performs melancholia on the level of form establish not only a relation of continuity, but also that of inadequation, even opposition. What I am suggesting is the following: in Bely's novel the melancholic expression combats the represented melancholy of history.

A year and half before his correspondence with Ivanov-Razumnik, in a letter dated June 10/23, 1912, Bely had confided to Alexander Blok: "I have exhausted myself with the novel and I have promised to myself to refrain from any further depictions of the *negating aspects of life*" (*"otritsatel'nykh storon zhizni,"* Bely's emphasis; Bely-Blok 470). This confession deserves our attention for at least two reasons: first, it centers on affects—those experienced, those represented, and the interaction between the two; second, it implies that writing is meaningful insofar as it exercises its capacity to portray and thus challenge the negating aspects of life, albeit at the expense of the writer's affective well-being. But, what are these negating aspects of life? Why should Bely feel the pressure to depict them in the first place? And how can a literary text confront them? These are the questions that I engage in the following sections.

Melancholic Constellations (Fathers, Sons, and Mothers, Too)

In one of his vodka-generated confessions, Alexander Ivanovich Dudkin, a character in Bely's *Petersburg*, relates the symptoms of his mental disturbance to the protagonist, Nikolai Apollonovich Ableukhov. Dudkin enumerates "anguish ("*toska*"),[11] hallucinations, vodka, smoking, a frequent dull ache in the head and a queer feeling in the spinal cord." Such sensations, he says, usually come "in the morning" (*Petersburg* 59). Coupled with what we find out about Dudkin's condition a few pages earlier and later—that he recently experienced a loss, perhaps of an "old woman [...] chewing her lips" who passed away in September (13); that he suffers from insomnia (12) and cannibalistic phantasies (263 *et passim*); that he might have tried to kill himself (17); that "conversations with himself or with others always produced a feeling of guilt in him" and "a loathing" that "he would transfer to himself," but that he would also experience sudden bouts of verbosity where "he would go on talking to the point where he felt actual attacks of persecution mania" and the meaningless alliterative word "enfranshish" would appear to him (58)—this account presents an impressively accurate description of an illness Bely may or may not have experienced himself, but of whose symptomatology he is likely to have been cognizant: aggravated melancholia. Yet, even more remarkable is the continuation of the character's litany. Suddenly challenging his interlocutor, Dudkin exclaims: "You think I'm the only one? You're sick too, Nikolai Apollonovich. Almost everyone is sick [...] every Party worker suffers from the same sickness" (59). He proceeds to describe this common sickness as "a general thirsting after death" (60), and to associate it, specifically, with a sensation of void in place of authority (59).

That Dudkin extends his own condition to society as a whole and that neither he nor his listener finds this ascription problematic should not surprise us. Mark Steinberg has noted that such practice was rather common in Russia of the 1910s: the "affect talk" in early twentieth-century Russia "overwhelmingly concerned not the inward emotional self as a separate sphere but the intercourse between self and society," or the "public mood" (816). But Dudkin's diagnosing of his and his society's condition by the term "*toska*"—the recurrent word in the Russian Romanticists' discourse—merits further attention. In Russian the term "*toska*" encompasses a spectrum of interrelated affects such as inexplicable sadness, anguish, and restlessness, as well as their discursive presence, interpretation, and use in self-fashioning. Among the early twentieth-century Russians, the term "*toska*" was most frequently understood as a full or partial synonym for "*melankholiia*" and invoked to describe the purportedly fatal emotional climate of the age (Steinberg 820-21). The evocation of "*toska*, limitless *toska*" (as one student glossed it in his suicide note repeatedly cited in the contemporary press) was an integral part of a larger discourse on social melancholy and clinical melancholia that developed between the two revolutions, a discourse that also encompassed affective postures such as feeling of disillusionment, sensations of crisis and the tragic, and belief in the approach of the Apocalypse.[12] This discursive scope shapes Bely's *Petersburg*, suggesting that, in terms of the history of affects, the novel documents the post-1905 climate—the time of Bely's writing—rather than the presumably more optimistic and belligerent mood of the year 1905 itself.

In the years between the two revolutions this social mood was habitually interpreted within the heteroglot framework of melancholia, a framework that subsumed both the affective mixtures of despondency and ecstasy that manic depression commands, and the distinct kind of self-fashioning that generates and fuels social constructs like "melancholy of history." Discursively pervasive, "social melancholy" was addressed, with equal urgency, in intellectual "thick journals" such as *Sovremennik* and *Apollo*, church periodicals like *Tserkovnyi vestnik*, penny tabloids like *Gazeta-kopeika*, film and theater productions, medical reports, urban legends, and jokes (Steinberg 818 *et passim*). It filled conversations in middle-class salons, jam-packed with oriental style divans and Japanese chrysanthemums, like that maintained by Sofia Likhutina in Bely's *Petersburg* (38-41); it galvanized discussions in small gritty abodes on Vasilievsky Island, the workers' and students' quarter of Petersburg (59-60); and it provided a topic for deliberation in porters' lodges in the "many-chimneyed, smoke-columned" suburban townships like Kolpino (66-69). Social melancholy was used to diagnose the state of society and polity by both conservatives and liberals, educated and uneducated.

Contemporary observers routinely identified this structure of feeling in the metropolitan life of the imperial capital. Thanks to its turbulent history and the cultural-mythic association of the "Petersburg text" with the melancholic utterance, St. Petersburg became both the emanating center and the obsessive reference-point for the new discourse on social melancholy (Buckler 21). While acknowledging the continuity between the local "melancholy mood" and the general European climate of crisis, contemporary Russian commentators were especially keen to link the depressive states and postures to the current socio-historical experience in their own country and its representative city: to the sudden lowering of national self-esteem due to defeat in the Russo-Japanese war and the failed revolution of 1905, to autocratic monarchy whose legitimacy had been questioned, to hasty industrialization, unplanned urbanization, economic recession, social tensions, pervasive poverty, and alcoholism. (The latter set of vicissitudes got directly translated into the social causation of Dudkin's melancholia: his heavy drinking, poverty, grim habitation on Vasilievsky Island, where he would "sit in solitude and keep track of the life of the sow bugs" 63.) Interestingly, contemporary accounts also suggested the ubiquity of a contrasting symptom: displaced, compulsive insistence on amusement and laughter. Captured in the phrase "fun-loving Petersburg" ("*veseliashchiisia Peterburg*"), this manic gaiety was seen as being nurtured at Petersburg masquerade balls; in circuses, vaudeville theaters, and cinemas showing slapstick comedies; in comic strips and public hoaxes; and in press stories of the city's nightlife—the aspects of city life that Bely portrayed with much gusto in his novel. These early twentieth-century commentators overwhelmingly viewed the city's buoyant pulsation as false and eventually as symptomatic of social melancholy as the containment in the tragic (after all, the notion of artificiality is integral to the "Petersburg myth"). The two aspects of the social mood being seen as inseparable, their joint expression was identified in the pursuit of irony (Steinberg 825). In Bely's text, too, Petersburg's gaiety is matched by its despondence, and laughter is frequently (although not exclusively) wrought by irony.[13]

Because of the omnipresence of this manic-depressive cadence, however, contemporary commentators viewed melancholia as both a genuine social mood disorder and an artificial societal vogue. The same double evaluation is readable in Bely's text, in particular in its treatment of the father-son relationship as the melancholic metonymy of history. As I have argued elsewhere, the slain father-ambivalent son scenario was utilized by male modernists like Bely, Freud, Kafka, and Joyce both to negotiate legacy and to express formally the affects attendant to their aesthetic and conceptual projects ("'Full Fathom Five Thy Father Lies'" 3-20). This ambition was served well by the paradigmatic modernist fictional template, one that foregrounds the close etiological link between the dynamic of primal patricide and that of melancholia by staging an unsuccessful, or only partly successful, rebellion of youth. Bely appropriates this joint dynamic as the thematic pivot for his novel because of its serviceability: it is a singularly productive interlocutor for both his contemporaries' affective experience of the material world and his text's marked intertextuality. At the same time, he seems to be aware that the template, more complex and more universal than the above enumeration of names indicates, is also premised on problematic myth-making, including gender myth-making. So Bely simultaneously rejoices in exposing its fabulous nature to the reader.

While extensive narrative attention is paid to the melancholic symptoms of the two characters involved in the father-son scenario, the text at the same time parodies the characters' melancholic self-fashioning. The chatty narrator seems to be particularly impatient with the sometimes resoundingly artificial manifestations of the mood. It is through the shrouds of the comic and the grotesque, for instance, that the reader learns about Nikolai Apollonovich's melancholic pleasures: sleeping till midday, walking around in an Oriental dressing-gown, immersion in books, musing about life and fate, and engaging in the most extravagant expressions of melancholy love. Apart from being troubled by these proverbial excesses, Nikolai also has some specific melancholic concerns: his incapacity to move beyond the "dummy-wummy" picture of "little Kolya's dancing" on his father's knees (*Petersburg* 228) and inability to confront the circumstances of his coming into the world. The torments of the super-ego, Freud notes, are particularly intense in melancholia, and Bely is keen on comically highlighting them in the psychological portrait of his protagonist. Coming to terms with the task of parricide, for example, Nikolai feels that "from childhood he had been carrying within him the larvae of monstrosities" that was now set to explode in the twenty-four hours of the bomb's ticking (230). As a young adult, the narrator relates, Nikolai "transferred the shame of his conception to his father" and came to think of everything as "spawn." The belief that "people as such do not exist" but are "things conceived" (*"porozhdeniia"*) aptly likens the protagonist's personal melancholia to the general crisis of investiture and sense of insubstantiality thematized in the novel (229). Still, these are not entirely disingenuous concerns, and, as Bely knows well, to abnegate them by satire would cost the novel much. Seamlessly, as the tragic (the representation of *"tragizm"*) and the grotesque (the meta-textual view of *"tragizm"*) blend into the tragicomic narrative mode, Bely's jovial, parodic depiction of Nikolai's "melancholy" transforms into an image of personal and social melancholia of far greater gravity, to which he anchors the novel's poetics of shadows and shadowing.

It is through a similar fusion of modes that we are introduced to Apollon Apollonovich Ableukhov, the character whom the text repeatedly associates with the planet Saturn and the "saturnine [melancholic] mood."[14] We are presented with a half-parodic, half-tragic picture of the senator's sudden attacks of "unaccountable melancholy" (58) at the sight of paintings in his household, or forms and documents in his office, and at the thought of personally corresponding with someone (122). The sixty-eight-year-old senator is depicted as suffering from a particularly modern form of solitude. The epithetic variants of the stem *"odin-"* ("alone") repeatedly attached to this character inform the reader that Ableukhov is dishearteningly "lonely," "solitary," and "utterly alone;" and yet it is the encounter with the urban multitude that seems to terrify the senator most. The open spaces being the place where multitude reigns, the senator also suffers from agoraphobia: closed rooms (and, by extension, straight lines, cubes, and rectangulars—the

Apollonian "order") soothe him, while open and irregular spaces (and circles, spirals, disarrayed objects—the Dionysian "disorder") upset him. This fear of space and vast landscapes, the narrator hypothesizes, stems from an accident in the senator's youth when he almost froze to death in the countryside. The symptomatic link between fear of space and fear of death is fuelled by the senator's nightmares, in which he experiences visitations of a dead friend. But Bely likens this traumatic event to the arch-bureaucrat's hatred of provinces, his confinement to the "city-walls," and, finally (via a verse by Pushkin that torments Ableukhov), to his—and his institution's—alienation from Russia itself (53; cf. 307). This is a serviceable association, since much of the novel revolves around the generation shift and "crisis of investiture" in late imperial Russia, focusing, in particular, on the attenuated operation of those social rituals where symbolic investiture is pronounced—the rites of denomination, promotion, and public affirmation (Santner 12). The facets of the symbolic order to which the senator pins his existence are clearly a thing of the past, and the novel as a whole (insofar as it might be read as a psychological novel) tracks Ableukhov's gradual coming to terms with this fact. To keep the link with the symptomatology of melancholia alive, Bely furnishes his character with a plethora of symptomatic obstacles on the road to this realization. One of them deserves a special mention in the present context: since the crisis of investiture is the obverse of the crisis of patrilineage, Ableukhov's attitude toward his son's conception is no less complicated than Nikolai's own. Upon recognizing his son under the mask of the red domino, the senator ponders: "Was his son really of *his own blood*? [...] Only a *mongrel* could embark on *undertakings of this sort*..." (124; Bely's emphasis). It is in this symptom, which one may provisionally term "the spawn" or "the things engendered," that the father and the son meet.

The representations of the father-son relationship in modernist fiction customarily take irony as their chosen mode of enunciation and yet they paradoxically insist on immediacy of emotions. Bely's treatment is a case in point: we both commiserate with and laugh at the image of Nikolai desperately racing to his father's bedroom after the explosion of the bomb in Ableukhov's study. And, once "in" the bedroom, the reader appropriates Nikolai's affective gaze as he surveys his father sitting on the bed, "his naked little yellow legs pressed to his chest; he was in his undershirt; grasping his knees with his arms, he was bawling; he had been forgotten in the general din; there was no one to comfort him; all alone...." (289). Strikingly similar to a key episode in Kafka's contemporaneously written "The Judgment," Bely's scene unravels as follows: Nikolai rushes to aid his father's "helpless little body, the way a wet nurse rushes to a three-year-old toddler who has been entrusted to her" but "the helpless little body—the toddler [...]—up and jumps from the pillow and—up and waves his arms in indescribable horror and with a sprightliness that was everything but childlike" (289). There is much vulnerability, depicted and experienced, in this episode; and yet it is precisely the repetition-rereading of the key emotive phrase, "helpless little body," that brings about the text's ironic undoing—the realization that the reversal of roles is only momentary. This modal duality points to one specificity of Bely's treatment of the father-son relation. Rather than suggesting either the Hegelian master-slave dynamic or its simple inversion, the father-son template serves Bely to indicate a certain fixedness of categories, a situation in which both sides are allocated an equal share of weaknesses and strengths, in which both revolt and acquiescence are temporary, and victors and losers are the same. In the final instance, the poor success of Nikolai's rebellion is his gain—he is given money and liberty to travel to the Orient, for which he ardently wished. In a sort of symbolic exchange Ableukhov is given back his wife, peace and strength to retire in the countryside (the very place he had feared most), and the mature understanding that his "time" has passed. The intersubjective ground on which the relationship between the father and the son is played out may have been irrevocably transformed (after all, they will not see each other anymore), but the emotive score of their interaction has not changed: a share of love, a share of hatred. This final immutability of the emotive score can be intuited throughout the novel, in numerous glosses on Ableukhov and Nikolai's affective similarity and the mood disorder they share.

Unsurprisingly, then, the loss of the same love object subtends Ableukhov's and Nikolai's personal melancholias: the loss of Anna Petrovna, Nikolai's mother, and the senator's estranged wife. The mentioning of her name is carefully avoided in the Ableukhov household: for Nikolai, but also for Ableukhov, she is a "dead mother"—"a mother who remains alive but who is psychically dead" (Green 170), weighing on the protagonists and their diegetic cathexes like a toneless, distant presence. It is since his mother's departure with an Italian singer two years ago that Nikolai has been pacing his room in a Bukhara dressing gown, yearning "to return to his real home: the nursery" (*Petersburg* 220). And it is since her flight that the senator has acquired a habit of locking himself in his study, assailed by memories of Chopin's roulades she used to play. André Green's and Julia Kristeva's descriptions of melancholia as anchored in the loss of the mother figure are compellingly applicable to Bely's figuration of the protagonists' melancholia. But in the Russian cultural context, which so fervently cathects the link between the cultural-mythic image of the mother and that of the motherland (Russia), this represented loss acquires a further significance. In Bely's hands, this loss binds, once again, the realm of the individual mood disorder and the general *nastroenie*: the image of the lost mother—lost because unfaithful, and unfaithful because neglected—merges with that of "mother Russia," a motherland relegated, like Anna Petrovna, to that cryptic space in oneself where one stores those objects the love of which must escape extinction (Freud, *SE* XIV: 257).

As for the son and the father connected through this melancholic dynamic, their distinctions blur.[15] We can now identify them, together with Berdyaev, as one "uncrystalized, formless whole" (413): they are the symbolic image of a melancholic people "in a time of transition" (*Petersburg* 124), a people who contemplate meeting with the mother on new terms. The recovery of that mother—aged, heavier, outfitted with the souvenirs of the West, but as loving as ever—is a textual and historical necessity, Bely understands; and so he builds upon her return the most important self-society arc in the novel. But it is the realization that this return is only a new beginning (or a beginning of a new series of returns, or turns, or roulades) that closes the novel. This is *Petersburg*'s modernist legacy. This narrative move places Bely's novel firmly in the tradition of modernist texts which, as I have argued in chapter 1, conceive of subjecthood (including political subjecthood) in heterogenic terms, as a melancholic whole borne out of, and constantly reshaped by, its past and present object-cathexes. To appreciate this dynamic model of subjecthood—and thereby to identify with a multiethnic, politically polyvocal, present-past Russia—necessitates constant discursive reassessments and dialogues; or perhaps just a replaying of Chopin's "thundering roulades" (280).

Lest we are led to believe that such subjecthood is easy to achieve, dialogues are precisely what Bely's characters do worst. The melancholic organization of human relationships in the novel is glossed specifically through the characters' failure to *communicate*. The characters in the novel are repeatedly precluded both from establishing a dialogic relation (because of either temporal mismatching, as in the case of Nikolai and Sofia's love affair, or psychological mismatching, as in Dudkin's conversations with his many real and imagined interlocutors) and from expressing that relation symbolically. Inappropriate questions, mismatched responses, misinterpreted ellipses, prolonged silences, and other indicators of melancholic restructuring of communication pervade the discursive exchange in the novel. The greater or lesser failure of language's communicative function taints each dialogue, even between those characters who are not primary narrative carriers of melancholia (see, for instance, the dialogues between Sofia and Varvara). But it is the senator's ossified interpersonal capacities that are the major lever of Bely's sympathetic depiction of relational melancholia. Thus, among Ableukhov's many melancholic symptoms, aphasia, proclivity to move solely along the paradigmatic axis, is narratively foregrounded. Marked by the senator's continuous search for the "right word" and his tragicomically abortive puns, Ableukhov's vaudeville-like dialogues with his valet Semyonych are as sad as they are comic (cf., for one, 235). Whereas much genuine humor comes out of this deterioration of the subject's ability to communicate (and the senator's punning symptomatically improves after the return of his wife; 281), the melancholic nature of the condition is foregrounded in the text: the persistent verbal mismatching at once relays the difficulties of interpersonal relations and suggests that the subject's battle with the symbolic collapse cannot be fought alone. The characters' agonizing attempts to communicate testify to Bion's claim that the "container" for experience can be afforded only by an "other" in symbolic and communicative relation to the experiencing subject (6). This is why Bely's characters do not cease trying to express their thoughts verbally; melancholic communication paradoxically pins its hopes on its own persistence. As a communication strategy, this might not be entirely wrong. Clashing as they are, these voices do create a polyphonic whole—on the page and for the animated reader. The latter now becomes implicit in this working through, if for no other reason than for the comic restitution that the engagement with one such text promises.

But before proceeding with the examination of the consequences of Bely's heterogenic turn on the formal features of the text, I should like to return to Dudkin's uncontrollable melancholia whose purpose in the novel, try as we might, exceeds the scope of the interpretation as it has unfolded so far. In terms of narrative economy the gravity of Dudkin's condition appears gratuitous: it goes beyond the narrow requirements of diegesis (for instance, the killing of Lippanchenko could have had a simpler causation) and its symbolic purpose is unclear. Dudkin, who admits to intoxicating himself with "the general thirsting after death" (60), is represented as suffering from obsessive "negating attitudes" and delusions concerning nonexistence, depersonalization, and decorporealization (Dudkin imagines his bodily parts fragmenting, exploding, or opening up, 64 *et passim*); from hallucinations related to the ideas of persecution and demonic possession; from megalomania, hypochondria, inhibited capacity for emotional resonance, and troubled sexuality; and, finally, from the delusion of an expansive, de-corporealized brain-activity, of "consciousness detaching itself from the body" (17). All these symptoms specifically link Dudkin's condition to the symptomatology of the Cotard syndrome ("*délire des négations*"), a sub-type, or a particularly severe form, of melancholia.

The syndrome was named after Jules Cotard, who first recorded a case of this type of psychotic melancholia in his 1880 study of a 43-year-old woman suffering from what he described as a "marked tendency to deny everything."[16] Thanks to the sensational nature of the illness (as well as to the perfect timing of its record in intellectual history), the Cotard syndrome attracted much attention in clinical and lay circles in Europe at the turn of the century. It was invoked in Russian psychiatric circles particularly frequently during the period of the "epidemic of suicides" in 1906-1914, and its symptomatology provided good material for the sensationalistic reports that filled the Russian daily papers of the time.[17] As described by early twentieth-century psychiatry, the Cotard syndrome entails nihilistic delusions, which may appear as a belief in one's depersonalization and decorporealization (the belief that one, or one's organs, do not exist, or are about to cease to exist, but that the person in question is condemned to live eternally in the form of consciousness rather than a body) or a more general conviction that certain visible qualities of the world have disappeared, or that the world itself does not exist—that the only thing left in the world is the observing function of the patient's disembodied self. Linked to depersonalization, there occur delusions of persecution and demoniac possession, of being pursued or "inhabited" by another person or immortal being (such as the equestrian statue of Peter the Great); ideas of guilt and damnation, frequently deriving apocalyptic imagery from texts like the Book of Revelation (Dudkin's favorite reading, alongside Nietzsche); and megalomania.[18] Nowhere is bipolar symptomatology as negating, as intensely focused on the denial of the self and the world as in the Cotard syndrome. And nowhere is the merging of defiant motion and stooping depression more pronounced, and its consequences graver, than in this condition. This is why the metonymic association between the character of Dudkin, a Cotard sufferer, and the notion of revolution-as-revelation is so unsettling for the reader.

The reader's disquietude would be significantly alleviated, indeed contained, were it only Dudkin who suffered from the Cotard syndrome in the novel. If such were the case, Bely's novel would meet the reader's generic expectations with greater ease, as either a realist story about social maladjustment, or a romanticist story about the mad and the doomed. In any case, the "wholeness" or coherence of the character would not be questioned. But Bely destroys his characters as he builds them. It does not take long for the reader to discover that, for all the careful development of melancholic portraits, Bely's protagonists are indices, traces, fragments of each other and the space that surrounds them, rather than "rounded" characters. Consequentially, as the characters melt and fuse, "passing over" into each other (Berdyaev 413), the Cotard syndrome becomes contagious—so much that it finally becomes a free-floating metaphor. Like Dudkin, Ableukhov suffers from a sensation of his organs missing or being dysfunctional, as well as from persecution mania (*Peterburg* 117); Nikolai's delirium in which "a little elastic blob" transforms into a spherical fat fellow called, onomatopoeically, Pèpp Pèppovich

Pèpp, is comparable to Dudkin's encounters with Mr. Shishnarfne; Nikolai is credited with the "Cotard" intellectual delusion that "people as such do not exist" but are "things conceived;" and Dudkin's victim, Lippanchenko, is likewise no stranger to "ineffable melancholy" and persecution mania (*Petersburg* 261, 263). Other symptoms of aggravated melancholia are also liberally dispersed throughout the text. Most notable among them are symptoms associated with incorporation and the porous borders between the inside and the outside: nausea, cannibalistic phantasies, voracious ingestion of food or its traumatic expulsion.[19] And the "dilatation of the heart" (first mentioned in *Petersburg* 14), the physical symptom most commonly, if questionably, associated with melancholia at the turn of the century, eventually becomes a property of all the characters in the novel. In the text's final ruse, everyone is melancholic.

This symptomatology, and, in particular, the cluster of symptoms coalesced in the Cotard syndrome, permeates the novel's most arcane, self-contradictory, and disconcerting sections, those concerning Dudkin's maniacal killing of Lippanchenko. Preparing the narrative ground for the murder to ensue, the first of these sections insists on the sharing of affective experience (and thus also complicity) between the narrator, the characters, and the reader. The narrator invites us, readers, to imagine ourselves "blown to bits," and "the planets circulating freely in the voids of [our] molecules;" to picture ourselves with our "detached organs [...] separated one from another by horrible billions of miles" and points of our bodies "rarified into gaseous state;" to experience the accretion of "Saturn's masses in the spine" and "the diseased joltings of the heart," while our consciousness "expands to a horrible extent," knitting together "a blatant and hideous monstrosity which at the same time lacks wholeness" (*Petersburg* 262). This disconcertingly physical description of what, the narrator says, presents our "overcoming spaces while becoming spaces"—or "rising up" the initial stages of the life of the soul—combines the symptomatic imagery scattered throughout the novel into a syndrome of negating one's body. But its purpose is to announce the exact opposite: the haptic reinscription of the (dead, debased) body in the text. Closely mimicking the progression of the imagery in this episode, the next section sees Lippanchenko's body being ripped open, sliced as a cold suckling pig, in the likeness of Dudkin's psychotic hallucination, and finally being mounted by its murderer, leaving the reader with an image suggestive of homoerotic necrophilia. This murder is bizarre and repugnant, and, as Olga Matich argues, the novel mobilizes this excess of repulsion to create a space in which a renegotiation of the reader's aesthetic, sensual, and moral values could take place (282). At the same time, the replay of the imagery alarmingly links this violent death to a sense of spiritual accomplishment that, also ambivalently, informs the previous section. Lippanchenko is no more; but "the monstrous periphery of [his] consciousness sucked the planets into itself, and sensed them as organs detached one from the other. The sun swam in the dilations of the heart; and the spine grew incandescent from the touch of Saturn's masses..." (*Petersburg* 263). Whatever focalization we choose (Dudkin's, Lippanchenko's, the narrator's, or our own as the fourth entity whose presence in Lippanchenko's cockroach-filled room is commanded), such associations are difficult to make, disturbing to contemplate, impossible to interpret.

These two sections—one that meta-textually invites the reader to enjoin an affective and mystic experience, the other that records the same experience as a murder of a character (and possibly postmortem violation of his body), and both giving mixed messages about the experience in question—affirm what Emery has articulated as the hermeneutic problem faced by every reader of Bely's *Petersburg*: that "the text contains no internal barriers to meaning" (83). Vital to this free-floating of meaning and its affective resultants in the sphere of reading is the conceptual range of melancholia—as a discourse, an actual psychological condition assisting characterization, and an assortment of symptoms used as representational strategy. While Bely's utilization of melancholia attaches no fixed value to the condition, one effect of this performance should be noted: by engaging the clinical pathology of the gravest form of melancholia and disseminating it among all the characters and discursive domains Bely's text paradoxically battles against the pervasive "social melancholy." Whatever romantic notion of intellectual gain or social innocuousness of this condition-posture-discourse we might have had is challenged by Bely's graphic description of its manifestations and consequences. Bely's affective ordeals while writing *Petersburg* did indeed pay off: his text exerted (and still exerts) far greater power to disturb than those reports on melancholy and clinical melancholia that, by 1913, had already become naturalized in Russian society.

The Language of *Petersburg* as Vocalization of Melancholia

As we have seen, the power of Bely's text to *negate* "the negating aspects of life" crucially depends on the modernist strategy of fragmenting, melting, and merging characters—as well as authors, narrators, and readers. But this strategy is part of a larger disseminating drive that saturates the entire text with the symptomatology of melancholia, critically reshaping the language and organization of the novel. Rather than being confined to any particular set of symbols or emblems, or attached solely to particular characters, melancholia spreads perpendicularly through the layers, or aspects, of the text, including those that signal comic restitution.[20] In chapter 1 I have argued that modernist novelists were less interested in the depiction of melancholia than in its aesthetic enactment. The case of Bely's text, where melancholia seems to be at once represented and performatively articulated, is especially intriguing. As we have seen, Bely does provide the reader with a penetrating image of an age of "social melancholy" and convincingly correlates this image to the psychological figuration of his characters. But Bely's novel is neither Tolstoy's nor Dostoevsky's text. As befitting the novel that appropriates the tropes and figurative strategies of the nineteenth-century novel only to deconstruct them in intertextual play, Bely's "melancholic portrait" curiously relies on its own formal undoing. For example, no sustainable typology of either social melancholy or clinical melancholia has been developed in the novel because the characters not only merge among themselves but also fuse with their environment—precisely in the fashion the borders between the subject and its others, and between interiority and exteriority, are challenged in melancholia. Bely has planted quite a few meta-textual pointers to this strategy in the novel itself, and I shall take up the one that most conspicuously brings together the realms of melancholia and formal figuration of the text.

In the section titled "Revelation," the agitated Nikolai asks Dudkin to help him elucidate the reasons for the deterioration of his mental health. Dudkin, a specialist in the area of mental pathologies, advises Nikolai that his "states of mind have been described [...] in fiction, in poetry, in psychiatry, in research into the occult" (183). While, Dudkin says, a psychiatrist would call Nikolai's condition "a pseudo-hallucination," "a modernist would call it the sensation of the abyss, and he would search for the image that corresponds to the symbolic sensation" (183). Nikolai objects: "But that is allegory." Yet Dudkin instructs:

> Don't confuse allegory with symbol. Allegory is a symbol that has become common currency. For example, the usual understanding of your "beside yourself." A symbol is your act of appealing to what you have experienced there, over the tin [an invitation to experience artificially something that was experienced like that, *Petersburg 1916*, 353]. A more appropriate term would be the term: pulsation of the elemental body [...]. According to the teaching of certain schools, the experience of the elemental body transforms verbal meanings and allegories into real meanings, into symbols. (184)

Moving from the could-be-psychiatric description of Nikolai's state to modernist aesthetics and, further, through anthroposophy, to Bely's own conceptualization of the symptom, Dudkin's explanation is just a fraction too ambitious, too meta-textual, and, eventually, too didactic. But its richness is a great asset for the interpreter. Through the voice of his character, Bely first reaffirms "the sensation of the abyss" (melancholia being symptomatically allied with this sensation) as the overarching topic of, perhaps even impetus for, his novel. He already glossed the concept of the abyss as one of the modernists' preeminent concerns in his 1907 essay "Stamped Galoshes" ("Shtempelevannaia kalosha"). There, he parodied the "abyss," obsessively invoked by the Silver Age writers, as a ubiquitous yet ultimately ineffective concept (344). To this exhausted metaphor, the "new" symbolist wave counterposed another concept: the masquerade, or the grotesque-carnival (Hansen-Löve 17). While both conceptual frameworks gesture the *mise en abyme*, the reconceptualizaton of the abyss as masquerade emphasizes the ludic, experimentation-ridden, articulation of the trope as we find it in *Petersburg*. Not surprisingly, the conceptual scope of masquerade correlates with the way in which a modernist, according to Dudkin, would treat the topic of the abyss: he or she would search for the "image" corresponding to this symbolic sensation (183). Here "image," or embodiment, should be understood in the context of the refractive relation between art and reality: a modernist work of art, Dudkin suggests, does not mirror but "corresponds" to, or "embodies," the sensation of abyss.

Yet, as I have cautioned earlier, when interpreting Bely's discourse on embodiments and symbols, one should be careful to disengage oneself from the usual meaning of image as a definite emblem. This is precisely what Dudkin warns Nikolai, while imperceptibly slipping from "image" ("*obraz*") to "symbol" ("*simvol*"): one should not confuse allegory and symbol. Whereas allegory is a fixed emblem, a symbol is an act of appealing to a certain experience, or, rather, a generation of an artistic expression that allows the reader "artificially to experience" a particular event, or affect (the extended version of this sentence in the 1916 edition comes to our aid here, 353). For Bely, we have seen, symbol presents a "new language" (it could be a phoneme, word, sentence, style, or a particular set of artistic stratagems) deployed to invoke the affective contents of reality. What Dudkin is saying, then, is nothing less than what I have claimed to be the tendency discernable in the modernist representation of melancholia in general: modernists invoke the affective experience that they deem paradigmatic of historical reality by *performing* it rather than representing it in the form of emblems or types.

It is critical to heed Dudkin's warning, positioned as it is at the climactic point in the book, for Bely's *Petersburg* could easily be interpreted solely in terms of melancholic characters and references that, as we have seen, proliferate in the novel. But the ludic over-distribution of melancholic indices suggests that the matter should be approached from a different perspective—one attentive to the "embodiment" of melancholia in the very form of Bely's text, in the "new language" Bely was creating. The following discussion concerns the distinctive features of this performance, and I shall start by attending, first, to actual language—words, signs, and their omissions appearing on the pages of Bely's *Petersburg*. For melancholia announces itself, first and foremost, in language; and it is in language that the symptomatology of melancholia could be most readily mimicked.

When Lotman defined Bely's artistic project as an attempt to make his text into a "great word" (439), he may or may not have had in mind another symbolist engaged in a similar project—Mallarmé and his efforts to create a "total word," a new word out of the words and enunciations available in the mother tongue, but foreign to that language itself. Julia Kristeva has described the latter's project as an artistically fortunate negotiation of melancholia. Incomplete mourning, Kristeva writes, "revives the memory of signs by drawing them out of their signifying neutrality. It loads them with affects, and this results in making them ambiguous, repetitive or simply alliterative, musical, and sometimes nonsensical." Such language, Kristeva continues, seeks to "become alien to itself in order to discover [...] 'a total new word' [...], for the purpose of capturing the unnamable" (*Black Sun* 42). The excess of affect has "no other means of coming to the fore than to produce new languages—strange concatenations, idiolects, poetics" (42); and Bely, like Mallarmé, invents a "new language" for his work. Kristeva's further description of the artistic "melancholic language" also corresponds well to the actual language Bely created for his novel. Bely's textual idiom in *Petersburg* is best described as a linguistic performance of melancholic disarray in the normative functioning of language: it is a neurotic language, where swift, repetitious, syntactic fragments alternate with slow-paced passages of poetic lucidity, and where subjectively overvalued colors and sounds are interlocked with ellipses and omissions.[21] This idiom, I propose, should be viewed as a deliberate narrative strategy, deployed to embody the era's inexpressible "culture of the death drive" in the novel, but also, surprisingly, to combat this very climate by a sublimatory reinvigoration of words, colors, and sounds.

To say that Bely's hardest-won achievement in *Petersburg* is the articulation of the language of melancholia is not an overstatement. For the literary language that purports to convey, or perform, melancholia is an impossible language: it has to run counter to the established laws of discursive ratiocination, even counter to the customary expressive embellishments that accompany a speech or writing act. As a "successful" language, it should be meaning-generative; as a "melancholic" language, it should obstruct meaning-production. In *Petersburg* Bely insists on just such impossible language. Much of it is a function of the flighty, capricious narrator (perhaps, narrators) whose linguistic purpose in the text is to ventrilo-quize the melancholic's thinking when in manic phase. The narrator's paroxysmal speech displays all the properties of cognitive-linguistic behavior that psychiatrist Emil Kraepelin, Bely's contemporary, associated with manic thought: "heightened distractibility," "tendency to diffusiveness," and "a spinning out the circle of ideas stimulated and jumping off to others" (Kraepelin in the 1921 edition of his widely used manual *Psychiatry*; Jamison 106). More recently, these characteristics of manic thought have been linked to obsessive combinatory thinking and passion-ate juxtaposition of "percepts, ideas or images in an incongruous fashion," distin-guishable in melancholia and absent in both schizophrenic and normal thinking. The product of such thought process is a shifty, heterogenic discourse in which ideas are "loosely strung together and extravagantly combined and elaborated" (M. E. Shenton, M. R. Solavay, and P. Holzman in Jamison 107). It is this discourse that permeates not only the narrator's speech but also, seductively, the entire ver-bal space of Bely's *Petersburg*.

Manic-depressive speech, eruptive and inventive as it might be, is shaped by its own inconsistent momentum: by ungovernable clashes of thoughts, accentu-ated caesuras, and sudden halts. In modernist use the language of melancholia obsessively reflects, and reflects upon, the psychic void carved by melancholic incorporation. Such practice, as I have indicated in chapter 1, entails engagement with silence and its textual equivalences—ellipses and pauses. Perhaps the most salient feature of Bely's "melancholic language," especially in the 1922 version, is its emphasis on the markers of semantic omission: ellipsis, blank spaces, and dashes.[22] Thus traditional ellipses, those that break the discourse or indicate eli-sion, proliferate in the novel. Used most prominently in the characters' dialogues, these omissions designate, I have argued, the gaps in human communication. Surprisingly, however, many of the narrator's comments, even those with a purely descriptive purpose, are marked by similarly unrecoverable elisions. The narrator's curtailed description of Nikolai and Apollon Apollonovich's going to bed ("A hand trembled...two fingers," 82) or the closing sentence of the "Charcoal Tablets" epi-sode ("At this point he took a tablet..." 235) are fitting examples of what Kristeva has described as a typical feature of melancholic discourse: to "utter sentences that are interrupted, exhausted, come to a standstill" (*Black Sun* 33). The intro-duction of such "spaces of void" in Bely's text reflects the melancholic's urge to approach the inexpressible (*Petersburg* 119). This "inexpressible," psychoanalysis submits, is a reflex of an unutterable loss; ardent desire to articulate this loss stems precisely from the melancholic's hyper-awareness of the limitations of language, which I have likened, in general terms, to the symbolist project itself. Comparably, the reader's immediate impression of Bely's elaborate typography of ellipses is the invocation of something to which the means of communication at one's disposal are not commensurate. Ellipses, for example, accompany almost every appearance of the "sad and tall one" but also every direct engagement with the material realities of the 1905 revolution in Bely's novel.

This poetics of semantic incompletion is enhanced by two typographic practices Bely appropriated for his novel: radical indentation of the sections that he regards as key moments in the narrative (for example, each materialization of the "sad and tall one") and graphic segmentation of the text by adding extra space (the 1916 version), or a series of eight dots (the 1922 version). Sometimes, the use of these graphic contrivances is a pure game, or a rhythmic device. The greatest blank space in the novel, for instance, accompanies the fragment describing Ableukhov's realization that the money he sent to Granada has not been received by his wife (267). And while Bely's typographic divisions usually suggest a temporal, visual, or epistemological occlusion, they also frequently inflect the narrative somewhat "falsely" so that it appears disjointed even when it follows a clear logical progression (for instance, in the section describing Likhutin's attempted suicide, 132). More commonly, however, Bely's use of blank space and segmenting dots is multifunctional. In the episode entitled "Pèpp Pèppovich Pèpp," for example, Nikolai's realization of "the horrible contents of the sardine tin" is accompanied by a string of anticipations concerning the explosion of the bomb, each prefaced by a dash and flushed right, and a sizable portion of blank space is introduced on the left side of the page (163).[23] Establishing a dialogic relationship between the printed word and the blank space, this radical indentation signals the mid- and culmination-point of the novel, but it also symbolically summons the themes of death, annihilation, and absence. The interaction of typographic elements on this page also presents in graphic form the disorienting merger of narrative viewpoints and the ego splits we are witnessing. It visually adumbrates Nikolai's dream—a textual interstice— appearing on the next page. In this dream the character will "feel" his ego splitting into "I" and an occluded "I," a shadow of the object whose death Nikolai foresees and mourns in anticipation. In this dream Nikolai will finally identify his father as another incorporated love object, and another donor to his heterogenic identity (165-168). The occluded love object and the deed itself are, however, first presented through a graphic tension between the printed and the blank.

As these examples indicate, Bely's hollows do not so much disrupt the narrative as punctuate it with gaps. Their general purpose is to include the notion of gap in the perceptual, and printed, world. Therefore their operation is inextricably linked to both the figuration of characters and their inner spaces and the functioning of the fragmented chronotope itself. They segregate in the textual, printed, world, some sheltered cavities: gulfs, vacuums, voids, vortices, and standstills in the unfolding of historical time-and-space (this is also the function, we shall see later, of Virginia Woolf's stases). But the value of Bely's linguistic and typographic cavities, one grasps, is ambivalent: they could be spaces of revelation as much as spaces of doom; and, as with any other space generated by the clash of incompatibles, these linguistic-chronotopic cavities also operate comically. It is left to the reader to decide whether "the inexpressible" (ontological, historical, subjective) or yet another mask inhabits them.

The gap-effect is reinforced by Bely's emphatic use of colons and dashes, and his idiosyncratic paragraphing. As separators, such punctuation signs suggest semantic omissions. Yet their eccentric use also generates comic effects. These lessen the tension established by a discourse replete with convolutions and agglomeration of adjectives. The following sentence, in which Nikolai reflects upon the vicissitudes that brought him to the threshold of parricide, captures both the convolution and fragmentation of melancholic language and their comic sub-print:

> And thus it [his word to the party] consisted of the promise that had come into being at the Bridge—there, there—in a gust of Neva wind, when over his shoulder he had caught sight of bowler, cane, mustache (the inhabitants of Petersburg are distinguished by—hmm, hmm, certain qualities!) (229).

By no means the most fragmented or convoluted sentence in Bely's *Petersburg*, this semantic unit "weighs" upon the reader: its meaning is "evasive, uncertain, deficient, quasi mutistic" (Kristeva, *Black Sun*, 43) and its infraction by dashes, commas, parentheses, and, in Russian, even a colon and an ellipses, is disconcerting for the reader. The repetition, shift of tenses, use of expletives, and the surrealistic accumulation of objects under Nikolai's gaze (a presumably human subject to be assembled from "bowler, cane, mustache"), all "swirl" the sentence into epistemological collapse. Yet, the clashing of narrative viewpoints, discrete temporalities, and semantically over-cathected words also creates a comic overtone that contrasts the overt narrative context, demarcates the ludic chronotope, and, eventually, imparts meaning to the sequence. Here the absurd and humor affectively support countermourning in language.

Similarly contradictory is Bely's performance of melancholic repetition. As in the quotation above, Bely's stalled sequences are frequently bent by repetition-games; these conspicuously ally the language of *Petersburg* with that of the melancholic. Connected to the workings of the death drive, repetition of words and phrases, or their reiteration by incessant substituting, is a marker of the melancholic's incapacity ever to find a "satisfactory" signifier. Much of Bely's language relies on hyperactivity with signifiers: on simple repetition and on repetition-games such as the invention of synonyms and homonyms, catachreses, and puns. It is a broken metonymy of desire that subtends this performance and becomes visible in repeated subtitles, preposterous short phrases like "And—yes, yes!" and "But, and—but!" that inundate Bely's text, and the repetition-with-revision of key sentences in the text. The same harrowing sound of 1905 "sounded softly in the suburban fields of Moscow, Petersburg, Saratov" in the section "Arguments in the Street Became More Frequent" (52) and "it sounded softly in forests and fields, in the suburban spaces of Moscow, Petersburg, Saratov" in the section "Noble, Trim, and Pale of Mien" (76). The ensuing question posed to the reader is punctuated in the first section as follows, "Have you heard this October song: of the year nineteen hundred and five?," whereas the later section enigmatically omits the colon— "Have you heard this October song of the year nineteen hundred and five?"[24] Such minor recompositions are not inconsequential, and they do indicate the extraordinary care with which Bely framed his verbal performance. But equally important is the circumstance that neither of these enunciations suffices. Bely needs a sound—oooo—to embody (*"obrazhat'"*) the historical events of 1905.

To substitute for semantic occlusion, the melancholic language customarily recourses to alternative elements of speech such as sound, rhythm, and intonation. This rerouting suggests that meaning has not entirely disappeared from the melancholic's language, but is "concealed" in phonemes. Like many contemporary writers and theorists (most notably, the futurists and the formalists), Bely claimed the epistemological preeminence for phonemes, and famously tried to dramatize the purported consonance between sounds and referents in his poem-treatise *Glossolaly* (*Glossaloliia* [*sic*], 1922). In his coincidental work on *Petersburg* sounds and sound-relations came prior to the creation of the plot content, Bely argued (*Masterstvo Gogolia* 306). The allegedly preexisting phonic instrumentation included, for example, the use of the phone /l/ to designate smooth, exact ("Apollonian") forms; the speech sound /p/ to signal the pressure created by repression, or covering of a surface; and the sound /r/ to ring out an impending explosion—a roar—beneath the covering. (The combinations, then, generate phonemes with further meanings: for example, the sound-value of "pr" conjures up detonation.) More preposterously, perhaps, the aspirated, accentuated phone /k/, Bely argues, was used in the novel to denote insincerity (as in Nikolai's name, or the phrase "lacquered parquet"), whereas the prolonged /s/ purportedly stood for "reflection" (1934: 306-307; *Petersburg* xvii). The reader may play along and try to "discover" the affective value of other speech sounds featuring prominently in the novel: to identify the onomatopoeic /u/ ("oo") with the ominous sound of wind, of the vast space swirled into a historical vortex, as well as to connect Dudkin's phonemic phantasmagorias concerning the speech sound /ʃ/ ("sh") with the semantic framework ranging from forcibly silencing, through hissing, to outpouring in a sudden torrent (*Petersburg* 58). Or, the reader may regard with reserve Bely's claim of a semi-mystical origin of the novel in the first place, cautioned, perhaps, by Mallarmé's equally idiosyncratic assessments of phonology in his *English Words* (1878).

By asserting that sound generated the content of his novel, that is, that some affectively overvalued phones (or phonemes) were preexistent to formed thoughts, Bely deliberately walks the melancholic tightrope. In his case study of one "depressed-persecuted" patient (a psychotic melancholic in psychiatric terminology deployed above), Wilfred Bion refers to the patient's speech as hyper-cathected sounding that precedes thought formulation. Not qualifying as verbal communication, this speech could be best described, Bion suggests, as "doodling in sound, rather like tuneless and aimless whistling [since] the words employed fall into an undisciplined pattern of sound." But "this pattern the patient believed he could see," Bion remarks, "because the words and phrases that he uttered were believed by him to be embodied in the objects in the room." It is because of this unwarranted symbolic ascription and the non-existence (or, rather, unrecognizability) of the pattern behind it that this sounding "could not be described as speech, poetic speech, or music" (38). Bely equivocates, too. The same habit to endow sounds with affective-semantic value that Bely credits as generative of his novel reveals itself as leading to delusion in the diegetic world: notably, to Dudkin's fear of the "persecuting" sound /ʃ/, and his racist insistence on the Oriental properties of the sound /y/ (*Peterburg* 89; *Petersburg 1916* 118; exc. in the 1922 edition).

Regardless of the circumstances of its inception, however, if *Petersburg* is to be legible—Bion's case-study teaches us—it must present itself as an intelligible pattern of sounds. Otherwise the text runs the risk of plummeting into a semantic abyss; and it is precisely this danger that is thematized and performed in Bely's novel. To configure the novel as a performance of the melancholic challenge to stable semantics and yet also as a kind of verbal communication (in other words, to make *Petersburg* into a countermourning text), Bely focuses on suprasegmental features of language: he "studies rhythms, movements, pulsations" (*Petersburg* 184). As a rhythmic whole, the novel alternates the "manic" tempo of questing, pressured speech (frantic fragments, short dynamic clauses), and the decelerating stretches of contemplation (interior monologues replete with lengthy, adjective-ridden sentences); the 1922 text significantly privileges the first mode. As evidenced in the description of the "noxious October" and Nikolai's recollection of his promise that I have quoted earlier, the visibility and intelligibility of these rhythmic patterns is assured by repetition and variegated intonation. But it is also supported by Bely's strategic insistence on rhythmic patterning of phonemes endowed with what the writer may have regarded as a hidden articulatory symbolism: the obstruent articulation of labial explosives such as /p/ and /b/ and dental-palatal fricatives like /s/ and /ʃ/; the vibration of /r/; the indistinct position of the marginals such as /l/ and /y/; and the free-flow of sonorants like /u/ and /m/. Much as it impedes decoding (and makes resonant, if anything, the impossibility of ever fully "deciphering" the novel), such rhythmic patterning is crucial to the figuration of meaning in *Petersburg*: it keeps the torrent of words from submitting to the death drive; it guards excessive symbolization from becoming asymbolia. Foregrounding the production of art as physical act, this playful exploration of sounds and rhythms surprisingly revitalizes the links between the work of art and the material world. It transforms Bely's novel into an exciting, surprising piece of prose that challenges not only the limits of verbal representation but also the very product of that representation—the melancholic world represented in the novel.

Representation as a Cerebral Play—The Spatial Syntax of Melancholia

Given that "melancholic language" is the operation that unites all other aspects of Bely's narrative, I would like to start this inquiry into the chronotope of the novel with a linguistic observation. Probably the most frequently used stem in the novel is "*pro(st)-*," which comes from the words "*prostor*" (space) and "*prostranstvo*" (vast open space). In Bely's novel this stem ramifies into a series of words that denote space or spatial expansion such as "*rasprostranenie*" (expansion), "*rasprostraniat'sia*" (to extend, to expatiate), "*prospect*," "*prostirat'sia*" (to span, to occupy) (see *Petersburg* 297). The ubiquity of words derived from "*prostor*" is instructive, for Bely's novel is, indeed, a narrative of space. Like the "*pro(st)-*" stem in the novel's linguistic space, the fictional space is endowed with emphatic motility and transformability. Rather than serving as a static backdrop of action, the space in the novel expands, extends, swirls, rushes, and collapses.

This space-mobility is a function of the general peripatetics of the novel, which includes as much the characters' and the narrator's physical and psychic repositioning (the perambulations and transformations of their "a-selves") as itinerary of Bely's language, under whose "shifting" the signified direction continually changes. The use of linguistic itinerancy simultaneously to develop a sense of time-space and obstruct it is inaugurated in the much discussed Prologue to the novel, excerpted below.

> This Russian Empire of ours consists of a multitude of cities: capital, provincial, district, downgraded; and further—of the original capital city and of the mother of Russian cities.
>
> The original capital city is Moscow, and the mother of Russian cities is Kiev.
>
> Petersburg, or Saint Petersburg, or Pieter (which are the same) actually does belong to the Russian Empire. And Tsargrad, Konstantinograd (or, as they say, Constantinople), belongs to it by right of inheritance. And we shall not expatiate [*rasprostraniat'sia*] on it.
>
> Let us expatiate [*rasprostraniat'sia*] at greater length on Petersburg: there is a Petersburg, or Saint Petersburg, or Pieter (which are the same) [...].
>
> But if you continue to insist on the utterly preposterous legend about the existence of a Moscow population of a million-and-a-half, then you will have to admit that the capital is Moscow, for only capitals have population of a million-and-a-half [...].
>
> But if Petersburg is not a capital, then there is no Petersburg. It only appears to exist.
>
> However that may be, Petersburg not only appears to us, but actually does exist—on maps: in the form of two small circles, one set inside the other, with a black dot in the center; and from precisely this mathematical point, which has no dimension, it proclaims forcefully that it exists; from here, from this very point speeds the official circular. (*Petersburg* 1-2)

Leaping from tridimensional places to dots on maps, and vectoring from real cities to their mythistorical images, the narrator's opening address paradoxically depends for its flight on the arrest of meanings related to its subject—the city of Petersburg. Multifunctional in its melancholic wavering, this garrulous address at once demarcates and destroys the spatio-temporal features of the novel's chronotope; it simultaneously establishes and obliterates the identity of the novel's protagonist-subject (the city of Petersburg), and, by analogy, it concurrently affirms and questions the identity of Russia. In short, the Prologue succeeds in rendering the features of the novel's chronotope as tentative as they could only be: it "proclaims forcefully" the simultaneous existence and non-existence of the created world. The latter circumstance led Lubomír Doležel to interpret the Prologue as inaugurating the "opposition between the *visible* and the *invisible* narrative worlds,*" which is to become the semantic base of the novel ("The Visible and Invisible Petersburg." 466). Doležel's interpretation describes accurately Bely's doubling of Petersburg-space, but it does not say much about the interrelation of the two realms, namely, their disturbing suspension in grotesque and melancholic modes. This suspension, I argue, is the quintessentially modernist (and melancholic) feature of the narrative. *Petersburg* is a modernist novel not because it depicts an ahistorical realm (be it the universe of symbols or the universe of one's mind), nor because it represents a "real world," but because it describes a tensional interaction between the two. In this context it is useful to remember Giorgio Agamben's advice that we should "accustom ourselves to think of the 'place' not as something spatial, but as something more original than space," that is, as a "placeless place," "a pure difference, yet one given the power to act" such that the site of non-existence, of unreality, becomes the site of future potential (*Stanzas* xviii-xix). Bely's introduction of Petersburg as both existent and non-existent serves precisely the complex function indicated by Agamben. Rather than simply polarizing the ahistorical and the historical, Bely uses the melancholic projection to bind the real and the unreal, presence and absence, in narrative friction, and thereby to set in motion a vision of history that is both disillusioned and hopeful; one that takes account of what is, what is not, and what might be.

To set the novel in St. Petersburg, a place whose semiosphere has been recently described as "obsessive melancholic utterance that refuses to complete the work of mourning" (Buckler 21), is singularly appropriate to such project. The time-honored image of St. Petersburg as at once a real city and a mytheme provided Bely not only with a superior embodiment for the ludic movement between representation and the represented (something Gogol discovered before Bely), but also with a suitably invested referent: one on which it was easy to hinge personal affective dynamics as well as general questions of national identity, political and economical fate of Russia, decline of Western civilization, and others.[25] In their recent study of Petersburg's "mental" architecture, Crone and Day argue that the writer's identification of his or her self with St. Petersburg has been remarkably productive in Russian literature (1). One of the possible meanings of this identification is relevant for my analysis: it refers to the writer's projection of his/her inner feelings onto the cityscape, with the corollary perceptual reshaping of urban sites. Crone and Day support this reading by explicit, if fleeting, reference to "Bely's sense of internalizing the outside world and externalizing the inner world onto the Petersburg cityscape" (67).

While Crone and Day's primary focus is the personalized city-pictures created in this way, this conceptual framework is close to what I have termed the
affective digestion of the material reality. This digestive dynamic is, I argue,
more complex than our customary understanding of modernist exteriorization
of interiority would have it. Aesthetic affective metabolizing presupposes an
outside-inside-outside move through which the affective experience of material
history becomes embedded in the formal composition of the chronotope. This
"reshaping" is synthetic, Bely observed: there is a continuity between the introjection of a perceptual image or experience, its affective processing, and its refiguration
in the material world ("Formy iskusstva" 343). Bely's narrative topography is best
understood in the light of one such metabolic activity, in which the material world
(the city of Petersburg) is first introjected, then melancholically "reshaped," and
subsequently exteriorized. It is not enough to identify the discrepancies between
the real Petersburg and the fictional place Bely created. Rather, one should probe
the nature of the affective inflection itself. If approached from this perspective, the
represented space-and-time is revealed as a capture of the melancholic fluctuation
of the psyche: it is an uncertain, protean, space, where distinct sites and temporalities merge and the "real" and "unreal" time-planes overlap.

To guide us toward this discovery, the novel abounds in miniatures of continuously redrawn space-and-time. These, as a rule, concern movement, as seen in the
following passage recording Nikolai's leaving the Summer Garden.

> ...the leaves stirred up from the spot. They eddied in dry circles about
> the skirts of the greatcoat. The circles narrowed and curled in ever more
> restless spirals. The golden spiral whispered something and danced more
> briskly. A vortex of leaves swirled, wound round and round, and moved
> off to the side somewhere, off to the side somewhere, without spinning.
> One red webbed leaf flew up and dipped to the ground. A darkish net-
> work of intersecting branches stretched into the steely horizon. He moved
> into the network, and as he passed, a frenzied flock of crows took wing
> and began wheeling above the roof of Peter's small house. And the net-
> work began to sway and murmur, and timid and doleful sounds winged
> down. They merged in an organlike swell. The heart felt as if there were no
> present...(99)

Similarly to what happens in Woolf's fiction at times, here the material reality
appears to dissipate in affective reconstituting of colors and sounds. The sketched
space continuously morphs, shifting and curling together with the leaves, swirling
time, too, in a vortex-like move between the historical and the supra-historical. As

the physical time-space withdraws and the metaphysical engulfs, the human subject also disappears, or merges with the swirling leaves. Yet the description painstakingly anchors itself upon a concrete architectural and historical object—Peter
the Great's summer house. And it returns to the human, only to vacillate between
the real-unreal natural world and its affective imprint for the rest of the passage.

One notable consequence of such melancholic redrafting of time-space is the
questioning of consistency of the material world. Specifically, the projection of the
unstable inner landscape onto the fictional cityscape renders the spatial stability of
urban objects suspicious. While, at first sight, Bely's novel might seem to be doing
nothing but restoring the Petersburg of 1905 to life—an impression reinforced by
Bely's obsessive incorporation of architectural details—scholars have noticed that
this image is a deliberately imperfect set-up. Admittedly, monuments and important public buildings are at their exact places, to which they remain more or less
fixed throughout the narrative. But all private and fictional buildings, as well as
some well-known public buildings and even the alignments of streets, fluctuate.
For one, the location—and thus identity—of the government institution for which
Ableukhov works remains elusive, even though the building in question is one
of the most elaborately described in the novel. Movable, also, are details of architecture, like the symbolically laden caryatid on the same building. Lest we think
this is due to the writer's negligence or his poor knowledge of the city, this playful motility affirms itself in the central location of the diegetic world: during the
course of the novel the fictional house of the Ableukhovs comes to occupy three
different locations in the city.[26] Whereas these incongruities might be linked to the
shifting of perspectives, they frequently occur in descriptions by the same focaliz-
ing entity, or within the same semantic unit. Hence, I would rather associate them
with the symptom-ridden metabolism described above. What is projected out is
not only a personal image of the material world but also melancholic indecisiveness about the world perceived.

The characters themselves are experienced as mysteriously generated by and
implicated in these fluctuations of space. This perception is common in melancholic recasting of reality, where the reinforcement of an impossible inner relation
with the lost object eventuates in the diminishing and blurring of outer relations.
Bely's characters are repeatedly described as "emerging" out of or disappearing
into the cityscape. They materialize out of "a foggy damp hung suspended" around
St. Isaac's Cathedral (this is the background against which Ableukhov revisions
the city as made of squares, parallelepipeds, and cubes; 10), or from the Winter
Palace lane in the light of the descending "crimson sun" (this is where Anna
Petrovna's shadow becomes a plump lady dressed in black; 101). They fade away

in the "darkish network of intersecting branches" in the Summer Garden (this is how Nikolai escapes Varvara at their mismatched "date;" 97) or evaporate in the "human myriapod" on Nevsky Prospect (this is where Dudkin disappears and reappears during his conversation with Nikolai; 179). Created by space and out of space, the inhabitants of Petersburg are also modified by the city's chimeric and artificial existence: they become shadows and maskers.[27] "Petersburg streets," we are told, "possess one indubitable quality: they transform passers-by into shadows" (22). Shadow, of course, is that rare entity that simultaneously invokes the presence and the absence of object, and, as such, it has been, since Freud at least, the symbolic epitome of melancholia. But a similar dynamic pertains to masks: they double identities in such way that both "selves" are endorsed while neither of them is seen as sustainable. The Red Domino and the White Domino are and are not Nikolai and Christ, respectively.

The play of presence and absence finds its structural embodiment in the movements of "patches" of fictional space, their collisions and juxtapositions in the shifting perspectives of a big city. These fragments sometimes comprise no more than a "Wh-a-at?!?" (159) or a question mark (147), and, at their lengthiest, they extend for three pages. The randomness of their positioning in narrative space is deceptive because the carefully mapped out perambulations of the major characters actually connect them, Peter Barta has argued (21). Some of these narrative transfers are not guided by a single character's stroll, though. Rather, they seem to be spatially organized by the narrator's putative affect or, perhaps, the affective state of the city itself. For instance, the series of spatial fragments that makes up the first half of Chapter 4 of *Petersburg* is orchestrated rather by affect-themes or sound-and-color associations than by their real proximity. The series starts with the failed love scene in the Summer Garden, then transfers to Sofia's bedroom via the love affair sub-plot, and, then, through analogy of affects, to the entry in the Ableukhovs' household when Anna Pavlovna arrives; the ensuing sound of the door bell at the Ableukhovs is followed by the tinkle of the doorbell at the palace where the ball is held. In other series, especially those that track the affect of horror, Bely deploys complex temporal leaps and perceptual shifts laden with competing visions of history and social reality. Earlier in this chapter I have suggested that the melancholic repositioning of the father-son-mother triad in Bely's novel eventuates in the postulation of a heterogeneous political subjecthood. I should like to propose now that this heterogeneous subjecthood is not unlike the fragmentary whole that is Bely's novel itself, a textual structure which, on this reflection, reveals itself as a structural meditation on political homogeneity and heterogeneity.

These are not easy matters, either for Bely or for Russia of 1905, and hence the diverse fragments that comprise the narrative could be conceived and presented only as abiding in some *in potentio* place, or scattered and suspended above, in, or under, a cavity. Not surprisingly, then, the void, or vacuous place, is the major spatial organizer in Bely's novel. An immense void is what is at the bottom and at the top of societal structuring, Dudkin says (59); sky is a "turquoise gap" (65); "a timeless void" is under Apollon Apollonovich's bed (93); "a kind of void [tears] off and [swallows] piece after piece" of Sofia's life (120); the clean-shaven Likhutin appears to Nikolai as "a pimply-looking void" (222); a void is behind the city walls, and under Petersburg itself, as corroborated by the myth that the town was built on hollow space; and, "beyond Petersburg, there is nothing" (12). As an artifice of literary topography, here the void gestures toward both psychological and metaphysical realms. It exteriorizes in the textual landscape a feeling of emptiness so frequently recorded in accounts of melancholia, that "hole in psychic sphere," which Freud made formative of our identity and Ronald Britton connected to "obsessive manipulation of space and time" (91). It is this very provenance that transforms the void in Bely's novel into a hyper-cathected symbol for the historically unknowable. As one would expect, the fate of Russia is explicitly connected to this dynamic of the void. Specifying the symbolic and historical space of the novel as that of suspended transition, Bely's narrator outpours, "Russia, you are like a steed! Your two front hooves have leaped far off into the darkness, into the void, while your two rear hooves are firmly implanted in the granite soil" (64). Playing around the void characterizes the present state of Russian history, and the gallop into that void and an apocalyptic "leap across history," the narrator prophesizes, will be Russia's, Europe's, and the world's future (65).

Only an inquiry into the void, the unreal, the *topos outopos*, Agamben has argued, is adequate for an exploration of the real-as-prospective (*Stanzas* xviii). It is a similar insight, I submit, that informs the perplexing coalescence of historical disillusionment and hope in Bely's melancholic chronotope. The conceptual scope of the void, like those of its allied symbols, the bomb and the apocalypse, purposely remains ambiguous in Bely's text. Similarly to the interiority of the bomb—a site of historical forces that is at the same time full and empty—the void in the text could be imagined as a "placeless place," at once vacuous and sated, terrifyingly obscure and promisingly unknown; therefore, a site that can harbor loss and destruction as much as some "unembraceable infinities" (*Petersburg* 59). If Bely's emphatic use of the imagery and "setting" of the void stems from an effort to exteriorize a comparable structure in the psychic sphere, then the contradictory meanings attached to this image render remarkably accurately what Britton claimed to be the dual potential of the melancholic hole: to be felt positively as a "space" that promises the return of the object or negatively as a "space" that obstructs the object's reappearance (111-2). In Bely's melancholic fusion of Revelation and Revolution, it is the reappearance of the object that allows the great leap across history.

These contradictory meanings are, literally, set in motion in the Summer Garden episode quoted above, where the vortex of leaves that surrounds Nikolai, swirls the reader, too, for a moment, in an unknown, terrifying direction. Throughout the novel, the image of the vortex evokes the uncontrollable spinning of the material world into a void. Yet the vortex also functions as the geometrical equivalent of the manic movement of the text itself—its own spinning into the abyss. As the novel evolves and "revolves," the spin of "spatial patches" accelerates (the narration becomes increasingly fragmentary and blank spaces come to dominate the printed page); the same pertains to the dramatic action itself (literally, the character's movements grow in swiftness, from walking to running to racing). This acceleration progresses up to the point at which the running Ableukhov finds himself in "the place that was comparable to no other" (*Petersburg* 289): the very hole created by the explosion of personal and historical forces that have driven the plot. The space in question (to which, by the way, access is denied to the running-after Nikolai) used to be the senator's study. Now it is a "huge gap from which smoke billowed" (288), a site of hissing gases, much like those stomach gases that Lippanchenko hears in the last seconds of his life. Narratively, entering this "void" signals Ableukhov's reconciliation with the idea of death—personal, public, and political. But this entrance also activates the meanings associated with another entry through a door, one evoked immediately before and in Nikolai's dream of astral journey, earlier in the novel. To the dreaming Nikolai, "everything that was beyond the door was not what it was, but something else;" for "beyond the door there was nothing" and "if the door were to be flung open it would be flung open onto the measureless immensity of the cosmos..." (164). Behind the door of the once-study is also one such "measureless immensity." Anthroposophically, the threshold crossed by Ableukhov is the exact point at which a body enters the astral realm, and, symbolically as well as psychologically, the space of revelation. Narratively (for this is the end of the text's whirlpool-like acceleration), this crossing is the ultimate point of the "zeroing" activity that is associated with the ticking of the bomb in the novel.

Bely's *Petersburg*, however, does not finish with this collapse into the void. The anti-climactic Epilogue brings yet another vertiginous reshaping of time-space, now in the form of a series of global frames: images of a village in Tunis and of "dust suspended in the air" in front of the Sphinx in Egypt, and a further reference to

Nikolai's visit to Nazareth. During these prolonged travels, we are told, Nikolai has brought his manuscript "On the Letter of Dauphsekhrut" to completion (292-293). This route mimics Bely and Asya Turgeneva's actual global itinerary immediately before the writer commenced his work on *Petersburg* (*Peterburg* 685). The end of narration is thus also its (hidden) beginning, as the embedded reference to Nikolai's own writing confirms. We are familiar with such endings in modernist fiction, especially in those novels marked, as Bely's *Petersburg* is, by insouciant challenging of the boundaries between biographical-historical reality, represented reality, and the act of representation. In chapter 1 I have suggested that such closures foreground the discovery of writing as a privileged method of mourning personal and general history, whereas their suddenness and the installed narrative aperture simultaneously draw attention to the impossibility of ever completing mourning. It is in this context that one should read the very last chronotopic picture in Bely's *Petersburg*, one reserved for Nikolai in 1913—for the 1913 edition of the novel. Back to Russia, Nikolai lives alone, roaming the countryside and sporting the peasant's look; he has been seen in church and people say that, of late, he has been reading the works of eighteen-century anti-rationalist philosopher Grigorii Skovoroda. He appears to be grounding his new identity on the values promoted by slavophiles and contrasted with those engaged in the melancholy and exuberant city of Petersburg: simplicity, close contact with nature and peasantry, physical work, recovery of tradition and national spirituality. But Nikolai's is not a contented reconciliation with either national identity or personal fate. A plethora of inconsistencies indicate that the protagonist is as muddled in thought and counterfeit in appearance as ever. Shrouded in a "camel-colored coat," Nikolai surveys the peasants rather than partakes in any work; and the 1910s saw Skovoroda's work, which Bely strategically plants into Nikolai's hands, denounced precisely for its imported pietism. This contradictory representation is presided over by the writer's insistence on his character's "gloom." To confirm the continued working of the affective disturbance that gave both the topic and the form to his novel, Bely describes Nikolai as observing the world around him "with gloomy indolence" ("*s ugriumoiu len'iu*"). The Russian word "*len'*" denotes indolence and sloth, and it is, like the adjective "*ugriumyi*," conceptually associated with the word "*unynie*." The last is Russian equivalent for "acedia"—the spiritual sin of melancholia.

Although, like everything else in Bely's ludic novel, the sincerity of even this affect is questioned, melancholia does seem to have the upper hand in the open closure of Bely's novel. The very last sentence in the novel, which suddenly inflects perfect into pluperfect, gives what might be decoded as a retrospective explanation for Nikolai's behavior: "His parents had died" (293). It is the possibility of this loss that has tormented the protagonist throughout the novel, and its inevitability is confirmed in the last sentence. The perceived (or experienced) loss of parents, the bearers of the primary object-cathexes, Freud proposed in *The Ego and the Id*, occasions in the child a stage of tumultuous melancholia whose consequences in normal psychic development are formative identifications with the lost objects and establishment of a critical agency; the forceful, sometimes injurious, activity of this agency reshapes the now heterogenized subject into a member of society as the melancholic crisis subsides (*SE* XIX: 28). Nikolai's poor integration bears witness to problems on this path; or, perhaps, just the stubborn insistence on an alterity-based subjecthood. The prominence of the parental loss on the last page of Bely's text indicates as much a closure of mourning as a confirmation of melancholia's continued life, and, perhaps, its eventual social functionality. Affixed to this melancholic extension, Bely's writerly countermourning, like Proust's relay of memories, is a kind of activity that could extend infinitely if only there were no end to narration. And, thus, to arrest this flight of words, Bely's rushes to underwrite—"The End" (293). Let me follow his suit.

3 "Schloßgeschichten Werden Erzählt?"

Franz Kafka and the Empty Depth of Modernity

Franz Kafka (1883-1924) was not impressed by anthroposophy. Unlike Bely, Kafka found no convincing anchorage for the modernist *a-self* in Rudolf Steiner's teaching. More important still, anthroposophy and its synchronization of the planes of the human and the spiritual could offer nothing to alleviate the contradiction of Kafka's own dual existence—living at once in the mundane world of familial and professional demands and in the ecstatic habitat of his slowly maturing art, those nocturnal writing-sessions comparable, he writes, to the clairvoyant states described by Steiner. Yet, surprisingly, Kafka not only attended one of Steiner's lectures, but also asked for a private interview.[1] This circumstance should be regarded as more than a piece of biographical trivia, as a similar destiny awaited all the other symbolic "anchors" that the continuously searching-and-doubting Kafka encountered or espoused in his lifetime, from his interest in Judaism to his series of fiancées. As if performing the privileges of tangentiality (at the time only mused about by Bely), Kafka—the man of low-scale mobility—repeatedly devised mental ways to remain "outside" while hankering to enter the "inside." The metaphoric locus of such existence, Maurice Blanchot has argued, is exile, a situation in which "we are not there, we are elsewhere, and we will not stop being there" (9). This liminal positionality, Blanchot notices, is exteriorized in the world of Kafka's characters: they are—like the Hunter Gracchus—the "living dead," imprisoned in the limbo between finitude and infinitude where meaning and non-meaning coexist and "nothingness might be just more existence" (8). Thus Kafka's paradoxical abode yields a paradoxical art form: one that exalts the uncertainty and flatness of the world, while constantly invoking certainties and the projected depth. If melancholia is, as Harvie Ferguson has argued, "the empty depth of modernity" (34), Kafka's fiction is its very spatialization.

To enter the realm of Kafka's melancholic performance in *The Castle* with a gloss on the competing poles of certainty and uncertainty is apposite, for the novel rests on a semantics of unresolve: Kafka's story about a (false?) surveyor struggling to get recognition from a (false?) castle captures the simultaneity of presence and absence, authenticity and falsehood, in a cognitive landscape that is both markedly ahistorical and historically overcharged. It is a text that simultaneously insists on the performance of mourning as an act of symbolic recognition (this is, after all, what K. strives for throughout the novel) and undermines all the diegetic paths toward such recognition (the postponement of mourning is what K. also strives for in the novel). To the extent such textual figuration could be captured in a description, I should like to call it a "countermonument."

The thematic particulars of this "countermonument" appear to have been developed over a course of years rather than during Kafka's eight-month outpouring of creative energy to which they are usually attributed. One may find the adumbration of a story concerning a royal palace and ordeals of gaining entry to it in Kafka's unfinished *Wedding Preparations in the Country* (1907-1908), and foretaste the representation of village life in his diary entries of 1914-1918, two sketches for stories in the Blue Octavo Notebooks (1917-1919), and drafts of early 1921.[2] But the writer's focused work on *The Castle* lasted from early January to September 11, 1922, on which day Kafka wrote to Brod that he was satisfied with the text (a self-praise unusual for him), but that he had to "lay down the castle-story forever" (*Briefe* 413). The extra- and inter-textual circumstances of this period could be gleaned from Kafka's correspondence with his translator and journalist Milena Jesenská, with whom he had a largely epistolary affair in 1920. One learns, for instance, that Kafka's readings during the production of the novel included, among others, Božena Němcová's *The Grandmother* (*Babička*, 1855), a novel which the writer had first read as a teenager, and to which he returned in April 1920, and Sören Kierkegaard's various writings, including *Fear and Trembling*, which Kafka reread in June 1921.[3] This particular constellation of texts merits attention for reasons that will become apparent, one by one, in the pages that follow.

Meanwhile, let me note that, insofar as each literary work is a monument, or a personal and historical memento, *The Castle*, a narrative that shares the unfinished and condemned-but-saved destiny with other Kafka's novels, also presents a textual countermonument *par excellence*.[4] Irrespectively of whether it was deliberately intended as such or not, this volatile condition of the text effectively warns us against what to Kafka might have appeared as the major danger for a literary work—its petrifaction into an aesthetic monument. It is thus no incident that animus against "finalization" informs the diegetic structuration of Kafka's last and, according to many, most ambitious novel. *The Castle* relates the protagonist K.'s indefatigable efforts to gain entry to, perhaps infiltrate, a "Castle" (an actual building and an inscrutable authority figuration) and to join the village community over which the Castle presides. As it happens in a world in which language forms truth, K. could but need not be what he claims to be—a land surveyor—and he may or may not have been summoned to work in the area. While he can obtain no intelligible information about his employment from the Castle officials, K. nevertheless keeps receiving encouraging messages that propel the largely static narrative. If there is any pattern in the Castle's reactions, it is to be read on the level of language itself: each enunciation—K.'s truthful or false statement about his condition—is followed by a prompt, albeit partly inadequate, "responsive action" on the part of the Castle. (For instance, K. claims to have assistants, and, soon enough, they arrive in the form of two bumbling helpers whom K. seems not to recognize.) Thus, as implied in Amalia's words that serve as the title of this chapter—"[Still] telling the castle-stories?"—the knowledge of the Castle and its very existence (and thereby K.'s own existence and the unfolding of the story) are contingent upon language and its use.[5]

Significantly, Amalia's question specifies the language-use implied in this hermeneutic activity: whatever we may or may not know depends upon the pursuit of *storytelling*. K.'s extended dialogues with the villagers and the Castle officials that comprise the major part of the narrative are function of this tale-telling drive. Setting in motion discourses that range from obfuscating bureaucratic speech to the half-silenced female speech, these conversations serve neither to enhance characterization nor to develop relationships in the diegetic world; rather, their main purpose is to relay stories. The diegetic veracity of these stories is never confirmed and thus this storytelling activity paradoxically perpetuates itself through a series of misunderstandings and misgivings. Like K.'s efforts to reach the Castle, which elicit a substantial amount of suspicion in the village community but also gain him a few friends and lovers, storytelling figures in the novel as an ultimately futile pursuit yet one that continuously carries glimpses of hope.

This dual affective move is embodied in what we today recognize as a surprisingly appropriate closure of the novel.[6] Kafka broke off his castle story in the middle of a sentence, a sentence in which the ever-present epistemological anxiety peaks: "She [Gerstäcker's mother] held out her trembling hand to K. and had him sit down beside her, she spoke with great difficulty, it was difficult to understand her, but what she said..." (*Castle* 316). What Gerstäcker's mother said will remain a mystery to the reader, and so will what the Castle official named Klamm really looks like. Like Klamm, whose very name indices delusion (the Czech word *"klam"* means "delusion" or "deception"), the novel itself is predestined to transform in each encounter. The writer's decisions to leave this novel incomplete and unpublished could therefore be tentatively understood as an (involuntary) reflex of an aesthetic practice immanent to the novel itself. *The Castle* truly *is* a countermonument, both exteriorly and interiorly: the textual condition of the novel as both unpublishable (by Kafka's expressed wish) and unfinishable (by Kafka's expressed action) presents an index to both its opacity and its status as a fragment. Kafka's narratives are figurations of countermourning, a mourning which, for reasons that I have explored in chapter 1, avoids healing or closing the space of the inner wound.

Because it is bound, interiorly and exteriorly, to this state of unfinishedness, Kafka's fiction sits uneasily in any finitude-bound interpretation, be it the praising of a "prophetic" Kafka, an oracle in the time of few, or the honoring of an "agnostic" Kafka, a living form of his age. Although it began its "life" with an attempt at formal "finalization" in a hermeneutic space fixated by Brod's authority (as well as by his literal possession of the manuscript), *The Castle*, in particular, has asserted itself as a genuine site of hermeneutic conflict. The novel has been approached as a religious or political allegory, or as an evidence to the contrary, namely, that Kafka's fiction, while it conspicuously rehearses the mode of allegory, cannot be subsumed under this discursive category; it has been read, equally convincingly, as a culturally specific memorial that reflects the contradictory ways in which Kafka related to his Jewish identity and a psychoanalytically informed treatise on universal refractions of language and desire; and it has been parceled into and equated with its narrative constituents such as, most rewardingly, so it appears, its protagonist. The figure of K. has been interpreted variously as a "revisionary" struggling against socio-political oppression; as a quester in search of a mythic totality, or divine grace, or community (or rejection thereof); as a mere linguistic strategy; and as Kafka's complicated double, an impostor whose identity shapeshifts under the regime of modernity—an entity comparable to what I have termed the modernist *a-self*. Being so hermeneutically productive, *The Castle* has gradually forced its critics to embrace the incomplete character of their own findings.[7] It is a symptomatic response to a symptomatic narrative. This "symptomaticity" needs to be preserved rather than "cured" in literary analysis, for, at its subtlest, Kafka's fiction teaches the critic a rare skill—that of "melancholic" reading, of the productive anguish of interpretation that operates on its own incompleteness.

This is also what makes Kafka's *The Castle* a particularly adequate text for the exploration of melancholic expression—an investigation that, by nature of its subject, activates the vectors of the unappropriable. The novel's specific resistance to appropriation could be traced to one of the more unsettling aspects of the melancholic symptom and, by extension, of the narrative practice that purports to embody it: namely, the challenge melancholia poses to the sanctioned vision and practice of community. This defiant—if potentially solipsistic—affect-attitude that pulses through Kafka's novel requires the support of a particular kind of novelistic presentation, one that both further develops and moves beyond the type of melancholic performance I have identified in Andrei Bely's text. The following pages are dedicated to the extra-textual vicissitudes and intra-textual properties of this countermourning performance: to the writer's melancholic reframing of the notion of historical engagement and his effort to "symptomize" three key areas of fictional expression, namely, characterization, language, and the chronotope.

Parades and the Eternal Torments of Dying

Like all good melancholic narratives, *The Castle* always harkens to but never pins down the actual loss that necessitated the melancholic performance. Thus, while scholars do not tire of repeating that Kafka's fiction provides us with the quintessential representation of the modern subject's existential condition, this "modern condition" and its representational effects in Kafka's prose are habitually defined through what they are not rather than what they are. Walter Sokel, for example, argues that the narrative of *The Castle* dramatizes "the fundamental situation of the modern man, for whom neither the world nor his own self is given and certain" (*Franz Kafka* 42). Of course, the representation of uncertainty and lack of givenness could be said to be a property of almost all novels, at least as far as young Georg Lukács is concerned (see *Theory of the Novel* 58-62). If that is true, then Kafka's *The Castle* is nothing more nor less than a paradigmatic novel in Lukácsian sense, a designation that Lukács himself would not necessarily oppose. But I have already argued, in chapter 1, that Lukács's early description of the genre of the novel applies particularly well to modernist fiction. Modernist prose foregrounds uncertainty and ungivenness as key modes of relation between the outer world and the subject, and this impulse gets exteriorized in the configuration of the story as a search for (irretrievable) home and organization of the text as a fragment, or an index to dislocation. It merits keeping alive the more specific link between Lukács's early theory of the novel and Kafka's *The Castle* as a paradigmatic *modernist* novel, though, since the *Stimmung* that Lukács termed "transcendental homelessness" is, the following pages will argue, the thematic and structural core of Kafka's text.

It is indicative, too, that Lukács, who admired Kafka as one of the greatest "realistic writers," was also the first to charge Kafka's work with historical solipsism: the mature Lukács objects to Kafka his succumbing to "a blind and panic-stricken *angst*" about material reality (*Meaning of Contemporary Realism* 77). In turn this objection reveals itself as an autocritique, a reproach to the mode of uncertainty and ungivenness that the young Lukács himself extolled and a censoring of the corresponding practice of reading. Defining Kafka's fiction as an "allegory of transcendent Nothingness" (53), the mature Lukács strategically overlooks the property of Kafka's novel to defy not only the mimetic-analogical but also the traditional allegorical reading. Much like reading modernity in Kierkegaard's text, I would propose, one can read history in Kafka's fiction (and any "nothingness" or "plenitude" that it might index) only by detouring; that is, by attending to textual modalities and moods, or to those details and dynamics of the material world that, affectively restructured, revalued, and reconnected, still worm their way into the diegetic world. Likewise, the affective value of this representation can only be established in detour. It is with this thought that I begin my discussion of Kafka's novel by recontextualizing, or restaging, the writer's (dis)engagement with the material world.

Biographically, Kafka seems to have been, or presented himself to be, genuinely disinterested in the historical turmoil around him. His failing health prevented him from participating in the First World War (the beginning of which he commented on August 2, 1914 as follows: "Germany has declared war on Russia—Swimming in the afternoon"; *Diaries* 301) and his correspondence and diaries indicate little interest in international politics. Comparably, Kafka might appear barely to have taken notice of the tremendous political changes in his own country—the proclamation of Czech independence and the constitution of the new nation, Czechoslovakia, decreed on October 28, 1918. Enclosed in a kind of mythic, or quasi-mythic, universe, Kafka's fiction similarly eschews all historical references. Yet, even without any references to current historical events, and bared to the representation of the universals of human interaction, Kafka's prose dramatizes an affective experience of contemporary history. This experience takes form of a weighed-down historical depression rather than the manic apocalypticism readable in the cultural climate of early twentieth-century Russia and in Bely's novel. *The Castle* is a case in point.

Because of the particular manipulation of narrative time about which I shall have more to say later, the reader feels, rightly or wrongly, that Kafka's fictional world—in sharp contrast to that created in Bely's *Petersburg*—knows neither apocalypse nor redemption. The representation of such supra-historical leaps, whatever value one may ascribe to them, would necessitate the use of prospective present, future tenses, or optative mood, and Kafka, whose prophetism is proverbially glossed, in fact rarely writes in the conventional prophetic mood. Rather, his preference for past tenses and indicative and subjunctive modes suggests a world to whose conundrums and anxieties there can be no future epistemological or psychological relief but which nonetheless commands the reader's active engagement with these unsolvables. For, Kafka's somber novels explore not so much historical impasses as our production of them.

The sense of historical enclosure decipherable in Kafka's controlled chronotope has been commonly associated with the cultural and political ups-and-downs of the Weimar Republic (1918-1932/33). This affiliation is actually misleading, and many scholars have found it more productive to interrogate Kafka's scepsis about history in the context of the writer's location at the cultural periphery of the disintegrating Austro-Hungarian Empire. In the rapidly urbanizing Prague of Kafka's time, Czechs, Germans, and Jews commingled closely, if anxiously, and the social climate was daily inscribed by both assimilatory and exclusionary passions. To Kafka, a German- (and, occasionally, Czech-) speaking Jew, this heteroglot space offered a fruitful clash of traditions, but also a repository of the feelings of displacement. While generative of the major themes in Kafka's fiction (the relationship between the margin and the center, authority and subalternity, and the like), these historical specificities, Stanley Corngold has suggested, corresponded well to the predicament and promise of Kafka's own situation as writer—to "the danger of becoming lost in impenetrable contradiction that finally flattens out into anxiety, apathy, nothingness; and the promise, too, of a sudden breaking open under great tension into a blinding prospect of truth."[8] So, when Kafka seemingly uncaringly juxtaposes the commencement of a global war with swimming in the afternoon, we are also reminded of the Central-Eastern European, specifically Czech, brand of toned-down satire that imparts on the (subjugated) subject a comforting chimera of superiority over historical circumstances. What becomes audible on this repeated reading of Kafka's casual remark is the special effort the writer puts in ironically dissociating himself from contemporary historical events. And there is a particular reason for this effort in 1914: a preservation of Kafka's "writerly being" ("*Schriftstellersein;*" *Briefe* 383) while he was drafting "Temptation in the Village," a sketch that adumbrated the narrative of *The Castle*.

Read in this context, Kafka's diary comments on the beginning of the war reveal, if not really a "political" writer, then a person deeply aware of the necessary relation between history and his own writing. On August 6, 1914 Kafka sketched a particularly suggestive report on history, one that closely connects the spheres of general history, personal (and group) melancholia, and writing practice. He records "[t]he artillery that marched across the Graben. Flowers, shouts of hurrah! and *nazdar!* The rigidly silent, astonished, attentive black face with black eyes."[9] With the image of a human face (Kafka's? the mayor's?), this report on the enunciation of the public sphere in a charged historical moment suddenly shifts to the writer's private sphere: his apathy, his aggressive self-accusations, and the lethargic rays of melancholia that occasionally spur on his current work on *The Trial.* This inner state is linked to general history through the motifs of the personal and social struggle. The beginning of an armed conflict sharply divides those who fight and those who, like Kafka, remain "passive." The latter—we shall also identify them in Woolf's *Between the Acts*—feel useless, weak, indecisive, petty: "I discover in myself nothing but pettiness, indecision, envy, and hatred against those who are fighting and whom I passionately wish everything evil," Kafka exclaims (302).

Immediately following this outburst of aggressiveness toward those who fight (literally and metaphorically), Kafka writes down one of the most frequently quoted yet rarely contextualized passages in his *Diaries,* a section that delineates the predicaments of the writer's dual existence (how his "talent for portraying [his] dreamlike inner life has thrust all other matters into the background") and relates his anxieties over the wavering nature of artistic inspiration. Kafka describes his writing agonies by a phrase that will soon find its artistic expression in his story "The Hunter Gracchus" (1917): "...it is not death, alas, but *the eternal torments of dying*" (*Diaries* 302; emphasis mine). And it is at this moment that an abrupt shift of narrative perspective brings us back into the public space; to the sardonic image of "patriotic parade," the mayor's shout "Long live our monarch...," Kafka's own malevolent participation in the event, and his concluding commentary:

> These parades are one of the most disgusting accompaniments of the war. Originated by Jewish businessmen who are Germans one day, Czech the next; admit this to themselves, it is true, but were never permitted to shout it out as loudly as they do now. Naturally they carry many others with them. It was well organized. It is supposed to be repeated every evening, twice tomorrow and Sunday. (302)

A curious textual effect may be noticed in this entry: the historical snapshots of the Prague Graben in 1914 insert themselves in the diary narrative, disrupting

Kafka's melancholic litany, but also interacting with it. The contagious "hur-rays" and "*nazdars*" glorifying the monarch of a crumbling empire form a sharp contrast to the silence of the observing writer searching for words and registers to articulate the happenings in the material world and his personal reactions to them. But the very juxtaposition of those who fight and those who observe entangles the two groups and their respective discursive spaces. While the public (and communal) intrudes into the private (and individual), penetrating the pores of the latter's discourse, Kafka's "interiority" and his "writerly existence" also go out and permeate the public space. This representational swinging back and forth blurs the borders between the "word" and the "world" to such extent that the reader no longer knows to which of these the attentive black face with black eyes belongs. In this way, Kafka's personal feeling of (irresponsible?) lethargy becomes interlocked with the anxiety of writing (will his inspiration return?), and both of them fuse with the sense of (avoided?) responsibility to address, or react to, an actual historically overcharged chronotope: the Prague of August 1914. However unassuming, the last two sentences quoted above stage the writer's "victory:" this is a prefiguration of Kafka's discourse in *The Castle*—brazen, mathematically pre-cise, pregnant with irony yet without overly explicit sarcasm with which Kafka started his diary-entry. It is an expression won by fist-fighting (this is how Kafka described August Strindberg's literary accomplishments the very next day; *Diaries* 302). Crucial here is the relegation of the notion of agency from those who fight to those who write, or a change in perception of what exactly constitutes the *telos* of historical engagement. Kafka's diary-entry at the onset of the First World War thus presages a more direct gloss in Woolf's diary-entry at the beginning of the Second World War, an insight, as accurate as uncomfortable, that "thinking is [their] fighting" (*Diary* V: 285).

If, for modernist novelists, thinking is their fighting, then we should conclu-sively take with us also the impression that writing and history (and even active politics) are inextricably bound together, even for writers as professedly disinter-ested in the material world as Kafka might have been. To "write" socio-historical despair, one needs to engage with it, and, also, to invent modalities of doing so. The meta-poetic statement quoted above suggests that Kafka's intervention in the genre of the novel concerns the question of exporting the "inner dreamlike life"—itself partly a product of social and historical vicissitudes—into a readable, thus, public form. This artistic inquiry appears to be closely linked to one set of socio-political issues with which, as the sardonic figure of the Jewish businessman of shifting identity in the fragment indicates, Kafka felt personally responsible to engage: the concepts and practices of social assimilation, segregation, and individuation. The scrutiny of these social and affective social dynamics forms the core of the novel whose earliest sketch Kafka may have been contemplating at the time—*The Castle*.

Assimilation and Identity

Kafka produced the first elaborate sketches of *The Castle* immediately upon rereading Božena Němcová's novel *The Grandmother* (1855), during the summer and early fall of 1920. Max Brod informs us that, whereas Kafka particularly enjoyed reading Němcová's correspondence, *The Grandmother*, Němcová's fictionalized memoir of her childhood in Northeastern Bohemia, was one of Kafka's favorite pieces of Czech fiction (Brod, "Some Remarks..." 251). One can easily identify the imprints of Němcová's narrative in Kafka's novel. Set in a Czech village neighboring a German estate/"castle", Němcová's Romanticist "youth narrative" unfolds through a series of realistic, folk-wisdom laden episodes, connected by the character of a granny; the latter's actions—above all, her storytelling—help her grandchildren to transition into adulthood. The grouping of characters (simple peasants, conniving servants/administration, and inaccessible nobility), the tensions that underpin Němcová's romanticized diegetic world, the emotive overvaluing of the activity of storytelling, and the episodic composition, all resemble closely the structure and affective targets of Kafka's novel.[10] While the novels have some conspicuous parallels of detail (for example, the cunning Italian servant Piccolo in *The Grandmother* and the clerk Sortini in *The Castle* share nationality, character traits, and even the type of narrative action), the chronotope, focalization, and miscellaneous motifs from Němcová's novel are taken over by Kafka as if in negative: Němcová's setting is an idyllic Bohemian village and its outskirts, extending toward the castle, Kafka's setting is a nightmarish Bohemian village and its outskirts, extending toward the castle; Němcová's protagonist is female and the narrative, concerning itself with the dynamic of desire, is focalized from a female perspective; Kafka's protagonist is male and the narrative, dealing with the dynamic of desire, is focalized from a male perspective.

While scholars generally agree on the existence of these and other links between *The Grandmother* and *The Castle*, they have had difficulties in interpreting the nature of the relationship between the two texts. Yet there must have been a special reason why Kafka turned to a rereading of this classic in 1920—apart from sharing the passion for the novel with Milena Jesenská. As the most widely read and most frequently exploited product of the Czech national revival literature, Němcová's novel, I would suggest, spoke compellingly to Kafka's increasing interest in the issues of national identity, cultural assimilation, and segregation, but also to his fears of political appropriation of literary text. Němcová's idealistic picture of the Czech countryside and its people—a nation with no land of its own—expressly helped the national awakening in the Czech lands and, more generally, contributed to the proliferation of the *Heimat* discourse in Slavic countries of Central Europe in the late nineteenth century. After the First World War, *Grandmother* was put into the service of the escalating Czech exclusionism, the rise of which Kafka witnessed firsthand during the anti-Semitic riots in Prague in 1920. This after-life of Němcová's novel is itself premised on a political appropriation, perhaps a misreading, of the kind dreaded by Kafka. Written by an author born in Vienna to Czech and German parents (and a woman active in the revival circles yet distrustful of nationalistic passions), Němcová's text itself actually counters the more didactic and zealously nationalistic discourses that dominated the Czech prose of the mid-1850s. The novel presents German nobility in a positive light; the anchorage of the novelistic action is not the struggle between the domineering Germans and the dominated Czechs, but the problems of non-existence of a common language and of the presence of harmful mediators—a horde of conniving servants and administrators that interfere in the apparently fulfilling relationship between the wise German rulers of the Castle and the good Czech peasants in the village. Of course, the novel could be read as a loophole stratagem, and it has been read as such by Czech nationalists; but Kafka arguably relished more those moments in Němcová's text when the romanticized image of nation suddenly turns self-ironical and where the matter-of-fact tone imparts the more sinister nuances to the text—a vision in language that may just as well be the exact opposite of the idyllic setting of the novel. Reading and admiring it in Czech, Kafka arguably recognized in the text's activation of multiple discourses a more complex message about national identity and social assimilation.

Quest for cultural distinctiveness, anxiety of a "minor" nation, displacements of angst, the dubious role of cultural mediators or cultural shapeshifters, the correlation of storytelling with psychological individuation and shaping of cultural identity—all these issues relevant to Němcová's novel and its public reception likely influenced Kafka's ambivalent treatment of the themes of cultural segregation and assimilation in *The Castle*. Significantly, several ethnic transfers occurred en route. The geo-cultural particulars of Kafka's home-place determined his melancholic contribution to the discourse about assimilation, a debate that agitated the Jewish intellectual scene at the time. The Prague Jews of the early twentieth century overwhelmingly aspired to assimilate in the domineering culture (German)— it was precisely this aspirational attitude toward the German "overlords" that was the major source of late nineteenth- and early twentieth-century Czech anti-Semitism—and, yet, in terms of the "affective everyday," they felt more connected with the dominated culture (Czech). As a linguistic memento to the complexities of this dual allegiance, they mostly spoke both German and Czech, while the use of Yiddish gradually eroded in the area. I invoke the issue of language here as it was vital for both general discussions about national identity in the fringes of Austro-Hungarian Empire (and, later, Czechoslovakia) and Kafka's own cogitations on identity. Bilingualism was the everyday occurrence in the Kafka household: coming from an upper-middle-class Bohemian family, Julie Kafka née Löwy, Franz Kafka's mother, preferred the use of German, whereas his father Herman Kafka, born and raised in the Czech speaking village of Osek, likely "remained happiest" when using "plebeian Czech" (Sayer 165). Franz Kafka himself spoke German with a Czech accent, a circumstance that immediately identified him as a Praguer; and his Czech was fluent and often used as affectionate language, but not "classical" and rich, he would complain. Most Prague Jews, like Kafka himself, were educated in German—at least until 1918 when, under the tide of nationalist tensions and political pragmatics, Czech Jews deserted German schooling and start sending their children principally to schools where the medium of instruction was Czech.

What it meant to be a Jew in turn-of-the century Prague, Derek Sayer comments, was in itself unclear and contested, both within and outside Jewish circles, and both in records and everyday life: Jews who spoke Czech frequently perceived themselves as Czech, and Jews who used German, especially those of the upper and middle classes, often declared themselves German (166). The census data are of modest help here, as categories such as Jewish, German, Czech or, later, Slovak, were not used, or were used in fluid fashion, and these identities themselves were not stable. The specific context for Kafka's engagement with the issues of assimilation and segregation in *The Castle* could then be read in that mordant image of "Jewish businessmen who are Germans one day, Czech the next" (*Diaries* 302), a representation that well communicates Kafka's doubts about the cultural authenticity of the group to whom he himself belonged—the assimilated Jews.[11] The issue of assimilation became even more complex in the late 1910s, when, under the changed political framework of a new nation, the relationship between the Prague Jews and the Czechs (and Slovaks) became tense and the intellectual-emotional connection between Jews and the German culture began to attenuate. In these years Kafka often spoke openly against what he regarded as the "cultural snobbery" that governed the assimilated Western Jews' feeling of ascendancy over the non-assimilated Eastern European Jewry. In turn, the lives of non-assimilated

Eastern European Jews appeared to Kafka—rather subjectively—as more authentic and more fulfilling than those of the perpetually self-questioning Western European Jews.

To contextualize Kafka's position within the conceptual framework of the present book, one may juxtapose it with the response to the Jewish assimilation debate by his Austro-Hungarian co-citizen, Sigmund Freud. Openly promoting an "assimilationist" stand for most of his life, Freud also addressed the issue of assimilation and nation loss covertly in critical texts like his 1915 essay "On Transience" (*SE* XIV: 303-8; see Jonte-Pace 164-7). Written at the same time as "Mourning and Melancholia," this essay contrasts three walkers' different responses to the sight of nature in bloom and the thought of its transience: a "revolt against mourning" observable in his friends (the poet's aching despondency and the taciturn friend's preposterous "demand for immortality") and the thinker's own posture—mourning progressivism, or the endorsement of transience. Under Freud's terms, Kafka's favoring of non-assimilated Jews reveals itself as a paradigmatically melancholic reaction. But it is rather plausible that Kafka was aware of the melancholic nature of this condition: he observed it around him and within him. In his psychoanalytical (and partly self-reflexive) assessment of the position of young Jewish authors writing in German at the beginning of the twentieth century, Kafka describes these writers as "fastened, with their posterior legs, to their father's Jewishness," and unable to find a new ground "with their waving anterior legs." Like Freud in his 1915 essay, Kafka correlates these melancholic struggles of ambivalence with creative work: the despair of this impossible positionality became, Kafka argues, these writers' "inspiration" (*Briefe* 337). Kafka's mental picture of young Jewish writers as quadrupedals "stranded in the present" (as Peter Fritzsche termed this particular brand of historical melancholia) is curiously consanguineous with Andrei Bely's representation of Russia as a steed whose rear hooves are firmly implanted in the soil, and whose front hooves wave above the abyss (*Petersburg* 64; see chapter 2 of the present volume). In both cases, the image should be read as much as an index to a specific historical and artistic situation—that of coming to terms with a passage into the future and the prospect of cultural assimilation—as a representation of "modernist modernity" itself. It is such affective imagining of history that informs, then, Freud's and Kafka's ultimate elevation of the question of Jewish assimilation onto the level of a universal societal conundrum. For Freud, the question became one of living in a future-oriented present versus abiding in the past/eternity. For Kafka, it metamorphosed into an interrogation of the relationship between individual and society, of the existential givens of isolation and cohabitation, and—a non sequitur with which Kafka's work is replete—of the conditions of segregation, exile, and cultural assimilation.

Nowhere is Kafka's pursuit of these issues more focused, more tenacious, and more inventive than in *The Castle*. The first thing we learn about the protagonist of *The Castle* is that he is an outsider, unassimilated and potentially inassimilable in the community that he enters. It is characteristic of Kafka's text, however, that the traditional acceptation of the verbs denoting entering, exiting, and, generally, moving from one place to another, is challenged at every stage of the narrative. This semantic game concerning actantial categories of movement commences at the very beginning of the narrative, that is, with K.'s "entry" in the village. Arriving on a late winter evening, K. seems to be both cognizant and incognizant of where he has come, which imparts a narrative impression that the protagonist is both coming to an unknown place and returning to a place he has visited before. K. is immediately informed that he needs permission to stay in the village, which is first denied and then granted by the Castle authorities; unexpectedly, K. takes the eventually favorable decision as a proof of the Castle's inimical intentions. The same kind of indecisiveness about the circumstances of K.'s arrival at/return to the village and his position in the village will accompany K. and the reader throughout the story. But that K.'s chief interest may lie somewhere else than in merely gaining the permission to do his work, or even entering the Castle, is suggested early on. To the landlord's hurried attempts to transfer him to the Castle on the first morning of his stay, K. responds by expressing his preference for life in the village: "if I'm to work down here, then it would make more sense for me to live here, too. And I fear that the life up there at the Castle wouldn't appeal to me" (*Castle* 6).

From the very start, K. appears to have an "irresistible urge to seek out new acquaintances" (10), but the villagers, while inquisitive, display a surprisingly direct lack of trust and hospitality. The landlord of the Gentlemen's Inn informs K. that even officials are not able to bear the sight of a stranger (33). The tanner Lasemann explains it forthrightly: "There is no custom of hospitality here and we do not need guests" (12). K. swiftly concurs, but also recourses to an intercommunal argument: " 'Certainly,' said K., 'what would you need guests for? But every now and then someone is needed, such as me, the land surveyor' (*Landvermesser*)."[12] K.'s response implies that, in order for a society to function well, an outsider is occasionally needed, a surveyor who would measure anew (*vermessen*), and thereby reposition, perhaps reaffirm, the community in question. Not that the villagers are unaware of this circumstance; this is why they treat K. as an unwelcome, yet somehow indispensable, guest who will measure—perhaps, mismeasure (*vermessen*)—their lands and themselves. As an entity of such order, the villagers reason, K. belongs to the Castle. But it soon becomes obvious that K. does not belong to the Castle either, as the exasperated landlady explains to him: "You're not from the Castle, you're not from the village, you are nothing. Unfortunately, though, you are something, a stranger, one who is superfluous and gets in the way everywhere [...]" (48).

It is not difficult to identify the politics of this preposterous relational logic. It reads a familiar scenario: an outsider enters a closed, well-running, albeit in actuality dysfunctional, community and attempts to set up a habitat there; his assimilation is barred by the distrustful community and the authorities presiding over it. Many readers have observed that the villagers' behavior could be easily linked to the traditional forms of anti-Semitism (see, esp. Arendt; Robertson). But this behavior could also be interpreted within a more general framework of the fear of the cultural other, the actants and parameters of which are rather unorthodoxly disseminated in the text. Indeed, lest we are deceived by the apparent one-sidedness of segregation taking place in *The Castle*, an opposite relation is also established at the very beginning of the narrative: by virtue of the villagers' overly frank pronouncements of inhospitality, it is the village community that is also textually configured as an outsider. If abiding by the laws of hospitality distinguishes between "the civilized" and "the barbarians," as ancient Greeks believed, the unwelcoming, eccentric village populace, who are not only consistently inimical to foreigners but also professedly ignorant of the "civilized" legal basics (ambivalently embodied in the Castle), are a cultural outsider to the presumably civilized "measurer" K. and, perhaps, the Castle itself.[13]

Indeed, to elevate K. as a sole victim of societal exclusion is to miss the major point about this character: Kafka's protagonist is self-assertive and opportunistic, and his behavior often borders on aggression and abusiveness. There is little evidence in the novel that K. genuinely wishes to belong to the village community; he even claims, rather pompously, that "he had not come [there] in order to lead a life in honor and peace" (153). At the same time, there are repeated clues, especially in the first half of the novel, that K. is interested in becoming a villager mainly in order to accrue favors with the Castle, to which the village community is then counter-posed as subaltern. K., for instance, develops the following paradoxical strategy:

> It was only as a village worker, as far from the Castle gentlemen as possible, that he could achieve anything at the Castle, these people in the village who were so distrustful of him would start talking as soon as he had become if

not their friend then their fellow citizen, and once he had become indis-
tinguishable from, say, Gerstäcker or Lasemann—this must happen very
quickly, everything depended on it—all those paths would suddenly open
up, which if he were to rely solely on the gentlemen above, on their good
graces, would always remain blocked and invisible too. (24)

K.'s anxious rumination is, normally, overdetermined. Hidden under the sentimental image of "if not a friend then a fellow citizen" that may lead one to interpret
the passage as bespeaking the predicaments of a cultural outsider, there lies a less
apparent cunning strategy that sheds a different light on the surveyor's pursuit. For
all the animosity that he occasionally displays toward the Castle, the protagonist
is driven by a distinct wish to become part of this structure of power—in fact, it
is that wish that propels the narrative. Along these lines, David Suchoff has suggested that K.'s attempts to gain recognition from the Castle may be interpreted as
an attempt not to overpower but to become one with the holders of power (136-
177). The character's assimilation plight may be genuine, but it does not prevent
him from having opportunistic aims, or, indeed, from the occasional use of the
means that are unjustifiable from the perspective of communal ethics. It is noticeable that, while seeking the recognition of his own individuality, K. conspicuously
disregards others' claims to the same treatment. Unable to distinguish between his
two assistants, he decides to call them both "Artur." When they object, K. insen-
sitively retorts: "Why, of course! [. . .] it must indeed be unpleasant for you, but
that's how it's going to be" (Castle 19). Here the critical point, highlighted by the
failure of K.'s communion with Frieda, is that Kafka's protagonist is simultaneously
interested and disinterested in community and bilateral relationships; he wishes to
commune but "to be free at all times" (6). Freedom of this kind is, of course, dear.
As K. experiences when he is left alone after his attempt to waylay Klamm, "there
[is] nothing more senseless, nothing more desperate, than this freedom, this waiting, this invulnerability" (106).

What the novel problematizes, then, is the split identity of one who longs for
assimilation (to enjoin what Kafka saw as the Western Jewish "inauthentic" existence) yet desires to remain isolated (to live the purportedly authentic life of the
Eastern European Jews). The impasse of this personal and group situation is obvious. The only possible means of "authenticating" such historical existence is by
recognizing and accommodating its melancholic prerogatives. It is for this reason,
one may add, that K., his opportunistic aims notwithstanding, seeks rather a communal recognition of his predicament than a full integration in the community. The
surprising goal of K.'s laborious struggle to reach Klamm is simply to "be standing

there opposite him" (85). Insofar as this is also the objective focusing the narrative material, *The Castle* is a product of maturing, and, perhaps, mellowing, of Kafka's attitude toward assimilation and interethnic co-existence. Elizabeth Boa argues that this affective development may have been informed by a sudden improvement in the political position of the Prague Jews in 1922, when Tomáš Masaryk, the first president of Czechoslovakia, granted the Jewish minority the constitutional rights as a recognized nation in the new country.[14] It is possible to interpret the villagers' inconsistent behavior and the ambivalent messages K. gets from the Castle as Kafka's anxious probing of alternative destinies for Czechoslovakia, the new multiethnic and multilingual state about which he was both melancholically apprehensive and hopeful. Like Němcová's novel decades earlier, Kafka's text gestures that the problems and potentials of coexistence, or cultural translatability, are "the proper stuff of fiction."[15]

Yet it is worth reminding the reader, by way of concluding this section, that *The Castle* is devoid of references not only to Jews, or Czechs, or Slovaks, or their languages, but also to all distinguishing features of class, religion, or ethnicity. This is so because, like Freud's, Kafka's interrogation of the problems of assimilation is grounded in an enduring fascination with "the anthropological absolute" (Dowden 119). As the novel prolongs itself through K.'s series of failed attempts to establish rapport with either the Castle officials or the villagers, the reader becomes aware that, rather than belonging to any particular ethnicity, or being an ethnic subject as such, K. is the narrative carrier of Kafka's wider melancholic insight about the tragic duality inhering in the relationship between the individual and society: the simultaneity of one's desires to assimilate and to remain autonomous. Alternatively subject to the anguish of belonging and the torment of freedom, K. (like the reader) does not know if such dual existence—being a member of a community and a vigorously independent entity—can ever be lived. Still, he melancholically probes its logical possibilities. What focuses the novel is precisely K.'s effort to establish this dual existence through an inconclusive series of actantial variants. Above all, exclusionism and inclusivity appear in Kafka's text as a dual contradictory predisposition of the human subject itself; a disposition that passages, sometimes with grave consequences, from a particular existence into the set of relations that constitute the material world. But the reflection on this dual disposition appears to be enabled in Kafka's texts only under conditions of well-nigh abstraction, where the particulars of both one's singular existence and one's situatedness in the material world are exceeded, and where what Fredric Jameson has called Kafka's "inexhaustible inventory of alternatives" can be examined through a substitutive series of logical permutations, or gestural possibilities, such as the self and the other, isolation and community, independence and belonging (96; see, also, 100). This volatile, inconclusive structure cannot but constellate a comparable chronotope. The melancholic inflections of the latter will concern me in what follows.

The Novel between Two Deaths: Countermourning in Action

It is difficult to ascertain the "where and when" of the land surveyor story. Focalized predominantly from K.'s perspective, *The Castle* unfolds in a compact, claustrophobic, and tantalizingly abstract space-and-time, a formal feature that many scholars correlated to the sense of historical despair that the text appears to emanate.[16] The parameters of the novelistic space are deceptively clear—a village at the foot of a hill with a castle on the top—but this space continuously contracts and transmogrifies: roads, like one leading to the castle, arbitrarily emerge, veer, and vanish, and the village houses fail to establish legible spatial coordinates. The reiterated ambiguity of these paths makes the Castle simultaneously distinct from the village-town and integrally related to it, an impression reinforced by Kafka's description of the Castle as "a rather miserable little town" (*Castle* 8). The circuitous paths also multiply the images/functions of the Castle as a tower, a castle, a private residence, and, as later revealed, an administrative seat:

> The tower up here—it was the only one in sight—the tower of a residence, as now became evident, possibly of the main Castle, was a monotonous round building, in part mercifully hidden by ivy, with little windows that glinted in the sun—there was something crazy about this—and ending in a kind of terrace, whose battlements, uncertain, irregular, brittle, as if drawn by the anxious or careless hand of a child, zigzagged into the blue sky. (*Castle* 8)

Many have reasonably assumed that the writer modeled this projected chronotope on Old Prague and the castle that he observed on an everyday basis; at the same time, it is only fair to admit that such direct parallels between the material world and Kafka's fiction are more serviceable in tourist guide books than in Kafka criticism. Curiously, though, the interpenetration between Kafka's castle and its surroundings, the multi-functionality of the building itself, and the unusual blend of the monolithic and the irregular that one reads in the above description of it all do correspond to the specific architectural and political context in which Prague Castle found itself in the 1920s. Soon after coming to power, Masaryk hired

Slovenian architect Josip Plečnik to reconstruct and redesign the decaying castle and the surrounding area (Hradčany), which now hosted both the presidential seat and his private residence. Plečnik started his work on the castle and the environments in 1920—the time of Kafka's early drafts of *The Castle*—and, although the president's and the Castle architect's statements of intent, drafts, blueprints and requests for permission were circulating in Prague between 1920 and 1922 (and were subject to much public debate and bureaucratic obstacles), it was only in the summer of 1922—at the closing peak of Kafka's work on the novel—that the scope and nature of the project became visible to the public.[17] It is then that the work on, initially, the First Courtyard began, and Plečnik's unique architectural vocabulary, characterized by insouciant eclecticism of neoclassical and preclassical styles, use of excursional elements such as terraces and steps, incongruent placement of monuments, asymmetry, and openness began to transform the once monotonous, monolithic structure. Masaryk's professed intention was "to reconstruct Prague Castle, a purely monarchical structure, as a democratic building," where the division between the castle and the town would attenuate in urban continuity (quoted in Jelavich 262). Yet, according to his private correspondence, he and his main confidante, his daughter Alice Masaryková, also envisioned a more spiritual function for the building; as reported by Masaryková, the castle was additionally to become a "sacred acropolis," a structure that would connect the political, earthly, and the eternal, spiritual ("City of God"), outside the reified practices and nomenclature of the Catholic Church.[18] Masaryk could not find a better suited architect for such a complex, interiorly divided vision than Plečnik, whose interventions on the castle from 1920 to 1935 spurred much public discussion about the new nation's identity and the relationship between the seat of power and people. While, to the extent that I know, nothing has been documented to suggest that this monumental project exerted a direct influence on Kafka's late fiction, the political and architectural context and public debates described here could indeed be related to some strategic decisions about the description and operation of the Castle in Kafka's last novel. If inconclusive and indirect, such an association is nevertheless useful, as it illuminates the specific way in which the material world appears in Kafka's text: neither as a verisimilarly represented set of objects nor as a direct symbolic parallel, but summarized, or synthesized, in an anthropological conundrum.

Comparably to Plečnik's redesign of Prague Castle, Kafka's novel layers temporal planes in a clashing yet eventually harmonized continuity. The feudal setting of Kafka's novel may connote medieval societal relations, but the low level of religious practice equally implies more modern or more ancient times (Dowden 60). And, whereas Kafka's narration is mostly confined to the past tense (except when an

odd present tense points to the presence of a narrator whose focalization is different from that of the protagonist) and it is propelled by a desire that, as desires go,
addresses itself to the future, there is actually little or no sense of the past or the
future in the novel. Rather, the world of Kafka's *The Castle* is a cognate of Rilke's
project to render the past and the not-yet as "the present to the ultimate degree"
(*Gesammelte Briefe* V: 292). Confined in an accentuated present-configured-as-
past (or past-configured-as-present?), Kafka's undifferentiated time-space corresponds closely to the way in which temporality is experienced in melancholia.
Startlingly, however, this containment of the narrative time is breached by the
apparent historicity of some objects thrown into this ahistorical present. Indices of
urban modernity randomly punctuate the narrative, suggesting the chronotope of
a secluded time-space in the midst of modern life: a few photographs, a telephone,
an "automated phonogram" and, finally, the electric lights—a mordant displacement of the divine light and an incursion of material history in the isolated village community. The incongruous modernity of these objects indicates that the
conflict between our experience of time as a collective singular and the need to
distinguish between the past, the present, and the future—what Ricoeur called the
aporia of the time of history—is the organizing concern of Kafka's text.

If this is true, then Kafka's novel provides a uniquely melancholic response to the
paradox of the time of history. Challenging linearity of the passage of time, Kafka's
narrative eventfully swells and folds unto itself, and, much like Klee's *Angelus Novus*
in Benjamin's reading, becomes a condition, or a state—a "catastrophe in permanence." Walter Benjamin has found an affective correlative to this state in spleen
(*SW* IV: 164), the specifically modern modus of melancholia in which, Pensky suggested, "the subject can no longer mournfully 'observe' the permanent catastrophe
of natural history, but rather, in a quite literal sense, *is* this catastrophe" (170). The
status of Kafka's text is comparable. Kafka substitutes the concept (and narrative
figuration) of history as a succession of events with what Agamben once described
as "the paradoxical image of a *state of history*" [Benjaminean *Standrecht*—SB],
a state "in which the fundamental event of the human condition is perpetually
taking place" (*The Man without Content* 113; emphasis Agamben's). In *The Castle*
the strategies of spatial-temporal containment transform the chronotope of the
village into one such state of history—abstracted, ritualistically conditioned and
thus made adequate for Kafka's melancholic probing of human action. Within this
chronotope, history is symbolically focused through the continuous happening of
one specific event that both stands in for and is fundamental aspect of the human
condition, and perhaps, also its ultimate catastrophe. I am referring here to the
melancholic organization of Kafka's text as a narration of *eternal dying*.

Commenting on the fateful self-containment of Wagner's music in a 1963 lecture, Adorno associated the "catastrophe in permanence" with myth, and with myth's tendency to reprise ("Wagner's Relevance..." 599). For the same reasons Kafka's fictional world has frequently been described as mythological. Although Kafka's use of myth is unsystematic, inconsistent, and based on the condensation of dream-work rather than the epic or fantastic elaboration appropriate to myth, the structure of his fictional world is paradigmatically mythic. It eschews recognizable spatio-temporal specifiers, and characteristically brings together two domains, or two modes of being (natural and supernatural), fusing them into a hybrid semantic whole where repetition rules.[19] One aspect of this mythic framework deserves special attention in the context of present inquiry. As readings of the novel attentive to its mythic components frequently emphasize, Kafka's *The Castle* repeatedly invokes death or symbolic equivalents for death.[20] The novel's dark and cold winter setting supports such emphatic invocation. In the village, Pepi informs K., winter is "long" and "monotonous," and while spring and summer do come, "in one's memory [they] seem so short, as if they didn't last much longer than two days, and sometimes even on those days [...] snow falls" (*Castle* 312). This perpetual winter shapes the text as the site of death, an adequate figuration for what Kay Jamison argued to be the obsession with the theme of death in the depressive phase of manic-depressive disorder (127). The eternal winter is also a uniquely appropriate setting for the stalled movement of Kafka's novel itself. This slow-paced series, I propose, gestures rather a prolongation of dying than the death itself. The novel unfolds through the same state of "eternal dying" that Kafka artistically examines in the story "The Hunter Gracchus;" it is the state that he links to creative activity in the diary entry of August 6, 1914, and to the eternal "singing of one's last song" in a 1922 letter to Jesenská (*Letters to Milena* 209).

I am aware of the charged legacy of the above claim. My use of the concept of "eternal dying" in reference to Kafka's work benefits, but also markedly differs, from several previous assessments of the issue, most influential among which are Maurice Blanchot's and Theodor Adorno's respective meditations on Kafka. Each of the last two inscribed his own philosophy in Kafka's text, and did so with substantial poetic force. Blanchot's exploration of the experience of "impossibility of dying" (an impossibility of all possibilities) focuses on the act of writing as dying and the artwork as deathlike inscription of limits, both of which he reads in Kafka's "The Hunter Gracchus."[21] At the center of Blanchot's cogitations is the relationship between duration and symbolic closures, and it is at this point that his interpretation could be complemented by the anthropological-psychoanalytic perspective that I introduce below. The same pertains to Adorno's retrospective interpretation of Kafka's fiction in the light of the Third Reich, where the "inability to die" of Kafka's characters like K. of *The Castle* or the hunter Gracchus is associated with a zone of concentration camps, "inhabited by living skeletons and putrefying bodies, victims unable to take their own lives" (*Prisms* 260), those who are destined to die not as individuals but as specimens.[22] Insisting that such a zone extends beyond the confines of time-place of concentration camps, Adorno perceives Kafka's characters as embodiments of the anguish provoked by banishment from the world of the possibility "to die after a long and full life" (*Prisms* 260); his interpretation controversially (if not without precedents) imparts a prophetic status to Kafka's fiction, and, while seeming to contextualize it historically, effectively relativizes its specific contexts and textual strategies. This reading is at once concordant with and opposed to my revaluing of this limbo-zone as the site of "countermourning" enactment of possibilities (an activity that in itself harbors potential for agency) and my identification of the general melancholic affect that shapes Kafka's text. Without lingering on the merits and shortcomings of Adorno's use of Kafka, though, let me note what is most valuable in it for my present purposes: Adorno's forced hermeneutic bridge affirms the activity of reading as an act of ethical intervention. I should like to retain the right to engage the readerly powers invoked by both Adorno and Blanchot—as well as the text's efforts to resists them—without having recourse to an over-extension, or over-amplification, of interpretation. My reading of *The Castle* is at once more specific (text-bound) and more modest (text-and-context informed) in its claims. And so I would like to start with specificities: what exactly makes Kafka's *The Castle* into a narrative of eternal dying?

In the course of the novel as it has come down to us, K. spends six to seven days in the village, yet there is no diegetic indication that the protagonist's stay in the village would actually come to an end. To underscore that the novel thematizes eternal dying—rather than a temporary or phase-bound visit to the underworld, which the Homeric undertones might suggest—Kafka repeatedly uses the attributes denoting perpetuality, most frequently when describing K. or the form and purpose of K.'s dealings in the village. In his first telephone conversation with the Castle, for example, K. is addressed as "the eternal land surveyor" (*Castle* 21; "*der ewige Landvermesser*," *Schloß* 31, perhaps also alluding to the expression "*der ewige Jude*," the Wandering Jew). K. does not need much to be persuaded that this is indeed an appropriate description of his pursuit. Like the hunter Gracchus, he starts referring to his plight as an "endless journey" (59), a turn of phrase determined by the time-honored association of the metaphor of journey with the passage to death. One may find an early action-image for this eternal journey, and the novel's chronotope of eternal dying, in the description of K.'s failed attempt to reach the Castle on the sleight of Gerstäcker, a coachman whose name, Richard Sheppard has noticed, invokes the German word for graveyard, "*Gottesacker*" (*On Kafka's Castle* 105). The sleigh drive, which leads K. back to the inn rather than to the Castle, is slow, monotonous, and punctuated by the coachman's coughing; it lasts the whole day but feels like a few minutes (16). The only memorable event that happens during this long drive is the sudden tolling of bells:

> The Castle [...] receded again. Yet as though he still had to be given a cue for this temporary parting, a bell up there rang out cheerfully, a bell that for a moment at least made one's heart tremble as if it were threatened—for the sound was painful too—with the fulfillment of its uncertain longings. Yet this large bell fell silent and was followed by a faint, monotonous little bell, perhaps still from up there, though perhaps already from the village. This tinkling was better suited to this slow journey and this wretched but implacable coachman. (15)

In the context of the first chapter, "Arrival," whose purpose is to demarcate the time-space of the novel as the time-space of death, the sound of the tolling bells confirms K.'s entrance in the realm of the dead. But one should not overlook the distinction between the two bells: the large bell of the Castle and the small bell whose sound comes—Kafka is keen on keeping temporal and spatial ambiguity alive—"perhaps still [*noch*] from up there, perhaps already [*aber schon*] from the village." It is not difficult to recognize in the sonorous sound of the Castle bell the tremble intimating the cessation of life—one's heart trembling because it *is* threatened—or the bell tolling announcing a burying ritual. As soon confirmed in the parallel between K.'s struggle to gain entry to the Castle and his childhood efforts to climb the churchyard wall and enter the graveyard (28-29), to aspire to reach the Castle means to desire death. Accordingly, the realms of desire and death are bound together in Kafka's description of the Castle bell and we are presented with two options for how to relate to this death-desiring sound: through the affect of cheerfulness or that of pain.

The novel itself is replete with the symbolic associations of the decaying Castle and death, the most productive of which is the index-image of "ivy" that "mercifully" hides part of the crumbling Castle (8). Kafka scholars have customarily interpreted this image within the Christian subtext of the novel, glossing it as a representation of humanity's need for divine support. But the special value of the index-image of ivy, whose symbolic use could be traced to Egyptian, Greco-Roman, and Christian texts, lies in the fact that, taken by itself, it already summons opposite meanings—eternal life and death/mortality. This ambiguity is important since it reminds us, on the one hand, that the opposition between the town and the Castle may be rather a matter of gradation than distinction, and, on the other hand, that symbols in Kafka, like ivy, "cling" to the signified (here, the Castle) rather than completely hide it or represent it. One way to resolve such ambivalences may be to read the "symbol" of ivy as a passage to death, a passage that may involve dealing with infinities; and, alongside, to insist on the interpretation of the Castle as a *humanly* produced symbol "sounding" such passage—an effect of language and a coalescing point for affects whose nature as projection-artifice is quintessential to the text. This expansion of interpretative framework leads me to the question that I have been postponing for some time: if, as so many narrative indicators suggest, the whole narrative unfolds in the time-space of death, how can the protagonist be already dead and still melancholically desire death?

In the economy of the novel, the resonant death announced by the Castle bell comes second: it is supposed to succeed a "temporary" or "small" or "provisional" death (a "pre-death") with which the novel begins, but it has not come as yet (and will not come in the novel as we know it). The tinkling of the other bell, one that "perhaps already" belongs to the village, is actually "better suited to this slow journey and to this wretched but implacable coachman" (15). (Not insignificantly, Kafka abandons the hypothetical form here; the literal translation of *"paßte freilich besser zu der langsamen Fahrt"* would be: this tingling "was of course better suited to this slow journey"; *Schloß* 26.) So, whatever meaning one ascribes to K.'s journey and his dealings in the village—that is to say, to the novel as such, insofar as the entire novel could be said to be contained in this image of "slow journey" constantly revisiting the same space in the pursuit of potential destinies—that meaning must be linked to the sound of the little bell. This sound is faint and monotonous, and there is no indication that it ever stops: while the large bell falls silent, the tinkling of the little bell may well follow K. throughout his stay in the village. The sound of this little bell, finally, is specifically related to Gerstäcker. This "wretched but implacable coachman" is the first person to inform the land surveyor that, while he may belong to the Castle, he cannot go directly to the Castle—or to the bell of the Castle—but has to take a detour of uncertain duration through the village itself (14-15). And if there is a promise that K. would ever reach the final bell of the Castle, it also abides with this ghostly coachman: a visit to Gerstäcker's cottage closes the novel as it has come down to us. On this reading, then, the Castle symbolically operates as the "fulfillment" of death, or as the "carrier" of the final death—resonant, ritualistic, perhaps resurrective; the end of narration. (It is due to Kafka's extraordinary skill in making us constantly aware that this symbolic carrier is simultaneously a human artifice that we intimate, from the very first pages, the lack of such resolution and the absence of the end.) But the village presents the text itself: a tormented, monotonous, perhaps eternal, state of preparation for the final event; an interval between the two "deaths".

The diegetic world of Kafka's *The Castle* is presided by a linguistic-symbolic epitome of this existence in between the two deaths: the ambiguous name/character of the lord of the Castle, Graf Westwest. The name "Westwest," commentators have suggested, is semantically linked to decline ("west" is where the sun sets; the German verb "*verwesen*" means "to decompose" or "to decay"); but "Westwest," as Richard Sheppard has noted, is also evocative of the noun "Wesen"—"essence;" or the verb "wesen," to be present (*On Kafka's Castle* 197-98). The name, I would add, is a repetitive: the Graf's name, which traditionally describes his geopolitical prerogatives, is "west" and—"west." In addition to being a lever of humorous, or satiric, release ("westwest" may be seen to operate as a pun that forecloses the carrier of the symbolic investiture through a comic relief), this repetition also function as a "trace" of the death-drive, a marker of compulsive repetition that Freud linked to the hyperactivity of the death drive in melancholia. In terms of its semantics, the repetitive "westwest" at once splits the word into two discrete semantic units—"west" as "decompose/die" and "west" as "be essential/present/ alive"—and unites their meanings in an interlock. Thus this compound recreates the ambiguous scope of the symbol of ivy glossed above. As Sheppard notices, the Graf's name summons "a paradoxical possibility that the Lord of the Castle is both dead and alive, a mere man and something more, a humanly created fiction that is in the state of advanced decay and yet the bearer of a metaphysical essence" (198). In the light of my unfolding analysis, the Graf's name is emblematic of the very state in which the protagonist finds himself and which the reader is invited to observe: dead yet still alive, in between the two deaths. This liminal existence in turn overdetermines Westwest's function in the novel. While the Graf may be a symbolic holder of metaphysical power—a (possibly dead) God, or a (possibly "killed") father—he is also, and without canceling the opposite, a humanly constructed effect of language: westwest. As the latter, the Graf operates as a partly foreclosed signifier, rather a function than a traditionally understood allegorical entity. His role is to be the mythic conveyor of death in language, the "grantor" and "guarantee" of the "final" death, or—to adhere to the Castle's terminology—the payee of the symbolic debt.

Kafka, however, ensures that his protagonist's "eternal dying" does not conceptually dwindle or affectively dissolve under this linguistic perspective. To this effect he introduces two further aspects of the state, both linked to the anthropology of rites of passage: the communal isolation of the protagonist (or the dying one) and his own inability to "understand" his death. In chapter 1 I have suggested that Phillipe Ariès's theory of the "invisible death" may further our understanding of modernist "countermourning." Ariès claims that the traditional attitude toward death (the so-called "tame death," characterized by the dying person's spontaneous awareness of the hour of her/his death and by the participation of community in the passage to death) was replaced in urban modernity by a practice and affective posture that he terms the "invisible death." By this phrase, Ariès signals the compound effects of privatizing, medicalizing, and bureaucratizing the event of death, which deprive one of the physical premonitions of death and remove from community the responsibility for the care of the dying. All this eventuates in a denial of death and diminishment of its legibility, for both the dying person and society. Its major social manifestation and consequence is the waning of mourning rituals. K.'s eternal and confused dying and his isolation from the community (which, to express its own perplexity, is alternatively welcoming and rejecting) dramatize precisely this modern attitude toward death. The villagers segregate K. because they cannot understand his intentions, and K. himself, indefatigable as he may be in his heuristic attempts, repeatedly misinterprets the signs around him, above all, those coming from the Castle itself. The bureaucratic conundrums of the Castle officialdom represent adequately the vicissitudes of modern death—medicalized, over-documented, deprived of actual communal functions and representative public rites, and, thus, incomprehensible. And Gerstäcker, an impassive but unrelenting "assistant" on K.'s endless journey, seems to possess no more means to bring about a public burial/"final death" than other characters.

Viewed from this anthropological perspective, Kafka appears to have shaped his protagonist as a paradigmatic limbo figure. K. is forever caught in what would normally be a transitional phase of unattachment to society, a phase that, according to Robert Hertz and Arnold van Gennep, respectively, is followed in traditional societies by symbolic confirmation of the deceased, a kind of "secondary burial" (see chapter 1 of the present book). The anthropological function of this ritual is to enable the deceased's return to, and remaining in, community, in the form of a memorable presence. The burial ritual grants the final *recognition* to the deceased person and provides him or her with the "second" home. Significantly, K.'s attainment of "final death" is consequential upon the performance of just such rite of investiture—the issuing of a confirmation that K. indeed belongs to the Castle and, by extension, to the community over which the Castle presides. These categories could also be translated into those engaged in a psychoanalytic theory of mourning profoundly consanguineous with this anthropological landscape: Jacques

Lacan's hypothesis about the two "deaths" of the subject, a physical and a symbolic one (Lacan 270-87). In Lacanian terms, K. is condemned to abide unendingly in the interval-space between the two deaths because he has not been paid (and he has not paid) the desired "symbolic debt:" the performance of symbolic rites.

That the dying/deceased enters the symbolic realm through one such ritual is also of ultimate importance for society itself, anthropologists and Lacan agree. The community's presence at death, burial, and performance of mourning rites serve to unite the society's "liminal" members (the deceased, the mourning ones) and the rest of community after a period of crisis. For this reason, the cohesion and functioning of community depends upon the symbolic act of burying/mourning the dead. Indicatively, however, K. is not the only one confined to the state of perpetual dying in the novel. The winter is everlasting for the villagers, too, and they all seem to abide in the same time-space of eternal dying. Yet, one may sense a relational distinction within this chronotope. If the villagers—save for the Barnabas family—have given up the possibility of entering the Castle, they seem not to have entirely abandoned the hope that one of them (or someone who comes along) will attain the "proper" death and thereby reconstitute the dysfunctional community, in the way the resolution of a "social drama" always does. On this reading, the messianic function of the surveyor, so frequently discussed by scholars, resides in his potential to reintegrate the village community. His mythic-ontological role is therefore linked to an attempt to resolve what both Benjamin and Simmel perceived as a quintessentially modern type of melancholia, one resulting from the social disintegration of community and the corollary decline of mourning practices (see chapter 1). Yet it is telling that this resolution never comes into being and that the villagers, themselves alienated from the experience of the "final" death, remain more suspicious than hopeful of K.'s attempts. For it is the villagers themselves—the destabilization of descriptive and topographical borders between the Castle and the village suggests—who should partake in, indeed perform, the symbolic rites necessary for the attainment of the "final death."

Interestingly, Kafka allegedly planned an ending for the novel that would grant the protagonist a "final," "symbolic" death. In the Afterword to the first edition of *The Castle*, Brod relates that Kafka once presented him with a possible conclusion of the novel. On his deathbed and surrounded by villagers, K. would receive the final equivocal message from the Castle; by this message, he would be denied the right to live in the village, yet simultaneously be permitted to stay in the village, or remain in community, owing to some unspecified circumstances (Brod, "Nachwort," 481-482). The intended end, with the villagers around K.'s deathbed and K.'s final admission into the community (with a simultaneous prohibition to *live* there), mimics the situation of the traditional, "tame death," as described by Ariès. Dying, Ariès argues, used to be a public ceremony: "[t]he dying man's bed-chamber [was] a public place to be entered freely [...] It was essential that parents, friends, and neighbours be present. Children were brought in..." (*Western Attitudes toward Death* 12). It is tempting to envision the end of *The Castle* as promoting one such powerful, if guarded, reintegration of community, a healing of the wounds that the melancholic split of experience afflicted on the modern subject. Still, one doubts that such ending would have made this piece of fiction into a superior novel. In the case of Kafka's *The Castle* the reader faces the curious situation in which the (perhaps accidental, perhaps forced, perhaps deliberate) unfinishedness of the text is also a perfect state-of-the text correlative for the inner logic of the novel itself. It is rather probable, I am inclined to think, that the writer preferred to let the novel hover in that time-space that succeeds "death" and precedes burial/symbolic death, thereby leaving unanswered the questions of reconstitution of society and reestablishment of the links between the individual and community. The chronotopic and symbolic suspension in the interval space of not-mourning (or before-mourning), which is readable in *The Castle* now, is both more convincing and sociologically profound.

According to anthropologist Victor Turner, the transitional phase in the negotiation of a crisis in society (such as dying) is of special relevance for the functioning of society: it is in this liminal phase that a conflict or societal crisis is made public and certain redressive mechanisms—from informal or juridical mediation to the initiation of performance of a public ritual (such as literary text)—are brought into operation to limit the spread of the crisis (38-39). Viewed from this perspective, the diegetic function of K.'s obstinate presence in the village is not so much to generate a crisis as to bring to the fore—time and again—already existing crises in community; his role is indeed that of a re-assessor (*vermesser*). This is also a good context for Kafka's novel as a whole. The text finds itself in the position of a deliberately imperfect redressing: it both initiates a writing-mourning rite and questions its validity, or effectuality, by suspending the actual performance of mourning rites. I have mentioned that the chronotope and the symbolic plane of the text, which concern the time-space between the two deaths, or a prolonged moment in which a mourning rite has been initiated but has not been completed, correspond, to a surprising degree, to Kafka's decision to arrest the text in the moment of its making; the novel thus appears to be a "countermonument" both interiorly and in the context of its production history. Without overestimating the importance of this coincidence, I remind the reader of the critical point: if everyone in Kafka's novel remains in the state of perpetual dying, the only person left to perform the mourning rites is the author himself. The author, then, is that invisible, liminal member of society, the (counter)mourning one, who simultaneously pays the symbolic debt to the lost and the dying through the only means of "struggle" he has at his disposal—writing—and withdraws his symbolic support in what he might perceive as a gesture of loyalty to the lost objects. With this positionality in mind, the question, "how Kafka countermourns," becomes the question, "how Kafka writes."

"Undoubtedly these were contradictions, so obvious they must be intentional"

One of the most fascinating properties of Kafka's prose is its capacity to uphold both hope and despair.[23] "Few texts are more somber" than Kafka's fiction, Blanchot notes, "yet even those [texts by Kafka] whose outcome is without hope remain ready to be reversed to express an ultimate possibility, an unknown triumph, the shining forth of an unrealizable claim" (7). Kafka's embrace of despair as category paradoxically filled with possibilities has reminded many of Kierkegaard, the thinker whose various writings Kafka knew well, with whom he felt a particular affinity—a kinship of spirit that the writer attributed to "melancholia" that he believed they shared—and from whom, for that very reason, he sometimes obsessively sought to dissociate himself.[24] Max Brod has claimed that reading Kierkegaard's *Fear and Trembling* supplied Kafka with the notion of "incommensurability between the realms of the human and the divine," an insight that morphed into the Sortini episode in *The Castle* ("Nachwort" 488). Scholars have revisited and contested Brod's interpretation (Kafka himself frequently challenged Brod's own reading of Kierkegaard), but some correspondence of thought between Kierkegaard and Kafka has never been doubted. The paradoxical behavior of Kafka's characters has been the most frequent point of entry for such inquiries.[25]

I would like to suggest here a complementary and, in the context of my discussion of modernism and melancholia, more productive way to correlate the two. What Kafka may have "learnt" from Kierkegaard is, first, the ambivalent potential of the melancholic symptom to be both an indication of illness and its very "cure" (According to Kierkegaard, the exacerbation of the subject's individual feeling of despair is necessary for battling the general state of despair.). Secondly and perhaps more importantly, Kafka was attracted by the poetics of Kierkegaard's text, and the implied assumption that, in order to be meaningful, an assessment of modern(ist) melancholia must be performative. His extensive reading of Kierkegaard may have furnished Kafka with an aesthetic insight: that the fragmented experience of the modern melancholic subject could sometimes be articulated more adequately through the structural inflection of inquiry than through the discursive weighing up of that experience.[26] And he effectively adopted a few discursive strategies for representing melancholia from Kierkegaard. These include the presentation of epistemological instability in language through the shift of arguments and bi-focalism ("*Doppelreflexion*"), fragmentation and defamiliarized partitioning of the narrative, textual and extra-textual devices that blur or question authorial power such as pseudonyms, eponyms, and other methods of epistemological distancing, and the use of humor and parody to vocalize the dual potential of despair.

It is the pervasive use of these Kierkegaardian strategies of melancholic performance that contrasts Kafka's *The Castle* to the previous aesthetic treatments of melancholia. Instead of providing us with a typology, or representation of melancholia in the behavior of an elect character (such as, for example, Hamlet's neurotic language), Kafka, gesturing toward Kierkegaard's vision of universal melancholic state, offers a world in which everyone suffers from the melancholic symptom of linguistic-epistemological impasse. The melancholic speech unites ages, genders, and societal positions in *The Castle*, since Kafka is disinterested in distinguishing between them: the child Hans's or the barmaid Pepi's speech acts are not structurally different from K.'s own musing, which, in turn, is not unlike the semantically ambivalent speech of the officials. The same ambiguity pertains to the rhythmic organization of transactions between the characters, which manifests itself as an unpredictable mixture of lengthy monologues and swift dialogic exchanges. As readable from these exchanges, the relations between the characters are equally subject to ambivalence; for one, the reader is never certain if K. loves Frieda or he clings to her because of her supposed former relation to Klamm.

This state of affairs is appositely summarized in Olga's metatextual remark about interpreting Amalia's speech: "It isn't easy to understand exactly what she is saying, for one doesn't know whether she is speaking ironically or seriously, it's mostly serious, but sounds ironic" (*Castle* 205). The same could be said about the novel as a whole. Operating through a broad conflation of genres and modes, the text activates two disparate enunciative modes, the comic/ironic and the tragic, each one necessitating a different approach to interpretation. The generic ambivalence of the text supports an unruly interaction of signifying systems, which problematizes the relationship between story and history: Kafka's "village tale" can be read as a religious allegory, a classical myth, a Gothic romance, or a social-political satire. Such hybridization of modes and genres, I have argued in chapter 1, presents a paradigmatic modernist strategy of "melancholizing" the text: it is a narrative exteriorization of the melancholic's difficulty in recognizing the genre, tone, and context of the utterance. But, since modal and generic indecisiveness is also a conspicuous feature of Woolf's *Between the Acts*, I will return to this problematic in the next chapter at greater length. Here, suffice it to point out that, rather than (solely) generating "melancholic types" or "melancholic situations," melancholia now affects the very form of Kafka's text.

This melancholic reconfiguration of narration is sensed first in the markedly slow and repetitious "pace" of the novel. Interestingly, the stupor that subtends the narrative of *The Castle* and relays the "sensation of dying" so frequently described by melancholic patients, results in part from Kafka's writerly routine: as the editors of the 1982 Critical Edition of the novel have established, Kafka wrote *The Castle* without a preliminary outline, simply by accumulating episodes (Pasley, "Nachbemerkung," *Schloß* 387). Still, it is worth remembering that the episodic structure is also another aspect of Božena Němcová's *The Grandmother* that may have attracted Kafka and contributed to the figuration of *The Castle* as a counter-mourning text. Comparably to *The Grandmother*, Kafka's novel unfolds through narrative variations on the same or similar theme, or alternative responses to the stated thematic problem, until this recording of gestural possibilities is broken, abruptly and mechanically, when the story-telling exhausts itself. Yet, unlike Němcová's text, which, however irreverently, still serves the template of *Bildungsroman* (the registering of actantial alternatives in *The Grandmother* somehow does help both the heroine's affective transition into maturity and the gradual establishment of the reader's rapport with the protagonist), the episodes in Kafka's *The Castle* effect little or no change in the protagonist's status and stimulate little or no affective development either on the diegetic level or on the plane of the reader's engagement with the text.[27] This stalled sequencing is a modernist response to the *Bildungsroman* pattern: Kafka's text depends less on a metonymic chaining than on filamentary substitution, on the workings of what Fredric Jameson described as "a machine for producing logical permutations"—an assiduous but neutral registering of the actantial possibilities imaginable in the situation at hand (99).[28] The stationary nature of this sequencing finds a manifestation in the diegetic world in K.'s constant difficulties in getting from one place to another and the persistent challenging of semantic categories related to movement in the novel. To help this game of repetition and substitution, there is an alienating tone of litany, audible in enumerable lethargic monologues, ranging from Hans's convoluted self-narrations to Olga's recounting of the Sortini affair. The meager expressive variation and scant punctuation of all this verbiage "tires out" the reader, much in the way in which the analyst becomes "exhausted" by the melancholic's litanies. The effect is pertinent, since *The Castle* is very much a novel about waiting, exhaustion, and the impossibility of moving, whether physically, socially, or psychologically. If storytelling is life-giving for both Němcová and Kafka, in Kafka's fiction it is also the formal correlative of an affective impasse, of the eternal torments of dying.

In this largely immoveable and solipsistic narrative space, some things, however, do move: the narrative progresses (for all the seeming repetitiveness of narrative actions) and the narrative perspective shifts (for all K.'s seeming monopolization of viewpoint).[29] This hidden mobility of perspectives and actions could be attributed to Kafka's interest in oral discourse, whose model of elocution is, pertinently, repetition-with-revision. Incidentally, it was the oral music of Czech that Kafka—who seems to have judged the success of his own fiction by the effect it had on the listeners when read aloud (Pasley, "Nachbemerkung," *Schloß* 390)—admired most in Němcová's novel. Němcová's Czech "music" ("*Sprachmusik*"), Kafka reflects, is, like Jesenská's, marked by "resolution, passion, charm, and [...] clairvoyant intelligence" (*Letters to Milena* 17). These and other affective evaluations of a language that was, for Kafka, both intimate and distant, "homely" and "foreign," appear frequently in his correspondence in the early 1920s (see, for one example, Kafka's probing of muscularity of Czech consonants and tonalities in a letter to Jesenská; *Letters to Milena* 21). Kafka's renewed interest in the tonal and articulatory properties of the written and oral Czech inspired, and was inspired by, his close engagement with not only Jesenská's writing but also writings by a number of young Czech authors at the time; these included, approvingly on Kafka's part, the texts by Vladislav Vančura, who was soon to become the most significant Czech modernist novelist (*Letters to Milena* 168). Thus I would venture here a suggestion that rereading Němcová's novel not only motivated Kafka's use of "oral expression" in an abstract sense of the term; for this, after all, he could have been inspired by any number of German texts; rather, Kafka may well have conceived of this transfer of oral style as a *translation* from a Slavic into a Germanic language. He may have posed it as an interlingual challenge to himself: how to translate the sustained intimacy yet anti-sentimentality of Němcová's Czech (or Jesenská's, or Vančura's more contemporary Czech) into a different but consanguineous orality of another language coexisting in the area.[30] As his letters to Jesenská repeatedly confirm, Kafka understood this affective translation activity—where one translates not so much words or sounds as rhythms and affects related to those sounds—as interpersonal "sharing," communal or individual (see *Letters to Milena* 24-35). The oral discourse of Kafka's *The Castle* presents itself as just such "embodied" communing in language: a record of an unrecorded inter-communal history.

This heteroglot discourse drives the *Castle*-narrative forward in the manner of a self-generative dialogue, where each speech act necessitates its elaboration in the guise of another speech act. But this fluid stream of recitations is warped by, indeed shot through with, the static bureaucratic speech. The latter speech, symptomatically replete with obiter dicta, instates an opposite affective framework: a sense of a heavily recorded but alienated community, idling in a historical interregnum; or, even, the absence of community. These two discursive styles, propelling and hindering narration in equal measure, interact with Kafka's simultaneous engagement of the stylistics of the German realist novel (emphasis on precision, long sentences, naturalistic description, apparent definiteness of meaning) and distinctive properties of modernist expression (convolution, suspension of meaning, metatextuality). To separate these discursive styles on the grounds of one of them being negating (petrified, obsolete) and the other one being creative (liberating, as-yet-unrecorded) might appear easy. Yet such a facile move is, as every Kafka scholar knows, impossible: these discourses can only be experienced in their uneasy interlock. This uncomfortable knitting of discourses, then, properly belongs to that series of linguistic strategies that "melancholize" Kafka's text. It contributes to what is one of Kafka's major accomplishments in *The Castle*: his invention of a fictional language whose epistemological qualities parallel the fixation in semantic ambiguity characteristic of the melancholic discourse.

Kafka's sophisticated strategies to suspend meaning and non-meaning in a narrative impasse might have been informed by one of the most widely experienced and recorded traits of melancholic discourse, namely, melancholics' proclivity to doubt their own assertions—their truth-value and their authority—the moment they are uttered. As if to approximate this melancholic semantics, Kafka infuses the narrative in *The Castle* with half-assertions, contrary promptings, concessions to a different point of view, renewed assertions, checked sequences, and other syntactic and dialogical patterns that communicate epistemological suspension. One may find their extensive use in the tale of the Sortini affair. In the course of telling and listening to this story, which spans five chapters, the picture of the affair continuously changes. Olga's and K.'s perspectives on the event shift and morph, always contradicting the assertions and conclusions reached previously: Amalia's refusal to respond to Sortini's lascivious offer is first seen by both as "heroic" (*Castle* 194), but then Olga sheds a negative light on the affair (197) and K. is led to describe it as "odd" (198); finally, K. has to admit that it is hard "to decide whether [the deed] was great or small, clever or foolish, heroic or cowardly" (198). This exchange gives a microscopic image of the operation of the text as a whole. To each and every proposition, a contrary meaning, or even a whole epistemological paradigm, could be adjoined in the novel's interrogation of possible interpretations. This comically dispirited heuristics culminates in the indescribability of Klamm and the fundamental undecidability of his very existence in the "mixture of sightings, rumors, and distorting ulterior motives." People say that Klamm looks "completely different when he comes into the village and different when he leaves," and that he is "different before he has had a beer, different afterwards, different awake, different asleep, different alone, different in conversation, and, quite understandably after all this, almost utterly different up there at the Castle" (176). No wonder, then, that Barnabas and Olga ponder the existence and location of the Castle itself: "[Barnabas] certainly does go into the offices, but are the offices actually the Castle?" (174).

The more microscopic look one takes the more palpable these interpretative impossibilities become. In an early episode in the novel, the chairman, having exasperated K. with his explanation that he is a file error which might have been prevented if there had been stronger control and his ensuing assertion that the operating principle of the authorities is that the possibility of error is not taken into account, proceeds to explain the role of control agencies in the following way: "Are there control agencies? There are only control agencies. Of course they aren't meant to find errors, in the vulgar sense of that term, since no errors occur, and even if an error does occur, as in your case, who can finally say that it is an error." To K., nothing else is left than to cry out, "That would be something completely new" (*Castle* 65). The chairman's vaguely expansive sequence and K.'s seemingly logical but in actuality mismatched response—lackadaisical about the logic, or coherence, of words precisely because K. utters them without believing in language—are typical of the way in which Kafka simultaneously builds and destroys meaning. Such problematic concatenation, borne out of simultaneous acceptance of and anxiety about the arbitrariness of language, is also characteristic of "depressed speech" (Kristeva, *Black Sun*, 52; see, also, my discussion in chapter 2).

Thus one is not surprised to find the same semantic suspension—melancholic impossibility to decide—replicated on the micro-level of sentence. In Kafka's language, connectives and disjunctives take center stage as carriers of affect: his sentences are rife with "but," "yet," "if," "albeit" ("*aber*," "*nur*," "*ob*," "*wenn auch*"). Kafka's older contemporary, William James, insisted that such seemingly peripheral elements of sentence are quintessential for the interpretation of affect. "We ought to say a feeling of *and*, a feeling of *if*, a feeling of *but*, and a feeling of *by*," James commented in "On Some Omissions of Introspective Psychology" (1884), "quite as readily as we say a feeling of *blue*, or a feeling of *cold*" (5). It is only our inveterate habit to privilege in analysis substantive parts of a sentence (subject, predicate, attribute) that prevents us from doing so, he complained. As if fulfilling James's missive, Kafka's sentences are replete with concessionary words and phrases such as "indeed...yet" ("*zwar...aber*"), "though" ("*allerdings*"), and "it must be confessed..."/"indeed..." ("*freilich...*"). The most habitually used among the qualifiers and quantifiers of this type is "to a certain extent" ("*gewissermaßen,*" also translatable as "in a manner of speaking"). Often positioned in the middle of a sentence, this phrase endorses the sense of ineffectuality of language—as it happens when, in his inspired pseudo-officialese in which every other sentence begins with a "but," Bürgel reveals to K. that, "however, there are, it must be confessed, some opportunities that are, in a manner of speaking, too grand to be acted upon" ("*Nur gibt es freilich Gelegenheiten, die gewissermaßen zu groß sind, um benützt zu werden;*" *Schloß* 327; my translation; the possibility of understanding and translating this phrase in a more strictly quantifying sense yields equally ludicrous results where the emphasis is placed on quantifying rather than qualifying precision: the opportunities are, then, "to a certain extent too grand to be acted upon"). Used for both somber and comic effects, such discursive whirlpools are, however, not restricted to the parodic rendition of bureaucratic speech. Tellingly, the chairman's equivocal perusal of (possibly) Klamm's signature and Olga's doubtful musing about whether Amalia is really indifferent to Sortini, both saturated with "*zwar...aber*" and "*gewissermaßen,*" belong to the same category of utterance—one where communicative function of language fails precisely due to the surfeit of information communicated. Ubiquity renders this type of utterance emblematic: "indeed...yet" and "to a certain extent/in a manner of speaking" become the mode in which the story and history unfold in Kafka's *The Castle.*

Ronald Gray concludes, somewhat harshly, that "writing like this cannot be defended on the grounds that the novel recounts a dream, or that the need for indeterminacy dictates it," but should be understood "on the grounds that Kafka himself did not wish it to be published, had not revised it and thought (however ambiguously) that it deserved only to be burned" (66). While Gray acknowledges that the repetition of phrases like "*zwar...aber*" "as no serious writer could allow himself" (67) is "characteristic of neurotic hesitation" (65), he overlooks the possibility that this neurotic reiteration may present a deliberate narrative stratagem. Kafka's introduction of concessionary or contradictory phrases in a seemingly coherent sequencing is, however, unmistakably strategic. These words serve precisely to reveal the implied coherence as false. Rather than bespeaking the writer's artistic inadequacy or his own mood disorder, these phrases foreground his conscious attempt to render in textual form a kind of linguistic disturbance commonly found in melancholia. It is, then, more than probable that Kafka, who argued in 1920 that "the therapeutic part of psychoanalysis [is] a helpless mistake" (*Letters to Milena* 216), embraced the "symptomatizing" of expression as an artistic opportunity. Like his "hunger artist," whose very performance depends on the melancholic refusal of nourishment ("A Hunger Artist," 1922), Kafka stages melancholia in language as a premeditated social-artistic stance. In this context, then, his installment of semantic ambiguity as a vital component of literary language is best described as a countermourning narrative strategy: Kafka performs a mourning rite (writing) but insists on its symptomatic impediments, and thereby preserves, in language itself, the painful workings of the lost object. How much aware of the social-political potential of such artistic practice Kafka might have been is likely to remain a mystery. Yet the most startling "side-effect" of Kafka's melancholized language is its palpable value as a societal critique, as a questioning of institutions and "rites of investiture," and of language's own capacity to capture and record these societal performatives.

Kafka on the Way to Home/Writing

The narrative strategies discussed above instate a sense of linguistic mystery, a maneuver that Kafka described as making everything sound "a bit uncanny" ("*ein wenig unheimlich*"; *Das Schloß: Apparatband* 275; see, also, Harman). Kafka had good reasons to use the word "*unheimlich*" to illustrate the enigmatic tone of *The Castle*, since everything in the novel subsists as at once "homely" (intimate) and "unhomely" (strange), just as the Freudian formula of "*unheimlich*" would have it (cf. *SE* XVII: 219-56). This attribute also helpfully gestures a more fundamental underpinning of the novel, of which the "uncanny" language, the chronotopic pursuit of "final death," and topics of assimilation and exclusion are but performative variants. This broader framework concerns the state and condition of being severed from one's "home."

That the home quest orchestrates the diverse themes and textual strategies in Kafka's *The Castle* is established early in the novel. The inaugural demarcation of the text's chronotope sees K. observing the Castle (and, possibly, its surroundings)—"a rather miserable little town"—and comparing it with his hometown. Although already invoked in my previous discussion, this comparison deserves quoting at length here:

> Fleetingly K. recalled his old hometown (*Heimatstädtchen*), it was scarcely inferior to this so-called Castle; if K. had merely wanted to visit it, all that

wandering would have been in vain, and it would have made more sense for him to visit his old homeland (*Heimat*) again, where he had not been in such a long time. And in thought he compared the church tower in his homeland with the tower up there. The church tower, tapering decisively, without hesitation, straightaway toward the top, capped by a wide roof with red tiles, was an earthly building—what else can we build?—but with a higher goal than the low jumble of houses and with a clearer expression than that of the dull workday. The tower up here—it was the only one in sight—the tower of a residence, as now became evident, possibly of the main Castle, was a monotonous round building, in part mercifully hidden by ivy, with little windows that glinted in the sun—there was something crazy about this—and ending in a kind of terrace, whose battlements, uncertain, irregular, brittle, as if drawn by the anxious or careless hand of a child, zigzagged into the blue sky. It was as if some melancholy (*trübselig*) resident,[31] who by rights ought to have kept himself locked up in the most out-of-the way room in the house, had broken into the roof and stood up in order to show himself to the world. (*Castle* 8; *Schloss* 17)

This breathless passage, difficult to exhaust in interpretation, follows the emergence of an insight about comparability of homes, old and new.[32] In the elemental world of Kafka's *The Castle*, the protagonist's putative community with his wife and child never figures as the "real" home. Rather, the affective configuration of home is reserved for the more general time-place where the chimerical fusion of the self and the world would seem to have still been possible through an extension of human labor into spiritual work—tower-building. At the same time, K., who refuses with ease Frieda's idea of emigrating abroad (*Castle* 136), perceives the Castle-village as not only the arrival point of his business trip, but also the place where he will settle for good. The Castle-village is the very completion of his life-travels; in short, a new, final, home. The opening juxtaposition of K.'s hometown and the Castle-village operates as much on the principle of similarity (hometown and the Castle-village are similar enough to be compared) as on that of dissimilarity (the church tower in K.'s hometown appears to have had "a higher goal" than the zigzagged tower in the Castle-village). If, from the first of these perspectives, the comparison inculcates the modernist insight that the end of the journey is not unlike its beginning, the other angle challenges this very supposition, asseverating that the beginning is qualitatively (spiritually) better than the end. K. introduces the existential problem attendant to this twofold vision through an agitated sentence in the subjunctive mood: if he had anticipated that he would not see anything new, or different from, his homeland, K. would have spared himself the effort of long wandering (8). The paradox of this double perspective can be easily resolved by translating, in accord with my previous argumentation, the motif of the home-journey into that of beginning, duration, and the end of life. Cast in this light, the end (new home) is indeed at once structurally similar to and qualitatively different from the beginning (old home).

But there is more to be said about these two homes and K.'s attempts to traverse the route between them, for the Castle-village not only invokes K.'s hometown but also invigorates his longing for any home or anchorage. When he first meets Barnabas and follows him in the hope that they will reach the Castle, K. finds himself in feverish reveries about his homeland. We are told that "due to sheer effort of walking [K.] could no longer control his thoughts" and thus "his homeland (*Heimat*) kept surfacing, filling him with memories" (28). One particular memory imposes itself on K.: the recollection of his success in climbing a wall around the church graveyard (few boys were able to do it, the reader is informed), an enterprise that ended in a hurt knee and scolding, after which K. "only with difficulty reached home" (*nachhause*) (29). K.'s memory of the ordeal of climbing the wall symbolically links death (the cemetery) and home (homeland and home-house). This knot finds an immediate corroboration in the diegetic present. Barnabas suddenly stops and, to K.'s surprise, starts descending. At this moment a peculiar misunderstanding is disclosed: " 'Where are we?' K. asked quietly, more to himself than to Barnabas. 'Home' (*zuhause*) said Barnabas in the same tone. 'Home?' (*zuhause*) 'Now take care, sir, that you don't slip. The path goes downhill.' 'Downhill?' " (29) K.'s discontent at being drawn into descent, instead of being elevated, when approaching the end of the journey—the Castle, death, "home"—is palpable. Yet, even bigger disappointment awaits him: Barnabas has led him to his own house. Realizing that "it was not they who were at home, only Barnabas was at home," K. concludes that the whole affair has been "a misunderstanding, a low vulgar misunderstanding" (30).

But there is no misunderstanding about the significance of the scene. The episode validates the link between the two homes, the Castle, and death, and it restates, if jocularly, an important conundrum: if K. has come to the destination of his life-journey, why does he continue to strive for the Castle/home at all? This seeming paradox may be explained, in line with what I have suggested above, as manifestation of K.'s urge to achieve the "second," symbolic death, using the rites of recognition and investiture appropriate to this goal. But in this particular episode search for home also signals a historically identifiable performance. Here, like elsewhere, the German words Kafka uses to denote "home" are either phrases *"zuhause"* and *"nachhause"* or, more frequently, the word *"Heimat"* and its derivatives. The term *"Heimat,"* whose discursive prevalence and social significance in the German-speaking communities in the early twentieth century have been widely recorded, denotes a physical and social location (one's home or native region) but it also operates as a conceptual blend through which one metonymically identifies with a locality or a social group. Socially and psychologically, an upsurge of *Heimat* discourse could be associated with the intensification of the feeling of "detachment" or alienation from one's local, or intimate, context. The paradigmatically melancholic nature of this social posture could be discerned in the customary activation of two major defense mechanisms: an emphatic engagement with the sentimental representation of the "lost" home and the zealous pursuit of a new home. Modeled on the latter template, and hosting a number of traditional features of the *Heimat* aesthetics, Kafka's *The Castle* presents itself as a text embedded in the social-ideational framework of *Heimat* discourse.[33]

This reading, however, deserves a few correctives. First, it is likely that Kafka understood the *Heimat* discourse as a framework of whose innocuousness one should be wary; the easy slippage from the adulation of home to the exclusion of the non-home is, after all, a masked target of Kafka's re-interpretation of Němcová's *Grandmother.* More importantly, as Elizabeth Boa underscores, Kafka's *The Castle* does not entirely conform to the *Heimat* mode of narration (78). In marked contrast with typical *Heimat*-narratives, yet in chorus with the modernist treatment of the theme of home, the search for home-place in *The Castle* is doubly foreclosed: K. is prevented from both returning to an old home and establishment of a new one. All K.'s attempts to found (or reclaim) a home in the village—ranging from his endeavor to find a permanent abode to his setting up of a nuclear family with Frieda—are doomed to failure. It is a lesson K. has to learn: there is no return to an archaic family/*Heimat* for a modern individual; and the desire of such return, whose coordinates are inscribed by our wish to belong or to assimilate, more often than not eventuates in manipulation.

A comparable interest in the subjecthood that anchors itself on a forlorn home-search could be identified in much modernist fiction. Kafka's unique response to the condition of transcendental homelessness, however, was to reimagine the protagonist as an effect of the fragmented, shifting subjecthood; it is an *a-self* coalesced, always only temporarily, by its goals. Walter Sokel has insightfully observed that Kafka's K. is "identical with his intention and nothing apart from that" ("Kafka und Sartres Existenzphilosophie" 271). Insofar as fictional characters tend to index depth, mental and physical intricacy, and informed social volition—or, what might be called, with more or less justification, an "identity" premeditated by the writer—K. is scarcely a narrative body. Rather, Kafka's hero is an effect of bodily drifts, or bodily momentum. K. can establish an identity only by creating it, and by treating this very activity of creating an identity as fundamental to achieving an opaque, in itself unattainable, goal: being home. It is for this reason that Kafka's narrative should also be read in the context of what Hermann Broch and, later, Charles Taylor, identified as the modernists' epiphanic quest for "unmediated unity" between the subject and the world (Broch 63-95; Taylor 471). Characteristically for the modernist negotiations of the loss of "unmediated unity," Kafka's text accommodates both longing for primordial unity and a critique of our desire to dissolve in totalizing collectivity. This contradictory affective framework corresponds well to the split experience of modernity Benjamin attributed to Kafka; to that melancholic figure of an ellipse whose "foci are determined on the one hand by mystical experience [...] and on the other by the experience of the modern citydweller" (Benjamin-Scholem 223). Thence comes the simultaneous similarity and dissimilarity of the two "homes" that K. compares in the passage discussed above, and the tandem working of the assimilation and individuation drives in the novel as a whole.

One could relate this ambivalent positionality to the psychoanalytic description of the experience of primal separation, a split that occasions the first tumultuous melancholia and is formative, Freud writes, of the ego. The attempts to revive in phantasy the primordial, or prelapsarian space, are deceptive but protective mechanisms, Freud has argued. These illusions enable the subject to deal with a loss that cannot be mourned insofar as it is already part of the dynamic existence of the ego itself. Freud allies such illusions and their regressive psycho-social constructions—the cluster that he calls "oceanic feeling"—with the protective phantasy of "an enormously exalted father" (*SE* XXI: 21). Kafka's *The Castle* conspicuously addresses itself to one such phantasy in the images of the phallically conjured Castle and the Graf Westwest, and their minute replicas in Klamm and Hans's father. Yet the projection of primordial home in Kafka's last novel actually foregrounds another space. It is the space of primal unity of the mother and the child—a stage-site that happens in the earliest childhood or, rather, never, since it presents the configuration prior to all the identified places and relations in which we have ever been—that is desirefully resuscitated in the novel's *Heimat* phantasy. For this reason, one would agree with Boa, the patriarchal world of Kafka's novel relies much on the subtending female figures of power, capable of granting (Frieda, Hans's mother) or refusing (Amalia) the dyadic nourishment (*Kafka* 243-86). The only place where K. feels "*zuhause*" and "*heimlich*" in the village is the community of Barnabas's sisters. More ambivalently, while making love to Frieda,

K. invokes the air of his "homeland" and compares it to that of these "foreign lands" (*Castle* 41), as one might juxtapose the fragrance of "mother(land)" with some other female smells. This intimate geography is revealing: underneath the veils of the paternal/symbolic significations, the dangerous excesses of which Kafka may have intimated, *Heimat* emerges as also the "*unheimlich*" space of the mother—a (psychological, political, cultural, and linguistic) site that is both "homely" and "uncanny." Projecting the ultimate fusion of the subject and the world, this maternal space, Kafka writes, is similar to yet qualitatively different from the end of the journey (8). It is only when this dynamic is translated in the terms of the finitude of psychological separation that one realizes that the return to home-space is truly impossible for K.

While the direct approach to this maternal space is precluded, home can still be approximated in phantasy, via a ritual. As it weaves a symbolic net around the gap carved by the primal separation, the literary ritual at once implicates the reader in a communal processing of the loss of unities and attests to the irrefragable division of the emancipated subject and the world. It is, perhaps, this ritual—which is both a mourning rite and a confirmation of the unfinilizability of mourning—that sheds the most rewarding light on the ambiguous treatment of *Heimat* and its suggested symbolic valences (home, death, nation, community, fatherland, and motherland) in Kafka's narrative. Constellating the literary ritual and home may help us glean an answer to the question that might have slipped from our horizon too easily: why, after all, and despite his disenchantment with where and what he is, Kafka's protagonist does *not* return to, or revive, his old homeland, but seeks a new one—a home that would be equal yet dissimilar to his old home-place. At work here, I suggest, is that faint but distinctive recuperative note that one occasionally intuits in Kafka's fiction: the prospect that, if one fathoms the negative, the latter might become the positive (Blanchot 7). For home operates in Kafka's novel not only as an irretrievably lost unity but also as *dynamei on*—what-is-(still)-possible—in the claustrophobic present. One might call this treatment of home a melancholic restoration of the new; or, simply, writing.

In a letter to Max Brod written while he was working on *The Castle* (July 12, 1922), Kafka postulates a close link between creative process and the search for an unattainable home: "And my writing? [...] I am away from home and I have to continuously write home, even if all that means home has long ago dissolved into eternity. All this writing is nothing but Robinson's flag placed on the highest point of his island" (*Briefe* 392). In these lines writing becomes a melancholic signal for an urge to return to/establish a home, or, even, the promise or sign of home itself. Activating the recuperative tendencies of the ego, creative activity, Hanna Segal has argued, presents "a re-creation of a once loved and once whole, but now lost and ruined object, a ruined internal world and self" (*Psychoanalysis, Literature, and War* 190). This re-creation generates a new condition (writing), new container for affects (a work of art), and a new communal experience (reception). It is for this reason that "writing home," even in the face of the evaporation of everything resembling home, presents an internal necessity for Kafka. If, as Freud argued, the creation of and enjoyment in the works of art is an auxiliary construction aiding us to resuscitate, illusorily and momentarily, a feeling of oneness with the world/object, it is certainly one of those necessary constructions. This is so because sublimation, a psychic and material performance that bears witness to the melancholic split, is simultaneously our main weapon in the struggle against the workings of the death drive and our only means to create home anew (*SE* XXI: 97). As Kafka's correspondence and diary indicate, the "strange, mysterious, perhaps dangerous, perhaps saving" activity of writing (*Diaries* 406) presented for him a primordial and perhaps only genuinely ethical mode of existence—"writerly being." To live this "writing home" was a matter of personal, artistic, and social responsibility for Kafka.[34]

Kafka, like many other modernists, seems to have understood what psychoanalysis also discovered at about the same time: the return to mother(land) is impossible, but precisely out of this impossibility, out of this severance, great art may emerge. This art—writing home—is created out of impossibility but oriented by what-is-possible (Kafka connoted both "home"). As such, "writing home" must capture both impossibility and possibility in the language it deploys. This language, in turn, becomes a fissure, or a cleft, signaling at once the impossible and the possible. Addressing the nature of the subdued yet persistent "hope-effect" in Kafka's fiction, Adorno correctly observes that, "if there is hope in Kafka's work, it is in those extremes [...] in the capacity to stand up to the worst by making it into language" (*Prisms* 254). Abiding at the conjunction of historical melancholia and its symbolic expression, the art created in this way appropriates the symptoms of melancholia as well as the inner sense of duty to voice it and, possibly, to move beyond it. The distinct social function of this unrelenting address to homelessness should be recognized even with writers like Kafka, whose historical solipsism has become proverbial. The paradoxical link between the "second home" and "second death" in Kafka's fictional world becomes fully meaningful only when one remembers that, anthropologically, the performance of "second death" is linked to the processing of social traumata; that its hidden purpose is the (re)integration of community. It may thus not be an overstatement to relate, conclusively, Kafka's "surrogate-home" in writing to what Ernst Bloch, a thinker who felt deep affinity with the writer, recognized as the radical potential of the awakening of the impossible into the possible on the last pages of *The Principle of Hope* (1938–1947):

> *True genesis is not at the beginning but at the end* and it starts to begin only when society and existence become radical, i.e., grasp their roots. But the root of history is the working, creating human being who reshapes and overhauls the given facts. Once he has grasped himself and established what is his [...], there arises in the world something which shines to everyone in childhood and where no one has yet been: *Heimat*.[35]

Melancholically to challenge any home-grounding and yet to keep this possibility always in sight (precisely because it grants us the gift of writing) may well have been the source impulse of Kafka's artistic project. The same belief in the capacity of writing to "invoke" or "be" home, but also, and more significantly, to "activate" home to its utopian potential, informs Virginia Woolf's last writing efforts.

4 Virginia Woolf and the Search for Historical Patterns

Between the Acts

It was in an agitated letter to Ethel Smyth, written on November 14, 1940, that Virginia Woolf (1882-1941) most directly addressed the relationship between the destructive work of history and the productive work of art:

> Another bomb in Meck Sqre; did I tell you? All the books down again. Did I tell you we half think of moving the furniture here? We brought down a car load last week. Then, to my infinite delight, they bombed our river. Cascades of water roared over the marsh—All the guls [sic] came and rode the waves at the end of the field. It was, and still is, an inland sea, of such indescribable beauty, almost always changing, day and night, sun and rain, that I cant [sic] take my eyes off it. Yesterday, thinking to explore, I fell headlong into a six foot hole, and came home dripping like a spaniel, or water rugg (thats [sic] Shakespeare) [...] Why am I much shyer of the labourer than of the gentry? I am almost—what d'you call a voracious cheese mite which has gnawed its way into a vast Stilton and intoxicated with eating—as I am with reading history, and writing fiction [*Pointz Hall*] and planning—of such an amusing book on English literature. Only room for exhortation: Write.[1]

The excerpt above is illuminating of the moods and strategies that shaped the piece of fiction glossed in the letter, *Pointz Hall*, or, as it was later renamed, *Between the Acts*. Situating herself and her creative activity in the dramatic context of air raids, the writer is self-mocking, but also troubled by her own response to history—her simultaneous fascination with and withdrawal from the culture of the death drive that governs the historical moment. And so she falls headlong into a six-foot hole, and comes home dripping. Reflecting on the event, Woolf associates history with an image of "indescribable beauty": that of the cascades of water "roaring" over the marsh. Following Kristeva's and Segal's appraisal of affiliation between melancholia and art, I have suggested, in chapter 1, that Woolf's synesthesias operate as the writer's strategy to avoid succumbing to the (inner and outer) hyperactivity of the death drive. To "aestheticize" the horror of such magnitude that it challenges our capacity for representation may be seen as ethically problematic (Woolf knew it too well), but the urge to do so actually inheres in the creative writer's battle with the culture of the death drive. Such "aestheticization" is the effect of the artist's effort to resexualize sublimatory activity in the face of death, Kristeva suggested (*The Sense and Non-Sense of Revolt* 60). In literature this effort manifests itself in two major practices: the sensualization of words, colors, and sounds, and hyper-concentration on the sublimatory act itself (60). Both are readable in Woolf's letter and they both target, courageously, the very blot of destruction—"a six foot hole" carved in by the workings of the death drive.

Woolf is not oblivious to the social problems attending this sublimatory resolution. Her aestheticized experience of the air raids eventuates in a real-world concern: class. This sudden turn of topic might be surprising, since the phenomenon of bombing should expressly deny social stratification. Yet it is precisely because the air raids force the question of social leveling that Woolf is made to reflect on the historical events in conjunction with her other intimate concern in the years surrounding the production of *Between the Acts*: her felt need to speak for all historical actants, irrespective of their class, and what she perceived (or fashioned) to be her impoverished capacity to do so. While this issue, together with the more general question of ethical ways to represent historical horrors, remains unsolved in the letter, this anxious self-reflection finds response in Woolf's creative writing. Not surprisingly, then, Woolf's letter to Smyth culminates in the extolment of writing as the only principled, perhaps the only possible, activity in the historical moment through which they are living. The very last sentence in the letter—"Only room for exhortation: Write" (*Letters* 445)—reflects back on Woolf's ruminations in May 1940, when she posed the problem of historical engagement in terms rather close to Kafka's cogitations on the matter at the beginning of the First World War. In her diary entry of May 15, 1940 Woolf records Leonard Woolf's decision to join home defense forces (a decision over which they quarreled but which would not materialize) and juxtaposes it to her own activity: her writing of a "fateful book," still replete with blank, unwritten, pages, and an urge, even a responsibility, to preserve what Kafka called one's "writerly being" (see chapter 3). Revisiting the division between those who actively fight and those who, like herself and Kafka, remain "passively active," the mature Woolf, then, specifies her own mandate: "This idea struck me: the army is the body; I am the brain. Thinking is my fighting" (*Diary* V: 285). Like Kafka, Woolf revisions the notion of historical engagement to include the meaningful activity of non-combatants, and to suggest—through a somewhat unfortunate organic metaphor—that the ultimate site of engagement with history might be somewhere else than the customary wisdom would have it.

Woolf knows that, if writing is to be reenvisioned as the ethically most appropriate way to engage with a catastrophic historical moment (and not only an individual's strategy temporarily to deflect the death drive), the question of representation, of what is written and how it is read, gains preeminence. The essential property of great art, she claims in "A Sketch of the Past," is the art's capacity to evoke a hidden pattern; a pattern that unites us all and that is itself ingrained in particular works of art. But what are the means and modes appropriate to representation of a history which, to its traversers at least, looks like "a criss-cross of lines making no pattern" (*BTA* 114)? To disregard reality in favor of a false harmony conflicts with the humanly and progressively informed understanding of life and art that Woolf advances. So her last novel shapes itself into a performance of what Freud deemed a particularly poetic form of melancholia—"anticipatory grief;" an impulse to foretaste mourning, melancholically to probe an impending historical catastrophe (see "On Transience," *SE* XIV: 306; and my discussion in chapter 1). At the same time, Woolf seems intent on rescuing meaning in the face of absurdity. In addition to performing "anticipatory grief," *Between the Acts* also stages a semi-hopeful search for intelligible patterns hidden behind "the doom of sudden death hanging over" (*BTA* 114). In this last respect at least, Woolf's mature aesthetic-ethic project is not unrelated, I would suggest, to how Nicolas Abraham and Maria Torok defined the mission of psychoanalysis a few decades later: as a meta-science whose task is to restore meaning under unintelligibility, to reinstall introjection (mourning-flow) against incorporation (melancholia). However, to Abraham and Torok's overly optimistic belief in the possibility of symbolic integration through concatenation, or patterning, Woolf counterposes a more moderate stance. To rescue signification through artistic language, her last novel suggests, may be a valuable effort—indeed the only authentic effort left to the artist in the present age—but its positive repercussions in the "real world" are hardly guaranteed.

Here the artist is faced with an almost impossible task: she needs to devise ways to represent historical occlusions and barriers, and yet forge an aesthetic whole that would meaningfully speak to whatever link is still binding people. To respond to the contradictions of this situation without falsifying the historical givens, one could examine the very frailty of artistic restitution, Woolf suggests. Such interrogation might ultimately engender a new mode of representation, one that would capture the simultaneity of loss (melancholia) and its therapy in language (mournful expression). The complexity of Woolf's self-assigned artistic mandate may be the reason why *Between the Acts*—a novel which, behind the appearance of a traditional narrative, abounds with fissures, gaps, and suspensions—unfolds in the paradoxical fashion that I have also identified, to various degrees, in relation to Bely's and Kafka's fiction: *Between the Acts* explores different models of "making sense," finding a "hidden pattern," or establishing a community, and yet, as all good fiction of countermourning, it simultaneously suspends the possibility of ever accomplishing any of these aims. Such writing entails both serving and obstructing the mourning ritual that is literature. As a text whose affective framework delicately oscillates between moderate optimism and despair, between the imperative of social action and the workings of historical melancholia, *Between the Acts*, then, may well present a paradigmatic case of countermourning fiction. The reappraisal of Woolf's last novel within this interpretative framework is valuable for several reasons. Such reframing sheds light on a hitherto neglected aspect of Woolf's art of fiction—namely, her strategic use of the melancholic symptom. In turn the context of countermourning fiction liberates the critic; the latter can now avoid straitjacketing the text into a single presiding affective-social mode. And it leads us, incidentally, to honor that feature of Freud's theory of melancholia which Virginia Woolf admired most: the notion of ambivalence of feelings.

Art, History, and the Foretaste of Mourning

In her 1939 description of the revelation brought about by mystical "moments of being," Woolf summarizes her mature philosophical discovery as follows:

> From this I reach what I might call a philosophy [...]; that behind the cotton wool is hidden a pattern; that we—I mean all human beings—are connected with this; that the whole world is a work of art; that we are parts of the work of art. *Hamlet* or a Beethoven quartet is the truth about this

vast mass that we call the world. But there is no Shakespeare, there is no Beethoven; certainly and emphatically there is no God; we are the words; we are the music; we are the thing itself. ("A Sketch of the Past" 72)

The feat of this insight coincided with Woolf's writing of *Between the Acts*, a novel that mounts an all-encompassing search for hidden patterns. At first sight, this epiphany appears to elevate an abstract mythopoeic aesthetic at the expense of history and agency. And, as such, it may seem to corroborate the charge of political escapism so frequently directed at Woolf in the late 1930s. Yet a closer reading suggests a different interpretation. The "ahistorical" or "universal" pattern Woolf describes is emphatically human, endowed with and generated by human agency and creativity. "The cotton wool," the text's sign for the everyday and the ordinarily human, extends into, rather than occludes or annihilates, the pattern hidden beneath it. Discarding the notion of genius and—ostensibly at least—that of God, Woolf also refutes any abstraction *beyond* the human. The "thing" is the human world itself; if there is a pattern, it must be inextricably bound to, indeed embodied in, the human. We are, then, both the creators and the very form of the "thing;" the outlines of our voices or gestures, of our veins and tendons, human creation itself, all partake in and shape this universal pattern, which is artistic. This promotion of the categorically human nature of art and creation, of the "inner harmony" that makes us all *Hamlets* or Beethoven's quartets, connects us in a global web of relationships that encompass levels from the mundane to the masterpiece. For all the utopian whiff of this passage (or precisely because of it), Woolf paradoxically assumes an active approach to history here. The passage responds to Woolf's pressing concern in the last decade of her life—namely, the capturing of the traces of life-giving, creative, agency in the world from which such activity appears to be withdrawing.

Already famed as the most prominent writer in the contemporary canon, Woolf nevertheless found herself in a precarious artistic position in the late 1930s.[2] The sometimes vitriolic attacks of the "Scrutineers" (J. F. Holms, Muriel Bradbrook, Q. D. Leavis, F. D. Leavis), Wyndham Lewis, Benedict Nicolson, and American critics such as William Troy and J. W. Beach, charging Woolf with escapist aestheticism and class detachment, were as uncomfortable for the writer as her own creative doubts, bouts of depression and disquietude, and the political anxiety that was steadily mounting throughout the 1930s.[3] The intimated sense of urgency spurred her work on devising new methods to conjoin the socio-historical and the mythopoeic, and on forging art forms that would have more immediate social impact. The antithetical coordinates of this last of Woolf's aesthetic shifts are

conveniently preserved in her own record, in the juxtaposition of her 1928 preference "for the windings of [her] own mind" (this is voiced in "The 'Sentimental
Journey'" 81) and her mid-1930s engagement with "a running commentary upon
the External" (this is how she described her enterprise of collecting newspaper
clippings on war and private life; *Reading Notebooks* 8). These modes shape the
mature Woolf's project to relay "combination of the external & internal"—to capture "the voice of fact" and yet to create a fictional text (*Diary* IV: 103; *TG* 30). But,
can history be narrated in both modes at once? The chasm between the "language"
of facts and that of fiction is irrefragable, Woolf acquiesces. "Let it be fact, one
feels, or let it be fiction," she exclaims, "the imagination will not serve under two
masters simultaneously" (*Essays* IV: 234). And, still, there exists an artistic and
historical necessity, so it appears to Woolf in the late 1930s, to dramatize both association and gulf between fiction and facts, between those "abstract words" and "the
photographs of dead bodies and ruined houses" (*TG* 85). Woolf shares this urge, a
vivid expression of the melancholic processing of history, with other writers I have
discussed here. The merger of the external and the internal is also the ultimate goal
of Bely's affective digestion of material history, as well as that of Kafka's translation
of an affective experience into the formal properties of *The Castle* chronotope. In
this aspect at least Woolf's last writing efforts meaningfully correlate with the very
different artistic-social expressions of Bely and Kafka.

The thematic structures of these novels are cognates, too. Similarly to Bely's and
Kafka's texts, *Between the Acts* revolves around the issues of personal-historical
loss and the relationship between the individual and community in crisis. The
novel renders modest temporal and spatial progression. Compressed within the
course of twenty-four hours of a June day in 1939, *Between the Acts* delineates its
narrative space against the background of the early days of the *Sitzkrieg*. Within
this moment of extended stasis, *between the acts*, several things happen: a family undergoes a subtly intoned crisis; a village pageant is performed despite the
vagaries of the summer weather; a family house transforms into a synergic point
for personal and socio-historical agons; and some strong correspondences are
established between private life and history. The pageant, a vision of a Miss La
Trobe, consumes much of the narrative space—as befitting the play's immoder-
ate aspirations, namely, to reenact both the entire English history and the history
of English literature. Surrounding it and interacting with it, a series of narrative moves unearths gaps in official, private, and literary histories, and underscores the inadequacy of the operative models of recording history. The ludic
attempts at mourning these gaps refigure the relation between fiction and reality
and eventually reshape the novel from a story about an English community under

conditions of catastrophe into a more general interrogation of epistemological and socio-historical crises.

This thematic framework has frequently been interpreted in the context of Woolf's response to the self-imposed directive of social engagement. Still, while *Between the Acts* is probably the most political of Woolf's fictional writings, indeed a "running commentary on the External," there is room to argue—together with Galia Benziman—that the novel is actually premised on a folding back into the private or subjective perspective of an individual mind-body, more specifically, an artist's mind-body (53). Rather than siding with either of these approaches, I should like to attend here to the transversals between these two perspectives, or writing-and-reading modes: for it is the routes, or continuities, between private perspective and social history that have been symptomatically activated in modernist novelists' use of melancholia. As I have argued elsewhere, structurally and thematically, Woolf's representation of contemporary history in *Between the Acts* suggests that the experience of material history has more to do with the *movement* from the "real world" to the "inner experience" (and back) than with either the material world or human interiority independently; and her most significant contribution to philosophy of history in the late 1930s resides in her reframing of two major psychological and epistemological practices, interlocked and, as it were, bound to this outward-inward movement: writing and reading.[4] If these hypotheses are true, then one is well advised to read Woolf-and-history in *Between the Acts* in the way she suggested we should read any artwork, that is, by attending to the affective routes that extend from the cotton-wool through the air raids to the novel itself.

The same routing—and route-reading—shapes the three projects in which Woolf was engaged in the late 1930s, presented here in order of generality: the interrogation of the relationship between art and history; a corollary inquiry in the relations between facts and fiction; and the inquiry in the possibility of substituting the "I" (focalizing-epistemological perspective enthroned in much modernist fiction) by a communal voice of "we" (cf. *Diary* V: 135). *Three Guineas* and *Anon* (1940), the two texts that encircle *Between the Acts*, write out the conflictual coordinates of these projects: *Three Guineas* delineates the social, cultural, and economic basis of women's oppression in pamphletic fashion, polemically allying the strivings of pacifism and feminism. But in the highly poetic prose of the *Anon* manuscript Woolf plunges into primeval time in order to forge an image of the mythic first creator, the singer whose "voice [...] broke the silence of the forests."[5] Anon, who might have been a woman, stands at the beginning of an alternative history, that of creative work. Yet, since Anon's voice both speaks for community and is part of that community (hers is "the common voice singing out of doors;" 1-2), the fragment suggests that, far from being autonomous, the "artistic history" participates in general social history—perhaps as its most productive part. Creation, after all, is the condition *sine qua non* of social history, its propeller, and its dynamic principle.

In an episode close to the beginning of the novel, *Between the Acts* stages a symbolic snapshot of the (now gendered) relationship between these two "histories." In the dining room of the protagonists, the Oliver family, there are two pictures hanging on the wall, we are told: a painting of "an ancestor" and that of "a long lady." The "loquacious" ancestor introduces the notions of genealogy and narrative ("he was a talk-producer, that ancestor"), more specifically, of official historical record ("he had a name," the narrator informs us) (*BTA* 36). The lady, on the other hand, has neither a name nor a narrative/history of her own. A being without social life, she is also an imaginary construct, a play of the mind; she abides beyond history, far beyond official narrative. "[T]hrough glades of greenery and shades of silver, dun and rose," this feminine emblem of art leads the spectator into the realm of silence, of timeless time, and of death itself: "[e]mpty, empty, empty; silent, silent, silent. The room was a shell, singing of what was before time was; a vase stood in the heart of the house, alabaster, smooth, cold, holding the still, distilled essence of emptiness, silence" (36-37). This silence, the incantatory fricatives suggest, is rather deafeningly resonant than quiet. And such is the encounter that unfolds before the reader. In real life the ancestor and the silent lady never met, the narrator hurries to explain; art and social life appear fated to remain irremediably disengaged. But this is a trick, one of those performative challenges with which Woolf's *Between the Acts* abounds, for the two *have met* somewhere: their meeting is staged—and endlessly restaged—in the narrative tapestry that Woolf is weaving. Opposite the window (a pregnant Woolfean symbol), hanging on the wall of the house whose mythic proportions the reader will soon discover, the two paintings/histories face an unknown spectator. Although their drama has never been performed, the very juxtaposition of the two figures produces a plot. Woolf tacitly summons up a dialogue, possibly confrontation, between the man and the woman. Enacting the different realms that they inhabit, she conjures up a dramatic action in an empty room, out of two pictures, all for the eyes of an attentive audience.

Narrating the troubled continuities between art and history, this episode speaks to Woolf's more general effort to forge her own contribution to the modernist interrogation of history in the late 1930s. Here Woolf's vision of history emerges as, above all, relational, and that in a twofold sense. Thematically, this episode, like the novel itself, sets up an apparent opposition only to reframe it and affirm "relation" as the sole personal and historical attitude that is productive. This stance is then reproduced in the act of relating itself, herein understood in its double meaning, as the production of a story and as the vibrant relating of the narrative's disparate constituents—genres, modes, types of sentences. Meanwhile, the semi-colon, the most frequently used punctuation mark in the novel, surfaces as the major carrier of meaning: the dialectic of broken links and their restoration, it says, gives form to *Between the Acts*. Correspondingly, the whole episode should be read as part of a carefully wrought sequencing wherein narrative parts inform and mold each other. The end of this section—the words that melancholically retard into the "distilled essence of emptiness, silence"—clashes, or, rather, interacts with the beginning of the next episode. There, a manic encroachment of silence occurs: a door opens and an indomitable influx of voices invades this sphere of quiet interaction. "Impetuously, impatiently, protestingly," heterogeneous voices set the stage for what might be a comedy of manners (37). Soon they will be joined by the veritable personification of loud, jubilantly disobedient, life—Mrs. Manresa—and, with her, the force of communing. She and her companion, the homosexual (perhaps) artist William Dodge, come uninvited, "lured off the high road by the very same instinct that caused the sheep and the cows to desire propinquity" (37). The empty space is now populated and the silent interaction of art and history is revaluated on the only stage that can give it meaning: the arena of discordant, cacophonous, human life. The intimation of death thereby transforms into a hopeful and gently comic vision of relation, restoring meaning under historical unintelligibility—if only momentarily. Though it is a memento to Woolf's disillusioned view of history, *Between the Acts* nonetheless tenaciously affirms life and creation.

We have seen that countermourning strategies, or the deployment of the melancholic symptom, accentuate the contradictory interpretative potential of literary texts. Woolf's *Between the Acts* is no exception. The novel's paradoxical affective tenor has been repeatedly engaged by Woolf scholars. One may read the novel, together with Mitchell Leaska, as "the longest suicide note in the English language"; or, with David Eberly, as the successful working through personal trauma by sharing it with the reader; or one may claim, together with Melba Cuddy-Keane or Christopher Ames, that the novel is not so much a trauma-narrative as a text enlivened by genuine, life-giving humor. Alternatively, one can speak of the novel from Joshua D. Esty's perspective as a mournful escape into the myth of national culture when confronted with a communal crisis—the demise of British imperialism and the threat of global destruction; or read it, together with Gillian Beer, as a semi-sarcastic narrative about reenvisioning a nation by a writer who long harbored mistrust of patriotic passions; or, celebrate it, with Christina Froula, as a superior fiction of an "outsider's patriotism." And, one can interpret *Between the Acts*, with Michele Pridmore-Brown, as a slap in the face of the death-driven troops that serve as its background, or, with Madeline Moore, as a frail withdrawal in the pantheistic utopia, bespeaking the writer's inability to either rewrite or forget contemporary history.[6] I myself am particularly intrigued, though, by Karen Smythe's suggestion that Woolf's novels should be read as "fiction-elegies," a form that engages the genre of elegy by mimicking, developing, or altering its conventions (64). Woolf's "fiction-elegy," Smythe comments, quests for a new verbal expression of grief, and thus a new (more "sincere") convention of mourning. She argues that Woolf's assiduous interrogation of affective processes in her fiction aims "to provide a repeatable paradigm, a model of mourning" (65). Smythe, however, omits *Between the Acts* from her consideration of Woolf's aesthetic work of mourning, and this exclusion is illuminating. It must have been evident to her that, unlike *Mrs. Dalloway* or *The Waves*, Woolf's last piece of fiction is a decidedly imperfect elegy. As a literary ritual, *Between the Acts* might offer aesthetic consolation, yet the incapacity to provide a successful model of mourning is actually endemic to the narrative, oriented as it is by both ineffective mourning of the past and grieving over future losses. If *Between the Acts* articulates a new model of mourning, the following pages will argue, it is the model that paradoxically relies on its own impossibility.

In contrast to the narrative configurations of Bely's and Kafka's texts (or the texts discussed by Smythe), the narration of *Between the Acts* is focalized by *anticipation* of a historical catastrophe. The narrative unfolds through probing of alternatives for the future opened up by the threat of Fascist domination: annihilation or continuation of life, paralysis or action, oblivion or memory. More generally, the novel could be said to investigate the ways of coping with the transience of things, which the war has brought into sharp focus. The trope of anticipatory grieving is familiar to us, as it may have been to Woolf. It was memorably described in Freud's 1915 essay "On Transience," his examination of the changes in humans' affective functioning occasioned by the First World War. Freud's gracefully written text records a walk in the summer before the war, a *Sitzkrieg* period strikingly similar to the one staged in Woolf's last novel. It describes a perplexing manifestation of "revolt against mourning" in Freud's walking companions, what he termed an urge to "foretaste mourning" (*SE* XIV: 306). Such anticipatory mourning, I have suggested in chapter 1, presents a particularly complex form of countermourning: one that protests against *future* losses and their *possible* containment in mourning. This melancholic "foretasting of mourning" binds personal and general history with creativity, since its very operation depends on an imaginative capacity to conceive of the present, or even unobtainable, objects as already lost (see, also, Agamben, *Stanzas*, 20). It is the latter capacity that drives Woolf's last writing efforts, too. The performance of anticipatory mourning subterraneanly reshapes the time-space of *Between the Acts* to signal the incipient and the ominous. This orientation is also readable on the micro-level of the text, in what Claire Kahane has identified as Woolf's use of anaphoric linguistic patterns to inculcate "the sense of incipient trauma" (226). As a countermourning text that orients itself toward the possible future fatalities while concurrently gesturing the past traumata (cf. Kahane 226-228), Woolf's novel also replicates the complex temporality of affects: what one grieves over is before one and yet—precisely because grieving emotionally reshapes the present and the past—it is already an existent part of one, one's history.

Another barrier to solidifying *Between the Acts* as a model mourning text inheres in the organization of Woolf's narrative. Elegies, like other traditional aesthetic models of mourning, tend to have a relatively stable, hence repeatable, structure, and they are molded as cathartic passages, or working-throughs, where the completion of the text brings (however equivocal) relief and a sense of closure. Woolf named the theme and structure of her last novel a "complete whole," a phrase that points toward her ambition to impart meaning on a grievous history (*Diary* V: 133). The text itself closes on a semi-relief note, yet this closure, like Anton Chekhov's inconclusive endings admired by Woolf, provokes rather "the feeling that we have overrun our signals" or that "a tune had stopped short without the expected chords to close it" ("The Russian Point of View" 176). More intricately, however, this "complete whole" is called into question *as it unfolds*: made of gaps, fissures, and heterogeneous narrative patches, the novelistic whole is constantly "scattered, shattered, hither, thither," then reassembled, reunited, made into a new whole out of "fragments" and "disparity" of contemporary history, only to be challenged again (*BTA* 74). Rather than proposing a new convention of mourning, then, Woolf's *Between the Acts*, much like Kafka's *The Castle*, ultimately defies transforming itself into any structure, or narrative convention, repeatable and amenable to societal appropriation—including the socially integrative activity of mourning.

On Water-Rugs and Genre Hybrids

In her letter to Smyth with which I began this chapter, Woolf compares herself—an inquisitive coming home limping from her encounter with historical reality—to a "water-rugg," a (maybe) animal to be found in Shakespeare's *Macbeth*

(III.i.93). The "water-rug" appears, amidst hounds, mongrels, spaniel curs, "show-ghes," and "demy-wolues," in Macbeth's catalogue of canines with which he greets the assassins whom he has just hired. The semi-ironic cataloguing underscores each breed's "particular addition" to "the bill that writes them all alike" and closes with a comparison between this unruly diversity and humankind (III.i.94-95). The comparison is not uninvited as "water-rug," like other breeds mentioned, has also traditionally served as a metaphor for a particular "breed" of humans, namely, sailors, or those who feel at home either on or in the water. In effect Macbeth's speech highlights the problems of taxonomy and calls attention to a variety of grades, modes, and experiences of what it means to be human; or animal, for that matter. Positioning herself as an animal—a shaggy dog, otter, or, even, alligator—or a mongrel breed, perhaps also a rain-bringing cloud, or a shabby human (for "water-rug" supports all these meanings), Woolf appears to be reflecting on the communal variegation and its resultant, the twine of unity and disparity invoked in the novel that she was writing at the time.[7] In *Between the Acts*, the juxtaposition of the animal and the human is a conspicuous formal strategy, one which effortlessly bridges the grotesque and the pantheistic. This figuration is compounded by the likewise Shakespearean insistence on the diversity of species and forms of life: the novel is populated by an endlessly variegated assortment of birds, fish, clouds, humans. The vital effect of these textual transfers across breeds, species, and forms of living is the inauguration in the novel of the qualities of relating, opposing, and, above all, abiding *in between* various modes of being or types of formal figuration. Everything in *Between the Acts* is in flux and in an unexpected, sometimes "illicit," relationship—phonemes, words, clauses, paragraphs, sections, as well as types of enunciation, kinds of address, and affective modes. The text shuttles between the genres (drama, novel, poetry) and modes (ironic, historiographic, lyric), and it markedly relies on the narrative devices that foreground the relational or hybrid status of literature (intertextual interpolations and free indirect discourse). One may read this poetics of the hybrid and the unclassifiable as formal expression of Woolf's insight that life and art, history and "supra-history," abide in a similar melancholic suspension; but it is also her purposefully ambivalent response to the cruelties of history.

How does *Between the Acts* operate as a mongrel text? Bafflingly to its critics, the novel advances a realistic-satiric representation while upholding a well-neigh mystic poetic sequencing. This merger of modes is a surface effect of a comprehensive hybridization of art forms that involves music, performance, and the written word. As the narrative segues from songs to tunes to ambience sounds, music measures and patterns come to permeate Woolf's syntax itself, whose melody alternates between the harmonious lines of assonants and the subdued roar of labials and fricatives. This rhythmic and expressive variegation transforms the novel into a historically charged operetta, comic and sad. To invoke the genre of the operetta is appropriate here, for Woolf's prosody in *Between the Acts* is conclusively inflected by the modalities of drama. Woolf nimbly plays with the *theatrum mundi* metaphor on a more general level, too, using the analogy between theater and life (and history) as both structural and thematic core of the novel. Taking on an inner form of an Elizabethan drama play, *Between the Acts* thus unfolds from the "evening before" preamble, through the morning act (curtain up), the acts covering, respectively, preparation for the pageant, arrival of guests, and the pageant itself, and the evening act (curtain down). The novel also presents itself as a formal scrutiny of the dynamics of the theatrical *agon* and its suspension *stasis*. Serving as a structural analogue for the way in which history unfolds, the shifts between agons and stases also organize the narration. They relate, analogically, the three planes operative in the novel—the Oliver family story (microcosmic structure), La Trobe's pageant (microcosmic substructure), and history (implied macrocosmic structure)—and further redistribute these planes across genre boundaries. In this way each plane of the text becomes a receptacle for elements or aspects of various genres.

While the pageant may be seen as the focal point for the fusion of genres in *Between the Acts*, it is not the actual locus of the novel's heterogeneity. Rather, La Trobe's symbolist-ritualist-Brechtian exercise functions as a signpost directing us to melancholic interlacing of genres in the interstices of time, *between the acts*.[8] The fictional space surrounding the performance is itself remarkably theatricalized and, appropriately, "put on stage" in the very first sentence in the novel: "It was a summer's night and they were talking, in the big room with the windows open to the garden, about the cesspool" (*BTA* 3). Introducing the topics, genres, modes, and even linguistic peculiarities of the piece to follow, the opening sentence ushers the reader/spectator into a parlor-scene of Shakespearean time ("a summer's night") and Ibsenian space ("the big room with the windows open to the garden").[9] This merger enables Woolf to introduce multiple constituents of her novel at once: its intertextuality; its simultaneously "naturalistic" and "supra-historical" chronotope; its curious rhythm and fragile structure; and, most importantly perhaps, its theatricality. This prominently positioned intertextual blend signals that the following discussion is a play, or, to be more precise (and truer to the Shakespeare reference)—it is a play within a play that is a novel. The immediate activation of the motif of the cesspool (raising the funds for the cesspool is the reason for organizing the pageant) renders the stage action satirical and binds it to contemporary history. Yet, the ensuing reflection on "scars" made by the Britons, the Romans, and subsequent peoples on the road where the cesspool is to be built cracks this intimate grotesque and recomposes it into a melancholic historical parable (4). Finally, the mood established in these few first sentences— smothered emotionality and atmosphere of waiting—signal yet another stage: like the tragicomic heroes of Chekhov's *The Cherry Orchard*, a play treasured by Woolf, the characters find themselves paralyzed "between the acts," an interval where little seems to be possible beyond the repetitious role-playing—blind beating of a butterfly on a windowpane or empty "chuffing" of the history-gramophone (17; 76; cf. *Essays* III: 246-248). At the same time hope (or a hope of comedy) glimmers in chant-like alliterations scattered on the first page: "county council," "gobble in the gutter," and "substance and succulence" (3). Their melody suggests that melancholic repetition, albeit bound to the activity of the death drive, may simultaneously condition a creative aperture.

The episode discussed above, like many other instances of heterogeneity in the novel, suggests Woolf's interest in a particular disturbance of vision found in melancholia: a difficulty in "reading" signs in their apparent speech genre context. In psychoanalytic terms, this receptive confusion occurs when the part of the melancholic's ego identifies with the renounced/lost object, and, as a result, the melancholic over-cathects, displaces and obscures the utterance of the other, relegating it to an unconstrained sphere of interpretation. This disturbance is a consequence not so much of unawareness of (speech) genre rules, or accepted principles of reception of addresses, as of their neglect, unconsciously calculated to protect the utterance of the introjected other. As such, it can have both negative and positive consequences for the melancholic recipient: in more severe forms, such receptive disorientation may preclude any understanding or interaction; in milder forms the relegation of the utterance into a zone where its speech genre can be liberally reinterpreted activates what Bakhtin called "actively responsive understanding" (as opposed to passive, or receptive, understanding) (*Speech Genres* 69). Woolf may have read an account of melancholic identification generative of this state in *Group Psychology and the Analysis of the Ego* while she was writing *Between the Acts* (cf. *SE* XIX: 108-110). Arguably, her decision to dislimn the boundaries between genres in *Between the Acts* was motivated by her enduring attraction to genre mixtures; but it is also likely that Woolf found in heterogeneity the most adequate formal correlative for the affective amalgams that marked her last years—in brief, a superior "melancholic strategy."

In her discussion of the relevance of Melanie Klein's theory of the depressive position for modernism, Sánchez-Pardo also likens the modernists' use of mixed forms to the dynamic of melancholia. She argues that generic mixtures in modernism bespeak the melancholic's problem with discernment of boundaries between the inside and the outside, or "the impossibility of ever securing the space where the psychic and the social converge" (213-14). I emphatically agree that modernist heterogeneity should be interpreted in the context of the melancholic symptom. However, rather than perceiving modernist generic mixtures—and the genre hybridism of *Between the Acts* in particular—as helpless confusion of the boundaries between the inner (the psyche) and the outer (the socium), I interpret them as the precise site where the psychic-individual and the social productively converge in the aesthetic act. Woolf's *Between the Acts* demonstrates the validity of this claim: it is through generic intersections such as the one discussed above that Woolf connects her narrative not only to general history, but also to strictly contemporary events and the concrete demands they pose to the modern subject. In this light, Woolf's problematization of genre boundaries needs to be understood as a premeditated narrative strategy through which she reassessed the presumed discrepancy between the inner and the outer, individual and group, experience of history.

The "problems of form and fictionality," Rachel Bowlby has noted, "undermine the certainties of historical actions and knowledge" (147). The inauguration of generic indeterminacy in a work of art is, of course, always a subversive move, since it precludes one from petrifying the creative act within a set of established rules. More complexly, heterogeneity obscures the signifying system within which one is expected to interpret the utterance (is it a lyric poem, a fable, a drama play, or a historical document?), and, by extension, challenges our presuppositions about particular adequacy of certain types of utterance to certain kinds of content; in Bakhtinian terms, this strategy forces us out of the comfort zone of receptivity into responsive understanding. Furthermore, as every genre sets up a relation between reality and fiction through which the recipient understands the utterance, the plurality of genres in a single aesthetic act powerfully questions not only the existing systems of representation but also the interpretation of reality itself—for good or for bad. And, if different genres present different negotiations of the interface of fiction and reality, it is plausible that heterogeneity has particularly strong implications for the form that most closely resembles, or purports to resemble, a reality/history-record: the novel. Cast in this light, genre hybrids in modernist novels such as *Between the Acts* may be seen as performing a conflict with the ways in which history is both narrated and interpreted. Specifically, the generic mixture of Woolf's last novel is inextricably bound to her effort to instantiate—rather than represent—occlusions in official historical record.

This fusion of genres can finally be associated with Woolf's relational view of life and history in the late 1930s. The writer's mature perspective foregrounds cathectic interrelation, possible and impossible, as both constitutive of the force field of history and vital for the figuration of story. In her diary entry of January 18, 1939, Woolf enthusiastically announced that, with *Between the Acts*, she "got at a more direct method of summarising relations" (*Diary* V: 200). The meaning of this laconic self-praise is not apparent, but its significance may be inferred from the brisk description of the novelistic language that follows: "& then the poems (in metre) run off the prose lyric vein, which, as I agree with Roger [Fry], I overdo" (200). Here, "summarising relations" is linked to genre interaction, between the poems in meter and (theatrically inflected) prose. In Woolf's self-assessment this pendular move between genres becomes a formal equivalent of affective and physical transfers, of routing through, and interrelating with, real, obscured and imagined objects.

Male Games, Female Games or, History as a Horse with Green Tail

One of the most compelling cases of hybridization of forms and modes of reading in *Between the Acts* revolves around gender violence. The two worlds of violence, general and private, converge as Isa reads in the *Times* the following:

> "A horse with a green tail..." which was fantastic. Next, "The guard at Whitehall..." which was romantic and then, building word upon word, she read: "The troopers told her the horse had a green tail; but she found it was just an ordinary horse. And they dragged her up to the barrack room where she was thrown upon a bed. Then one of the troopers removed part of her clothing, and she screamed and hit him about the face...."
> That was real; ...(*BTA* 20)

A miniature analysis of reading and reading habits, this episode examines the ways in which we make sense of historical and fictional texts: how we imbue them with the fantastic and the romantic until, unexpectedly and disturbingly, the interference of the real happens—a military gang rape. Stuart N. Clarke has validated that such rape occurred on April 27, 1938, and was recorded in the *Times* on June 28, 29, and 30, 1938 (3-4). In her recent rereading of the same scene Claire Kahane has suggested that the incorporation of this episode also has a reparative function, since it served Woolf to work through her own childhood trauma of incestuous abuse (235-37). Through a striking conflation of facts and fiction, Woolf makes this historical incident both a decisive marker of Isa's interiority and a general statement on masculine violence (and, if Kahane is correct, also an instrument of her own working-through). One of the nodal points for Woolf's interrogation of the nexus of art and history, this factual-fictional episode suggests that violence is gendered, and that the power structures of private and public worlds are comparable—that "the tyrannies and servilities of the one are the tyrannies and servilities of the other," as Woolf provocatively claimed a few years before (*TG* 258).

Commonly articulated in Woolf's fiction through the grouping of characters, this gendered analogy installs what might at first appear as a set of typified contrasts between men, who are distinguished by cerebral intelligence that may turn into an aggressive inclination toward analysis (separation), and women, who are emotive and creative devotees of synthesis (unifying). "Fighting," Woolf provokes, "is a sex characteristic in which [women] cannot share" (*TG* 194). For this reason, a group or individual perpetrator of violence in Woolf's writings is often—and more commonly so in her late work—gendered male. Woolf's female characters typically "heal" ruptures in history and collective memory through "unifying" activities such as knitting, sewing, painting, or directing a play, while men split, smash, or break in search for an analyzable core. This polarization is Woolf's regular device, but one that, as it will become evident soon, is not devoid of sophistication, self-reflection, and ironic distancing. So, before we accuse Woolf of stereotyping, it is worth tracing this binary thought to its less frequently recorded provenances. One such route would lead from Woolf's distinction between the analyzing male and the synthesizing female back to Freud's cogitations on the twin workings of the death drive and the life drive, a theory with which she was getting acquainted in the late 1930s. Freud first hypothesized the existence of opposing drives in *Beyond the Pleasure Principle* and he revisited this theory in many subsequent texts, including *Moses and Monotheism*, *The Future of an Illusion*, *Group Psychology* and *Civilization and its Discontents*, all of which Woolf read during her work on *Between the Acts* (see *Diary* V: 248, 249, 250, 252, 252n, 264; she may have also read *Beyond the Pleasure Principle* but there is no record of it). Modeling his distinction upon Ewald Hering's hypothesis of the two contrary types of biological processes, "assimilatory" and "dissimilatory," Freud allied the libidinal-life drive with "assimilatory," "constructive," and "creative" activities, one whose determinative action is synthesis (the life drive seeks "to combine organic substances in ever larger unities;" *SE* XVIII: 43), and the death drive with dissimilatory and destructive impulses (the death drive seeks to return to the preexistent by analyzing, breaking the wholes, separating the particles). In a remarkable gesture, Woolf appropriates Freud's distinction between the drives and utilizes it to her own (feminist) ends: the dissimilatory and destructive drive becomes the insignia of "maleness" whereas the synthesizing and creative activity gets cast as the dominant "female" trait.

The frequently interpreted "library scene" in *Between the Acts* is based on just such supposition. Bart and Lucy, brother and sister, a separatist and a unifier, an atheist and a believer, quarrel. (Or, rather, Bart "groans" and Lucy "flushes.") Their silent conflict has been prepared by Lucy's taking the hammer and nails without asking leave; it subtends their discussion on the weather, children, and superstition; and it eventuates in the disclosure that the issue of religion lies behind their permanent confrontations. The two characters are granted opposite personalities: Lucy's mode of existence is ecumenical and unifying, whereas Bart relates to the world in terms of separation and systematization. Her imagination is artistic; his—encyclopedic. The difference is in gaze, Bart thinks: "She would have been [. . .] a very clever woman, had she fixed her gaze" (24). The disparity might lie not in disposition but in perception, the narrator counters: "what [Lucy] saw [Bart] didn't; what he saw she didn't" (26). Finally, the difference turns out to be neither endogenous nor insurmountable: it is "not a barrier but a mist" (26). Thus determined by and encased in the field of (mis)perception, the distinction between an analyzing male and a synthesizing female now emerges as being perspectival, contingent on the assumption of positions, or roles, on the stage of life. The overarching theatricalization of the text confirms: it is the gender *performance* rather than any "essentials" of the sexes that the punchy representation of relations between women and men in *Between the Acts* thematizes. The same pertains to the symbolic correlatives of this gender performance: if the confrontation between Lucy and Bart also replicates the opposition between an England "whose values are feminine, pastoral, and literary," and an imperialist Britain "whose values are masculine, industrial, and expansive," as Esty has argued (259), one should bear in mind that these two geocultural tropes are, likewise, performatives.

This is a point to which I shall return later. Meanwhile, let me note that Woolf's treatment of this performance is nowhere more poignant than in her probing of the processes of male self-definition. Bart's game with his grandson at the beginning of the novel aims at just such gender identity-fashioning. Having masked himself with a newspaper crumpled into a beak, Bart springs out from behind a tree in front of the terrified George. Yet, the young seem not to enjoy the old confrontational game: George bursts out crying and Bart is disappointed (*BTA* 11-13). On closer reading of the Bart-George episode, one may discover that *three*

violent games take place: male identity-forming game that is soon to be seamlessly connected to the rape story (18-20), the agon of infantile cruelty, which sees
George shredding a flower with curiosity, and the war-game, signaled by the occasional appearance of an aeroplane. The link established between the three games
corresponds to the triple analogy governing the novel, one that connects play/
game, story, and history. It expresses the mature Woolf's vision that that there
is a continuity between gender self-definition games, assertion of sexual dominance, and corroboration of national identities; or, more generally, that "the gun
slayers, bomb droppers [...] do openly what we do slyly" (187). As also noticed
by Elizabeth Abel (although prompting different conclusions), Woolf's final gendered analogy is not unrelated to Freud's argumentation in *Moses and Monotheism*
and *Civilization and Its Discontents*.[10] For mature Woolf and Freud agreed most
profoundly where their shared position was most controversial: claiming that the
analogies and slippages between the individual and the group are omnipresent,
they treat confrontational games on which our experience of personal or national
identity rests as (dominantly masculinist) manifestations of the "pure culture of
the death instinct" (*SE* XIX: 53).

To heed these analogies is important, since gender (self-) fashioning is inextricably linked to the major question posed by *Between the Acts*—that of personal
and historical responsibility. For the reasons that become apparent in Bart's game
with his grandson, the issue of active participation in historical conflict torments
men more than women in Woolf's text. Giles is the novel's correlative for this affective conundrum. His participation in history is pitiably inadequate, Giles reasons;
he is "forced passively to behold indescribable horror" while the whole of Europe
is "bristling with guns, poised with planes" (60; 53). I have previously related the
character of Giles to Kafka's self-depreciative journal entry written at the beginning of the First World War, and suggested that the split between those who "fight"
and those who, like Kafka and Woolf (and, in the diegetic world, all the characters
in *Between the Acts*), remain "non-participants," is not only a social conundrum
posed with renewed urgency at the beginning of each war, but also one of the
key affective challenges that marked the period between 1914 and 1945. Insofar
as Giles is the carrier of this melancholic affective quandary, the character's primary function is not to signify an "aggressively virile masculinity's" collusion with
Fascism, as previously argued by Abel (109) and Zwerdling (308), but to embody
the dilemma of what constitutes active participation in history—a concern that
permeated Woolf's private and public writing in this period. As her final thought
on the subject, *Between the Acts* emphatically recuperates the role of the audience;
only gradually will the inhabitants of Pointz Hall and their visitors comprehend

the significance of the role assigned to them by Miss La Trobe—to participate in a communal effort.

But this expansion of the notion of "active non-participant" to an entire community also challenges the stereotypical division into male "violent participants" and female "active non-participants" that so obviously ripples the surface of Woolf's text. Pausing at this non sequitur, one may square this division with what Freud designates as final purposes of the death drive (dissimilation aiming to restore the state of primal inertia) and the libidinal drive (assimilation aiming to incite activity). Rather than jumping to—dangerously analogical—conclusions, let me note that, when she finally got to reading Freud, Woolf was a uniquely astute reader.[11] She doubtlessly noticed that the relationship between Freud's contrary drives is not one of simple opposition. In the closure of *Beyond the Pleasure Principle* and throughout *Group Psychology and the Analysis of the Ego* Freud hypothesizes that the drives eventually serve each other's aims in dynamic interaction, the evidence for which he finds precisely in the twin workings of melancholia-mania (more disturbingly, he would conjecture once, both drives might aim to affirm the deadly state of primal inertia). Judging by her reading notes on *Group Psychology and the Analysis of the Ego* Woolf understood this dynamic very well. I tend to believe that one of Woolf's hidden projects in the text she was writing at the time, namely, *Between the Acts*, was to probe not so much the opposition as the complementary working of the drives, their interaction and intersection at various planes.[12] In their intertwine, like in the myriad events of everyday life, she found—ambivalence. Indeed it is Freud's insight into this paradigmatic affective structure that Woolf particularly appreciated (see *Diary* V: 249). Armed with the concepts of ambivalence and dynamic interlock of the drives, Woolf extends Freud's discussion to her treatment of "gender" performance and thereby interrupts the gender analogies she has just established.

For even though the novel showcases "masculine" destructiveness and "feminine" creativity, one may notice a simultaneous tendency in the text to problematize the behavioral "precepts" and distinctions between the genders. What I have in mind here is not the challenge posed to the facile gender-based figuration by homosexual characters such as William Dodge and Miss La Trobe (in fact, *all* characters in *Between the Acts* cross, or blur, the boundaries between "masculine" and "feminine" positionalities and behaviors), but the circumstance that, irrespective of their gender, all characters also engage in small, mundane, acts of violence, in thought or in deed. It is vital to notice this complication of analogies, since the gendered performance of history in *Between the Acts* is also a narrative trap, a challenge to the reader. While the above examples might seem to indicate an unproblematic division of the diegetic world into male (dissimilatory death drive driven) participation in cruel historical games and female (assimilatory erotic drive driven) non-participation, it is more accurate to say that all the characters, regardless of their gender, are non-participants. Rather than being divided along the gender, participation, or the drive dominance lines, Woolf's characters in *Between the Acts* are split into those who are oblivious to the ongoing historical turmoil and those who reflect on it through various means at their disposal. It is the latter group of characters that Woolf shapes as dynamic conveyers of her insight that non-participation may still present an active work in history. She is cautious, though: a perspective liberated from gender analogies, Isa's ventriloquizing about the military rape suggests, must not blind us to the real existence of gender violence, or—to be more precise—violence as such. But it can perform something the narrator of *Three Guineas* was not able to perform: to speak to, or motivate, the vastly diversified whole that is humankind.

Between Community and Individuation: The Four-Dimensional Character

It is valuable to recast Woolf's figurative strategies in these terms, since she is in fact disinterested in polar typology in this novel. While certain "typological traits" are invoked in the representation of each character, the characters are nuanced and complicated enough to preclude any neat classification, let alone opposition. If anything, the proliferation of minor and major characters in *Between the Acts* testifies to Woolf's belief in what I have intimated in her reference to Macbeth's speech, namely, the inexhaustibility of categories of the human. In addition to the gender roles, the life-stage also offers some individual parts, to be played with effort or ease. The narrative suggests a range of them: tinker, tailor, soldier, sailor (Bart "counts"), thief, liar, gun slayer, bomb dropper, tyrant, slave (the metal voice of the megaphone announces), queen, or "girl in white" (Lucy feels like playing them both); or the roles of priests and lovers, village idiots and stockbrokers. Between the acts of history, there also remains a detritus of unperformed roles, unemployed "individual strings" (153). Sometimes it takes only a disguise to act out one's "hidden" part. Long after the pageant has finished, the actors "linger," reluctant to give up the historical roles that they were assigned for one afternoon (195). Others are self-reflexive: "What a small part I've had to play! But you have made me feel I could have played . . . Cleopatra!" Lucy exclaims. " 'You've stirred in me my unacted part,' she meant," La Trobe infers (153). Yet others cherish precisely the role they have been allocated. Mrs. Manresa can "[preserve] unashamed her identity" (186), for she alone embraces freely the artificiality of any identity-construction: she is the celebration of acting-life itself.

Just like professions, functions, and personas, Woolf suggests, classes are also incorporated roles. A comic failure to create a community by bridging classes and personal histories organizes the under-discussed, yet stimulating scene in which Lucy and Mrs. Sands prepare sandwiches for the pageant:

> Mrs. Sands fetched the bread; Mrs. Swithin fetched ham. It was soothing, it was consolidating, this handwork together. The cook's hands cut, cut, cut. Whereas Lucy, holding the loaf, held the knife up. Why's stale bread, she mused, easier to cut than fresh? And so skipped, sidelong, from yeast to alcohol; so to fermentation; so to inebriation; so to Bacchus; and lay under purple lamps in a vineyard in Italy, as she had done, often; while Sands heard the clock tick; saw the cat; noted a fly buzz; and registered, as her lips showed, a grudge she mustn't speak against people making work in the kitchen while they had a high old time hanging paper roses in the Barn. (*BTA* 34)

The episode stages an interaction of two "worlds" and thus, in Woolf's musical vision, two different rhythms. The strong regular beat of Mrs. Sands's activity and the lingering tendrils of Lucy's mental processes are juxtaposed and then overlaid by an interaction of a nursery-rhyme rhythm (the zero degree of narration) and an elaborate "writerly" rhythm. This rhythmic interplay is primarily intended for comical effect and character-miniature, but it is also historically and socially inflected: this interrelation of rhythms instantiates the different temporalities of the cook and her mistress, presenting the two as a dissonant whole, "consolidated" by this handwork. These different temporalities and their rhythms in turn draw the reader's attention to the fundamentally polyrhythmic organization of the novel and, analogously, to the polyrhythmic organization of our world. Yet, like in many similar instances of "working together" in *Between the Acts*, the final satiric twist reframes the episode. Lucy's attempt at reaching beyond the official social narrative turns out to be not only unsuccessful but also short-sighted: the unison of working rhythms is only ostensible. The episode comes to serve as a satiric reminder of Woolf's own "shyness" with laborers that she confides in the letter to Smyth quoted at the beginning of this chapter. More generally, however, the episode highlights that "togetherness" does not, perhaps should not, equal the vanishing of individuality, and thus points to a writerly concern that Woolf shared with Kafka. Like Kafka, Woolf conceives of the relationship between the modern individual and community as galvanized by its own impossibility. "Scraps, orts, and fragments" under a dissolved heaven (*BTA* 188),[13] modern humans will realize the "sweet joy in company" only in the moment of their dispersion (196). And yet the need to commune will remain, Woolf's text suggests in its final movements, because communing is life-giving.

This exploration of community and individuation through scrutiny of characters' "rhythms" is only one aspect of a unique figurative strategy that anchors Woolf's last text to the dynamics of mourning and melancholia. Despite the abundance of figurative types and life-rhythms I have listed above, Woolf appears also to be disinterested in entirely particularized characterization. In fact, one of the reasons why the text does not conform well to the pattern of elegy is that it offers very little "extensive study of characters" that Smythe calls for (64). The protagonist of the novel is a collective, or, rather, componential entity that may, but need not, represent England. Such collective figuration only seemingly facilitates a reading in terms of what scholars like Ian Baucom conceptualized as imperial and post-imperial English melancholia, that is, an affective construction of Englishness grounded in the exaltation of the locale and developing, in the post Second World War period, into a racist refusal to face up to the loss of empire. Even though it mournfully engages the issues of community, English national heritage, and tides of history (and, through the image of Bart, British rule in India), and it is set in an emotionally charged rural landscape (but neither a pastoral idyll nor a specific "redemptive locale"[14]), Woolf's last novel effectively precludes any interpretation in this vein. In his otherwise insightful study Baucom unfortunately conflates melancholia with nostalgia, and thus bases his assessment of pre-war English "melancholia" on a conceptual slippage that, as my discussion in chapter 1 made explicit, cannot be supported. *Nostalgia proper* is conspicuously absent in Woolf's fiction; despite all the introduced specificities, the site of narrative action and/or the locus of "lost home" are ultimately abstracted and the text consistently projects events from the local to general history. The writer's persistent, if delicate, undermining of the discourse of empire *in general* and ironic distancing from *all* historical victors reinforces such impression. And, if Woolf's communal protagonist, coalesced as it is around efforts to preserve and read national heritage anew, may be seen as stand-in for a nation, the nation in question appears as a markedly diversified, polyphonic, and self-reflexive one; and, ultimately, rather a *performance* than a stable entity. Most importantly, perhaps, mature Woolf, like Freud of *Group Psychology* and *Civilization and its Discontents*, is apprehensive of collective "ethos," and thus also wary of unequivocal enforcement of any form of mourning that homogenizes community and/or corroborates a national identity.

As a narrative focused through an emphatically "diversified" communal protagonist, *Between the Acts* is thus fated to shift between restitutive mourning
(what Joshua Esty calls "recuperative ideas of national heritage") and melancholic anxiety about community as such (Esty names it "fundamental wariness
about any kind of communal ethos;" both 257). Scholars like Cuddy-Keane (280)
and Pridmore-Brown (416-19) recognized in Woolf's postulation of a dissonant
and open collectivity her challenge to the traditional models of nationhood and
cohabitation; and Berman linked Woolf's handling of diegetic collectives to "an
oppositional cosmopolitan politics" (156). Melancholia often operates precisely
through such correctives: it establishes critical relation to the community based on
totalitarian models of mourning and nationhood. For this reason, the collective in
Between the Acts is a melancholic whole, comprised of divergent parts that could
be reconciled only temporarily, and perhaps only chimerically. Yet melancholia is
a dangerous master, too, a circumstance of which Woolf is more than aware: it may
lead one to relinquish community as such (cf. Forter). So Woolf fine-tunes her
representation: even such fleeting union as Mrs. Sands and Mrs. Swithin's working
together, when it occurs, is rendered precious.

This contradictory representation is not unrelated to what I propose to be
Woolf's ultimate figurative achievement in *Between the Acts*: the figuration of
the protagonist as both a singularity and a collective. Taking the form of a categorically heterogeneous group, Woolf's componential protagonist is also transient; no sooner has the "hero" been "assembled" through the affective work of
crisis, it already starts disintegrating from within, as an effect of the inner working of the ungovernable variation of its components. Such paradoxical figuration reminds one that, in 1937, Woolf envisioned her next aesthetic project as
an investigation of the "four dimensional character." What is this new narrative
entity? "Different aspects [are] to be given," Woolf explains laconically, "not the
one personal intensity".[15] But the four-dimensional character she is contemplating is neither simply a collective nor a tridimensional character shot through
with time—such figurations are familiar to us from Woolf's previous fiction.
Rather, this entity could be described, I suggest, as a note mirrored in the others, fragmented and fractured, like the scraps of personality in the finale of La
Trobe's pageant; it is a note that only exists in its relation to other notes and
their historical temporalities, and thus it has to accommodate more than one
"personal intensity." On this reading, four-dimensionality emerges as figurative
strategy that attempts to capture subjecthood as it is being constructed relation-
ally. To Kafka's painful probing of the relationship between the individual and
community, Woolf has responded by an impossible figuration: her protagonist

is both a community and an individual established in relation (including opposition) to this community.

Woolf's unique figuration of the protagonist as shuttling between individuality and collectivity confirms her interest in continuities, or permeable borders,
between an individual and a group. That this "four-dimensional character" replicates the melancholic structuration of the ego expounded by Freud in *The Ego
and the Id* and *Group Psychology and the Analysis of the Ego* is not incidental. Like
Benziman, I believe the description of group behavior in a season of crisis is not
the ultimate aim of Woolf's use of the melancholic symptom in *Between the Acts*
(cf. Benziman 64-65). Rather, Woolf's interrogation of communal relationships
serves to forge an image of the structure of the human mind. For Woolf (like, at
times, for Freud), I propose, the recognition of melancholic dynamic in psychic
structuring of community bounces back to the image of a single mind: if community is necessarily a heterogeneous whole, one that can establish itself only in
relation to singularity (as well as in relation to other, similarly diversified entities),
this is so because each one of us is a heterogeneous whole. This shift of perspective
on *Between the Acts* should not disappoint Woolf scholars keen on isolating in her
late fiction engagement with contemporary politics and reparation-work. If Woolf
examines group behavior in crisis in order to interrogate the "ordinary mind" as
melancholic structure—as an ever-diversifying whole continuously reshaped not
only by our interaction with others but also by our interaction with that expo-
nential agglomeration of irretrievable objects in ourselves (gaps in personal and
historical record)—it is because she believes that we can only start engaging with
the complexity of the world, and working in groups, if each first identifies such
structure in oneself.

Agons and Stases: History in Motion

Oriented by this melancholic protagonist, Woolf's novel can hardly unfold through
a horizontal stringing together of events as they happen to characters any more
than Kafka's *The Castle*—although both novels tenaciously uphold a chimera of
linear storytelling. The vertical accumulation of narrative elements is the only possible pattern for such narration. Thus *Between the Acts* unfolds spatially, through
the over-layering of narrative planes (history-story-theater play), mirroring stories (war, private war), and respondent casts (the three sets of characters, and two
gender categories). It builds its cackling melody on the vertical rather than on
the horizontal accretion of tones and tonal fragments, a literary composition that,

I have argued elsewhere, shows pronounced affinities with the chromatic extensions of melody, reinforced motivic repetition and polyrhythmic structure of
modernist classical music.[16] Based on the principles of repetition and covariance,
Woolf's *Between the Acts* is, we have seen, shaped by analogical relations—com-
parisons and conflations of the private and the public sphere, and correlations and
convergences between the group and the personal traumata, and between historical facts and their phantasmic extension in the characters' lives.

Hauntingly, Woolf's covariant structures repeatedly instantiate the same theatrical pattern: that of agonic exchange. Spanning the range from creative interrelating in a system of differences to violent conflicts, the dynamic of agon appears
in Woolf's novel as informing all human activity—linguistic, affective, and political. It is indicative, however, that this relational pattern becomes visible first in its
negative aspect, as conflictual exchange that calls into question any possibilities of
coexistence. The opening discussion about the future site for the cesspool effortlessly associates the historical scars made on the site by the battles of the Romans,
the Britons, and the Elizabethans with those inscribed by the Second World War
(*BTA* 4-5). This opening turns out to be a Benjaminean crystallization: it suggests
that, rather than being an exception, confrontation and destruction are the very
differentia specifica of history. From the battles of Lucy's "mammoths in Piccadilly"
to those of the "valiant Rhoderic," from Bart's years in colonized India to the
bombings of the Second World War, the agons of history seem to have produced
(at least to Isa, a little donkey in caravanserai) nothing but a Benjaminean "pile
of wreckages" (*SW* IV: 392). And so Isa, Woolf's "Angel of History," whispers her
valediction: " 'How am I burdened with what they drew from the earth; memories;
possessions. This is the burden that the past laid on me, last little donkey in the
long caravanserai crossing the desert' " (*BTA* 155). To relate Woolf's late cogitations
on history to Benjamin's contemporaneous thoughts on the subject is relevant,
I have argued elsewhere, because Isa is a female kin of Benjamin's Angel of History,
burdened by the past, troubled by the need to look back and beyond, to write
down the "indescribable horror" of history—"what we must remember; what we
would forget" (155)—while propelled forward by the momentum of an arduous,
dubious, and unavoidable journey.

Although the narrative material of Woolf's last novel is conspicuously focalized
through this melancholic intimation of cataclysmic conflict, and thus oriented by
a vision of history as a series of bloodbaths or piling of wreckages, the text projects
an ambivalent image of agon: agonic exchange in the text appears to be equivocal
in its affective, ethical, and existential purpose, agons span across genders, and,
notably, they are never-ending. Isa, the most poetic of abortive poets, is not only

the text's reflector on confrontational games and gender violence, but also a performer of agons herself: it is the agon played out between her and the heavily satirized Mrs. Haines in that opening scene and the other performed between her and Giles at the end of the text that demarcate the novel. It is through Isa, her witnessing, her engagements, behavior, reflections on the subject, then, that the pattern of agon is first isolated and then allowed freely to float across and against gendered and other analogies. Not incidentally, then, the novel closes with an agon that revisits the opening exchange. The ending returns the characters to the same (now more intimately lit) drawing room, Woolf's privileged site for delicate revelations.[17] Here, a whirlpool of tenses and modes affirms the agonic exchange as both primal and everlasting state of history, a state of history where "the dog fox fights with the vixen, in the heart of darkness, in the fields of night" (*BTA* 219). Left alone for the first time that day, Isa and Giles face each other, like Bart and Lucy earlier, in confrontation and love. "Before they slept, they must fight: after they had fought, they would embrace," the reader is informed (219; cf. 26). Their final embrace postulates that unison could operate within a system of differences. In such context, we learn, an agon may also be creative, indeed life-giving: "From that embrace another life might be born" (219). Insofar as the whole history of destruction is enacted by the present-day violence invoked at the beginning of the text, the whole history of love also replicates itself in Isa and Giles's confrontation at the end of the novel.

Thus agon emerges as a dynamic principle conjoining different planes of human interaction, love as well as hate. Such broadening of the semantics of agon reframes, retrospectively, the vision of history offered by Woolf's text. Rather than anchoring historical events solely in the notions of violence and destruction, Woolf narrativizes personal and general history as a perpetual series of agons, similarly structured, but with sometimes vastly divergent affective values and consequences. And, as these agonic games shuttle from the framing narrative into the pageant and back (*pace* Esty), the reader is reminded that the whole history of representational arts, insofar as it is always a history of representing, or "summarizing," human relations, is also premised on the pattern of agon. As all these love-agons and hate-agons reproduce themselves in the performative and historical time *ad infinitum*, there seems to be "no need to puzzle out the plot" (*BTA* 90). Succumbing to the work of the pattern with a semi-ironic smile, Isa reflects, "Surely it was time someone invented a new plot..." (215). But perhaps this is the only way the plot *can* unfold—not because there are no other plots, but because agon emerges to Woolf, in what DiBattista has called the writer's final panoramic vista (62), as that overarching pattern by which we inhabit and embody history.

I have suggested that Benjamin's mature vision of history speaks well to Woolf's own artistic project in *Between the Acts*. Writing the world/human in a moment of crisis, both argue that history itself offers instances in which its agonic structure may be grasped and evaluated. Those are the moments, often horrifying, when the series of agons ceases, when an agon both surpasses and annihilates itself—such as happens in one of the key "between-the-acts" scenes. Walking toward the Barn in an intermission during the pageant, Giles is presented as kicking a stone, while, in a fast free-association, his imagination makes temporal bridges from "a barbaric stone" to "a child's game" of stone-kicking:

> He kicked a flinty yellow stone, a sharp stone, edged as if cut by a savage for an arrow. A barbaric stone; a pre-historic. Stone-kicking was a child's game. He remembered the rules. By the rules of the game, one stone, the same stone, must be kicked to the goal. Say a gate, or a tree. He played it alone. The gate was a goal; to be reached in ten. (*BTA* 98-99)

Thus entertaining himself with the mental game of soccer, Giles revisits the history of England that has just been performed and connects it to his own life, forging somewhere in the Elizabethan England an analogy for his current condition.[18] Every kick is a different type of settling accounts with others and himself that Giles has to perform in order to not so much take action as impart meaning to the events taking place around and within him: "The first kick was Manresa (lust). The second, Dodge (perversion). The third, himself (coward)" (*BTA* 99). And when, in ten steps, he does arrive at the imaginary "goal," the latter proves to be both content-filled and emptied of meaning. The goal, or Giles's positionality, is a curled snake, choked with a toad in its mouth. Caught in the midst of movement, the snake and the frog have come to a moment of stasis: "The snake was unable to swallow; the toad was unable to die." Likewise stopped in motion, Giles watches the contraction of the ribs and oozing of blood; this is an abortive action, a "birth the wrong way round," he concludes (99). The whole agonic history has congealed into the absurd state in which Giles finds the snake and the toad.[19]

This snapshot corresponds surprisingly well to Benjamin's notion of the dialectical image, an image forged when, in an instant fraught with danger, the past and the present converge to disclose the real nature of history (*SW* IV: 391). In Benjamin's thought, the formula in which this concept partakes, that of "dialectics at a standstill," serves as both the definition of the historical impasse in which modern subject has found itself and a representational method of contesting this situation—a "dialectical image," he writes, is "only genuinely historical image" (*The Arcades Project* 463, 865). Under these terms, Woolf's tableau with Giles, the snake,

and the toad is, indeed, dialectical. As a kind of immanent critique, the consti-
tuting of a dialectical image gestures toward action, or dissolution of a certain
social coagulation into another series of agonic repetitions. Accordingly, an action
ensues in *Between the Acts*: "…raising his foot, [Giles] stamped on them. The
mass crushed and slithered […] But it was an action. Action relieved him" (*BTA*
99). Woolf dryly underscores the vicissitudes of this historical disclosure. Giles's
revelation of the nature of history tethers to both, an ultimately aggressive action
(killing of the animals) and an incipient erotic agon—Giles's acceptance of Mrs.
Manresa's flirting, for she is a person who "[makes] him feel less of an audience,
more of an actor" (108). And as we leave behind the comic-pathetic image of Giles
in his bloodstained tennis shoes, let me note in passing: by inserting singularity
whenever there is a danger of over-generalization, modal discontinuities such as
this abrupt closure—and there are many similar instances in *Between the Acts*—
also serve to unrest, intermittently, the very analogies that organize the novel.

One can imagine the dialectical stases of this kind to be used strategically,
though, just as Benjamin wished it, and La Trobe's pageant purports to offer a few
such revelatory experiences. The most memorable of these is the deliberate dramatic stasis entitled "Present Time. Ourselves," during which the dramatic action
is suspended in order to expose the audience to an accentuated present-time reality. In a moment of silence, the audience is given a chance to perceive themselves
in their historical situation, each on his/her own terms: Mrs. Lyn Jones revaluates
the Victorians; Bart inquires about the financial outcome of the entertainment;
Giles, unhappy with his role of spectator, grumbles in low voice; Lucy caresses her
cross; and Isa whispers her intimation of history as story of unacknowledged toil
and perseverance: "On, little donkey […] bearing your burden" (*BTA* 173-179). But
something goes wrong with this theatrical experiment. Every stasis entails a risk,
La Trobe realizes as the audience's intense despair engulfs her: one may become
overwhelmed by reality, fall into autistic stillness, or be driven into melancholic
asymbolia. If this static interregnum has revealed a dynamic of history, it has also
touched death: "This is death, death, death," La Trobe notes (180). Here the analogical bridge built between the play (stasis), the Oliver family story (stasis), and
history (war) is functional again: it discloses that war, despite its inherently ago-
nistic structure and the destructive energy that it employs—or, precisely *because of
it*—leads to, and paradoxically inhabits, the cruel and abortive stasis emblematized
in the toad and snake image. War is the "distilled essence" of transfixed negativity;
the cessation of life. For Benjamin the revelatory stasis is invariably a chance for
revolutionary change; for Woolf, it is also a moment of touching death, fittingly
heralded by repetitive phrases, scattered fragments of language and subjectivity.

These reiterative phrases, signs progressively hollowed of meaning, indicate that repetition may serve yet another purpose in *Between the Acts*, namely, to vocalize melancholic obstructions and recursions in (linguistic and historical) concatenation. While Woolf's linguistic repetition might be regarded, as many have viewed it, as a marker of a "female language," it is worth bearing in mind that such traumatic repetition of words or phrases, where modification (if or when it eventually happens) occurs more as a subtle modulation in tone, pitch, rhythm, or duration than as a change in content, is also the most commonly referenced feature of the melancholic discourse. Repetition, Woolf leaves us in no doubt, is "senseless, hideous, stupefying" (*BTA* 67). Tellingly, it is the repetitive chuffing of the gramophone needle that announces a malfunctioning of the machine of history.[20] Repetition signals that we may have broached something that surpasses our capacity for stable representation—a deadly stasis in history. It is also omnipresent: repetition lurks behind, or inheres in, a pleasing panoramic view, or, indeed, in a gratifyingly written sequence (such as the one describing how "the flat fields glared green yellow, blue yellow, red yellow, then blue again," a sentence that prefaces the above definition of repetition; 67). In Woolf's novel repetition is emphatically operative when the death drive asserts itself. Whenever the presence of death becomes tangible, the characters find themselves stuck in the melancholic circles of linguistic repetitiveness: Isa's "Ever, ever, ever" is a helpless marker of the presence of death announced in La Trobe's words on the same page (180). This sequence echoes the phrase "never, never, never" in the description of the empty library at the beginning of the novel. There we find the tortoiseshell butterfly "[beating] on the lower pane of the window; beat, beat, beat; repeating that if no human being ever came, never, never, never, the books would be mouldy, the fire out and the tortoiseshell butterfly dead on the pane" (17). The last litany-like passage correlates the notions of depopulation, self-destruction (the melancholic reiteration of "beat, beat, beat"), and the termination of voice, and suggests that repetition is, at bottom, an abnegation of speech; a stasis performed verbally.

Consistently, a cessation of agons always brings speech to a halt in *Between the Acts*. The image of the snake choking with a toad resides at the very verge of the representational plane, and, as such, it cannot be communicated—it can only bear a traumatic trace on Giles's tennis shoes. Unsurprisingly, then, Giles finds himself unable to command metaphor when he tries to describe the menacing approach of the war:

> Giles nicked his chair into position with a jerk. Thus only could he show his irritation, his rage with the old fogies who sat and looked at views over

coffee and cream when the whole of Europe—over there—was bristling like...He had no command of metaphor. Only the ineffective word "hedge-hog" illustrated his vision of Europe, bristling with guns, poised with planes (*BTA* 53).

This unsuccessful attempt to articulate a historical condition conforms well with Abraham and Torok's designation of the melancholic impasse as an anti-metaphor, an annulment of figurative language. Opposed to the life-giving and sense-giving activity of "metamorphizing" (i.e., introjection), severe melancholia "*entail[s] the fantasmic destruction of the act by means of which metaphors become possible*" (*The Shell and the Kernel* 132; the authors' emphasis). The cryptic immurement of his-torical loss gestured in the two Giles episodes cited above precludes the character from articulation and, thus—Abraham and Torok claim—cognition. The analyst/writer's task in the face of such incapacitating stasis is, then, to rescue traces, to recover the activity of metaphorizing and sense-giving. It is from an awareness of this task that comes, I suggest, Woolf's effort to follow such collapses of language by instantaneous affective recathecting of language through activation of colors, rhythms, and alliterations.

This process of resublimation is so immediate that it appears that the text repeatedly conflates the termination of voice with its triumphant rise. Rarely are we given the opportunity to observe their different functioning in succession, but one of the examples quoted above furnishes us with a metatextual comment on this dynamic. No sooner have we learnt that "repetition was senseless, hideous, stupe-fying," we hear Lucy inviting, "in a low voice, as if the exact moment for speech had come, as if she had promised, and it was time to fulfil her promise, 'come, come and I'll show you the house'" (67). Here the narrating voice ascribes to Lucy its own task of bypassing the stasis, of retrieving signification. To understand this intimate twine of speech and silence we need to remember that Woolf proposes the existence of three, rather than two, affective modes: "Peace was the third emo-tion. Love. Hate. Peace" (92). Peace is an affect of a different, "unagonic" register. It is an affective posture disquietingly cognate with death, Freud was wont to argue, and it should come as no surprise that "peace" read "death" in the early typescripts of Woolf's *Between the Acts* (*PH* 442). Silence and death are, however, repeatedly linked to art in the novel. Both the deadly peace of the empty library and the col-orful vista quoted above foreground the aesthetic allure as a condition that both symptomatically represents and mitigates the melancholic impasse. Comparably, the picture of the long lady, the emblem of art, leads us to death via the paths of repetition ("Empty, empty, empty; silent, silent, silent") only to resublimate, resexualize the language, and, perhaps more problematically, the death itself, in the final alliterative sequence: "a vase stood in the heart of the house, alabaster, smooth, cold, holding the still, distilled essence of emptiness, silence" (36-37).

Thus Woolf's conjuring up of a category of death-silence-peace is unorthodox: the latter always verges, holds onto utterance, or resublimation. A vision of intimate relationship between melancholia and language/art that emerges from this convergence is comparable to that developed by Melanie Klein in the 1930s and later expanded by Segal and Kristeva.[21] This vision holds that silence/stasis/emptiness is necessary for a sound or art to emerge. We hear the same insight vocalized in the mature Woolf's description of the beginning of history of creative work, where the initial movement of art-life is associated with Anon's voice that "broke the silence of the forests" (1). Great art, Kristeva argued decades later, emerges precisely at the junction between melancholic silence and mournful utterance. Rather than instantiating an unproblematic work of mourning, Woolf's fiction performs this very moment of passage, when the affect slips into the effect. It suggests, although by no means promises, a sublimatory outcome for our personal and historical paralyses.[22]

It is for this reason that Woolf insists on creative-erotic breaching of stasis. Nature itself aids Miss La Trobe in contravening another standstill, this one unplanned. Just as tense, compact silence engulfs the empty stage and slightly irritated spectators, one of the nearby cows starts calling out for her calf, and her bellow spreads to the whole herd. As Woolf expands this mundane event spatially and temporally, one realizes that we witness an axial moment in history: "The whole world was filled with dumb yearning. It was the primeval voice sounding loud in the ear of the present moment" (BTA 140). Not incidentally, this primeval voice is related to the libidinal drive. The cows vigorously lash their tails, toss their heads and bellow, "as if Eros had planted his dart in their flanks and goaded them into fury." Their primeval yearning sets history in motion: the bellow has "filled the emptiness" and "continued the emotion" (140-41). This life-saving, agon-propelling activity is revisited in La Trobe's deliberate dramatic stasis I discussed earlier; there, the breaching of silence is helped by a "sudden, profuse" shower (180). Together, the two episodes articulate Woolf's response to the modernist "wasteland paradigm"—her harkening to the symbolic figurations of fecundity to irrigate and fertilize the soil scarred by history. This life-giving measure will then be repeated in the twin ending of the novel, where the "primeval yearning" brings about a resounding affirmation of the creative work of Eros. While trying to forge the first dialogue between the two shadowy figures of her new play in a smoky pub, Miss La Trobe experiences a semi-mystical moment of creation: sensing that "the mud became fertile" again, she "hears" the first words of the play, words that will restore to life the dialogic mode of human drama (212). It is these words (which readers are not allowed to hear) and the invocation of fertility that, then, close Giles and Isa's last diegetic encounter.

In accord with the work of undecidability—or Freudian melancholic "ambivalence"—that nourishes the text, Woolf, however, offers one final corrective to this affirmation of the erotic and the agonic. Lest we be deluded by this overt faith in humankind's capability to rejuvenate itself, La Trobe's artistic revelation has a taste of drink, "the need of [which] had grown on her" (*BTA* 211), and Giles and Isa's concluding intercourse has to be prefaced by a fight. Likewise, the series of agons—productive or destructive, unifying or separating, comprehensible and incomprehensible—seem to resume not because they are always constructive but because history has to unfold. There is no more romanticism in this insight than in the image of Isa as the donkey who will patiently stumble its way "till [its] heels blister and [its] hoofs crack" (155) into what modernists—Woolf, Freud, and Benjamin alike—ironically called "progress." And, yet, these episodes seem also to adumbrate the perdurance-paradox that would be voiced at the end of Beckett's trilogy of novels: "You must go on, I can't go on, you must go on, I'll go on."[23] So why, I wonder, is the persistence on this road so important to Woolf?

The Form of Countermourning: Unrecorded Histories and the Syntax of Unity-Dispersion

The main function of narrative, Paul Ricoeur has claimed, evolves from "necessity to save the history of the defeated and the lost" (I: 75). There is indeed another reason why Woolf's "donkey" must endure on the stage of history. Like Benjamin's Angel of History, the "donkey" has a vital task on its voyage—the duty to record the unrecorded:

> She roused herself. She encouraged herself. "On, little donkey, patiently stumble. Hear not the frantic cries of the leaders who in that they seek to lead desert us. Nor the chatter of china faces glazed and hard. Hear rather the shepherd, coughing by the farmyard wall; the withered tree that sighs when the Rider gallops; the brawl in the barrack room when they stripped her naked; or the cry which in London when I thrust the window open someone cries..." (*BTA* 156)

For writing to be an active response to history, Isa's soliloquy suggests, it must address the anguish of the present moment in such manner that occlusions and gaps—someone's cry, the raped girl's fight, a shepherd's coughing—are rescued from the abyss of non-knowledge and brought to the sphere of meaning and social cognizance. To engage with melancholic history means, then, to expose the mechanics of concealment that subtends it. The text must become an obsessive address to the gaps in record, for only in this way the ambivalence of affects accompanying such history will also become legible. Readable in Isa's words is, then, an implicit poetics, one that decisively influences both the selection of narrative material and the unique operation of language in *Between the Acts*. The specifics of this performance merit special attention here.

In chapter 1 I have suggested that the modernist writers' habit to riddle their supple syntax by gaps and elisions is a calculated textual maneuver: by translating the structure of melancholia into an enunciating strategy, modernists signal a comparable organization of historical record. Woolf's frustration with recorded history and her life-long mission to reclaim, critically and artistically, the "Lives of the Obscure" (*Diary* III: 37) made her particularly receptive to the use of such devices. But the question that Woolf increasingly posed to herself in the late 1930s was neither one of the existence of historical and personal "gaps in record" (there she had no doubts) nor that of the need to represent them in writing; nor was she unaware that the symptomatology of melancholia could be used analogically to gesture such gaps. Rather, she pondered, not without urgency, the following question: How to weave a hyper-sign around and with the concrete historical gaps, and not occlude them or even lose them inadvertently in aestheticization of melancholia/mourning? To interrogate this representational conundrum, Woolf strategizes to include in her last novel both the (hi)stories of the "obscure" and typographical and semantic markers of occlusion as equally legitimate aspects of text-space.

The principal effect of Woolf's "playing around the gap" is the presentation of the historical record as deficient to such extent that its recuperation appears well-nigh impossible. With equal ruthlessness, official history fails to document peasants' lives and La Trobe's creative work, the gossiping of maids and the chirruping of birds; yet, precisely these alternative historical narratives grant continuity to history, Woolf's text insists. And so, from the moment when the voice of a "daylight bird chuckling over the substance and succulence of the day" (*BTA* 3) intervenes in the conversation in the parlor room and the reader's attention is drawn to an alternative history, incidents of which remain mostly "inaudible, invisible" to us, unspoken histories keep on proliferating in *Between the Acts* (14; cf. DiBattista 81-84). At times they succeed in sequestering the narrative space for a couple of pages; more frequently, they concede to the status of miniature but startling interpolation. One such encroachment striates the text in the scene in which young men and women decorate the barn before the pageant. First several intruders enter the narrative space: "A hen strayed in, a file of cows passed the door; then a sheep dog; then the cowman, Bond, who stopped" (28). Herein Woolf's narrative also stops in order to render the story of a character that would conventionally figure as an insignificant addendum to the plot. Readers find out that the "silent and sardonic" Bond "thought very little of anybody, simples or gentry." This realistic-satiric image rapidly transforms into a lyrical comparison, seemingly immaterial, per-plexingly over-cathected: "[Bond] was like a withered willow, bent over a stream, all its leaves shed, and in his eyes the whimsical flow of the waters" (28). The very next moment Bond cries for a cow and leaves the novelistic stage, never to mount it again, save for a brief appearance in the pageant. Still, this particular commotion of narrative space lingers in the reader's mind. This special rapport with the text occurs not only because a profoundly humane image of man rises from the page (we are accustomed to receive these from Woolf), or because these few sentences prove themselves extraordinarily functional (they summon both satiric and poetic narrative modes and introduce the text's major symbolic actants such as willows and cows), but also because Bond's passing by affectively recomposes surrounding elements of the narrative. Whatever is to happen in or around that barn, we feel, it will be mundane but emotionally overcharged; and its emotive content will be as varied, unstable, and unpredictable as "the whimsical flow of waters." It is through the affective refraction between "minor" stories such as this one and the major storyline that the narrative material of *Between the Acts* is focused.

The project of reclaiming the obscure, of course, lies at the heart of Miss La Trobe's play, where an unlikely cast purports to perform nothing less than the entire history of England and the history of English literature. These outsiders in the realm of theater are also outside the historical record, but Woolf makes their names, as well as the "orts, scraps, and fragments" of their existence, dis-coverable in a series of recognition scenes in which the villagers' private lives are comically contrasted with the theatrical roles they play for one night (the reader learns, for example, that the tobacco-seller Eliza Clark hides behind the mask of the Queen Elizabeth character in the play, or that the role of noble Flavia is played by the shop assistant Millie Loder; *BTA* 135). As history of private life vies with the official record, these deceptively light juxtapositions unsettle the narrative space and draw one's attention to other, more surprising instances of textual individu-ation. The same play of minor and major narratives is, for example, activated in the representation of sounds. The text acoustically foregrounds a number of previ-ously "obscured" sounds and transforms them into irreverent personifications: the room-shell "sings" (36), the plane "whizzes," "whirs," and "buzzes" (15), the cows "moo" (84), the breeze "rustles" (98), the cars "purr" (73), the gramophone "chuffs"

(76). Thus detached from a human producer and a human auditor, the sounds in the novel acquire a curiously autonomous status, indeed "stories" of their own: the characters' "voices impetuously, impatiently, protestingly [come] across the hall" (37); the music "wails" at the dispersion of the audience (97-98), and a popular tune "brays" and "blares" of its own accord (79). These and other textual individuations have a vital function in the novel: they instate a radical play of politico-historical possibilities. Readers find themselves immersed in a set of disquieting questions: Whose story is to be attended? Who has been given a voice? Whose voice has been subdued?...

Still, this seemingly egalitarian treatment of minor stories deceives the reader's expectations: no such story evolves into a leading narrative. Rather, Woolf's polyphonic world in *Between the Acts* emerges as constantly under threat of being censored or silenced by an authority external to itself. To gesture this condition, Woolf foregrounds the power of authorial intervention. Isa's poetic endeavors, for example, appear forcefully interrupted, as if their failure was governed not so much by diegetic needs as by the writer's, or history's, whim: "With a feather, a blue feather... flying mounting through the air... there to lose what binds us here...," Isa mumbles (*BTA* 15). It is interesting to note that, while semantically coherent, and sometimes even fluid, Isa's poetic syntax relies for its development on unmotivated elisions and unfounded caesuras. Both aborting and sustaining the poetic sequence throughout the novel, these bands of silence come to be experienced as punctures, or incisions (of a knife, of history, of poetry's limited capacity), crypts of the losses that cannot be articulated.

The use of bands of silence to gesture occlusions in "melancholic" history is most palpable precisely where the ostensible polyphony of the novel peaks—in La Trobe's pageant. Throughout the pageant, "a long line of villagers in shirts made of sacking" (*BTA* 77-78) contrapuntally passes in and out in the background of the "stage." As they enter and exit the stage, the villagers chant a rhythmic *parodos* recanting their own historical position and their work of "digging and delving" in history. At first the chant seems to promise jubilant recovery of verbal capacities and thus reinstallment of mourning-flow. Yet, as if reflecting the inner consummation of the communal ego, the peasants' song turns melancholic: half of their words are immured, inaudible. "Cutting the roads... up to the hill top... we climbed. Down in the valley... sow, wild boar, hog, rhinoceros, reindeer..." (78), the peasants saturate their account of history with pauses.[24] This communal cryptonymy deteriorates rapidly; it soon omits the epistemologically crucial connections between phrases and replaces them by gaps (ellipses) and half-adequate associative links, typical of melancholic speech: "Dug ourselves in to the hill top... Ground roots

between stones...Ground corn...till we too...lay under g-r-o-u-n-d..." (78).
Only "a few great names—Babylon, Ninevah, Clytemnestra, Agamemnon, Troy"
resound in this thwarted outline of general history, and before long the contrapun-
tal choir hears even these names dying away (140). The incorporation of silence
in the continuity of the chorus's sequence reveals that form is pointedly contingent on the shifting circumstances of the material world. Formally exteriorizing
the gaps and fissures of history, the peasants' song is structurally opposed to the
putative fullness of content (historical record or communal memory) that it purports to convey. If La Trobe's pageant is supposed to activate and sustain pastoral
memory, as argued by Esty (259), it fails at every step. The "scraps of the communal
and personal past" in *Between the Acts*, Gillian Beer has noted, emerge as recuper-
able "only as gossip and pastiche, a flotsam of significant fragments" (*Arguing* 156),
much like the historical debris growing skyward that Benjamin's Angel of History
contemplates.

The hidden political significance of the representations that foreground absence
and gaps in the perceptual field, Benjamin suggested in "Work of Art in the Age
of Reproducibility," lies in their capacity to operate as "evidence in the historical trial [*Prozess*]" (*SW* IV: 258). Woolf's pointers to the occluded social content
metamorphose the audience into detectives, melancholic interpreters of the traces
of the irrevocably lost. For a representation to function in this mode, the absent
content must not be semantically pinned down. Indeed the most intriguing feature of Woolf's syntax of gap in *Between the Acts* is not the political insight that it
ostensibly imparts—that the Hegelian whole of history is replete with holes—but
its resistance to inscribe these holes with a fixed meaning. While one can intuit
the structural content of these gaps (for Woolf, like Benjamin, it is "the anony-
mous" that hides in these crevasses), the actual referent and even the affective
value of Woolf's bands of silence remains undecided. Modernist writerly ethics,
I have suggested in chapter 1, is at its most profound when it refuses semantically to appropriate the "absent" or the "unrecorded" (that is, when it "melancho-
lizes" the historical content), while simultaneously gesturing its presence (that is,
"mourning" this content). Such performance is both desperate and hopeful; I have
termed it countermourning.

Does Woolf's vision in *Between the Acts* allow for a history beyond our fragmented, inadequately recorded, agonic history, though? If so, then Lucy is the sole
character who has been granted access to it. With her mind "given to increase the
bounds of the moment" (*BTA* 9), Lucy indulges in cross-temporal constellating, as
when she reads the dry prose of *Outline of English History*:

[She] had spent the hours between three and five thinking of rhododen-
dron forests in Piccadilly; when the entire continent [...] was all one; populated, she understood, by elephant-bodied, seal-necked, heaving, surging,
writhing, and, she supposed, barking monsters [...] It took her five seconds
in actual time, in mind time ever so much longer, to separate Grace herself,
with blue china on a tray, from the leather-covered grunting monster who
was about, as the door opened, to demolish a whole tree in the green steam-
ing undergrowth of the primeval forest. (*BTA* 8-9)

As if to gesture the homeless' search for "undivided totality," the thought of
Piccadilly summons to Lucy an imagined chronotope of the primordial kingdom
of swamp, an interest in which Woolf's characters sometimes share with Kafka's
and Bely's heroes. But Lucy is no homeless; she is, in fact, the only character in
Between the Acts who appears to have preserved the sense of immediacy between
the world and the self, the only one who can comfortably traverse history, and
probe its nature as a flux, or a string of constellations. In part, this singular capacity
should be interpreted in the context of Lucy's religiosity, but her cross-temporal
aptitude is also related to creative imagination, the only intellectual (or spiritual)
faculty, Woolf suggests, able to provide a response to the aporia of the time of history—history's simultaneous existence as collective singular and as dissociation of
the past, the present, and the future (Ricoeur III: 261; see, also, my discussion in
chapters 1 and 3). Lest we romanticize Lucy's metahistorical capacities, however,
the text is comically shrouded in the digressive functioning of her elderly mind.
So, as the episode draws to close another facet of this multi-temporal play gains
prominence: the conflictual cotemporality of personal and objective time, the concern with which, Ann Banfield suggests, guides modernists' experimentation with
narrative time (48). The comic corrective reveals Lucy as poorly equipped to deal
with the socium present, here emblematized in the maid, Grace. But the introduction of Grace, one of those significant "minor agents" in Woolf's narrative, merits
closer attention, since it engages the text in yet another set of temporal aporias;
these, so it appears to me, carry particular weight for the mature Woolf. While,
acting out the prerogatives of four-dimensional character, the maid dialogically
invades Lucy's mindscape and forces it to loop into present, Grace is also a cross-
temporal symbol—a reflection on the human being that she is. The last property
is conveniently preserved in her name. Given that the believing Lucy contemplates prehistory (and pre-Christian history), the shock of Grace's appearance,
with china on a tray, also signals the negotiation of a particular supra-historical
passage, or conflict, that Lucy is likely to consider at the moment—one between

the eschatological and geological time. The shape of this passage-chronotope is even less uniform than those of its individual components: like the insecure space where the self and the other face one another in melancholia, this is a morphing, fractured time-space—a room for dangerous thoughts.

Alongside this temporal fracturing, I am also intrigued by the particular "music" of this episode, the breathless agglomeration of phrases that, had they not been punctuated by surprising caesuras and finally bent by the comic twist, would have established a "whole" of history and might have even swept Grace into it. I have suggested earlier that, by its very structure, the protagonist-community in Woolf's *Between the Acts* is fated to mourn only partly successfully, and only in fragments. The textual model for such an impossible mourning rite can only take form of a multifarious structure, where expressive sonorous sentences alternate with anti-climactic (often ironic) phrasing and displaced caesuras. As the previous excerpt suggests, the functional harmony of Woolf's iridescent syntax always verges on breaking down; her sentences are led by their own chromatic contortions rather than by a fixed sentence-center, and are frequently halted by caesuras, fade-ins and fade-outs and shifts of descriptive mode. One may recognize the dominance of this syntactic patterning on the macro-level of the text, where narrative rhythm and unison are constantly refractured by caesuras, shifts of modes, elisions, fading in and out. The compositional problem that Woolf faces here is equivalent to that experienced by Miss La Trobe, as recorded in the holograph notes of *Between the Acts*: "And a damned ticklish [problem] it was: (...) they had to hear a discord; yet it must not break the harmony" (*PH* 521). The quandary was not new for Woolf. But it was the invention of the four-dimensional—individual-collective—protagonist in *Between the Acts* that enabled her conclusively to fuse the "uniting-fragmenting" mode of expression with her view of history. Establishing what I have termed the "broken music" of affects, here the disarraying of text effectively gestures a disjointed history, its sounds and its silences.[25]

This complex narrative strategy is most memorably articulated at the end of La Trobe's pageant, where the narrative both confirms and comments on the affect that has governed its structuring throughout. Freudian "conflict due to ambivalence" (*SE* XIV: 251) is here attached to the politics of community and translated into music. An optimistic tune opening the last act suddenly changes into a modern polyrhythm—broken, fragmentary, contortive—relaying, tightly overdetermined, positive and negative fissures of contemporary history: "The tune changed; snapped; broke; jagged. Foxtrot, was it? jazz? Anyhow the rhythms kicked, reared, snapped short. What a jangle and jingle! [...] What a cackle, what a rattle, what a yaffle..." (*BTA* 183) As the audience continues to listen to this playfully dissonant music, the children, "imps—elves—demons," come in, carrying mirrors of all sizes and origins. They reflect the mirror-sides toward the audience, performing the fragmentation of experience that is modern life but also forcing each viewer to experience its own Lacanian *méconnaissance* (Pridmore-Brown 418). The "infernal megaphone" halts the music and announces what has already been performatively suggested: that all we can ever cognize about ourselves is "scraps, orts, and fragments" (*BTA* 188; cf. *PH* 239). But a final change of music is pending. A Bach, Beethoven, or, perhaps, traditional tune finally seems to reunite the melancholic collective protagonist—"To part? No. Compelled from the ends of horizon; recalled from the edge of appalling crevasses; they crashed; solved; united" (189)—only to let it disperse again at the end of the play.

Thus, when the "triumphant yet valedictory" gramophone ultimately gurgles, "Unity-Dispersity" (201), it does have its needle on the right affective spot. But this phrase also metatextually comments on the reproduction of the same affective structure on all narrative levels of Woolf's last novel—from the figuration of time-space through syntax to characterization to dramatic action. By organizing her narrative through the concept of "a whole made of shivering fragments" (Woolf, *Passionate Apprentice*, 393), Woolf suggests that a similar structure informs all our affective behavior and interrelating. To a researcher in melancholic expression, this performance conclusively indexes the permeation of the text by human psychic structuring. Composed as interlace of dispersion and unison, *Between the Acts* exteriorizes its own melancholic protagonist: the novel becomes a "'We'...composed of many different things...we all life, all art, all waifs & strays—a rambling capricious but somehow unified whole" (*Diary* V: 135). To identify with, or even merely to relate to, this rambling whole is difficult. Yet, like primary identifications according to Freud and Klein, this task, tethered as it may be to melancholia, is simultaneously the sole life-giving and sense-giving act in the face of separation and loss.

And so the end of *Between the Acts* leaves us, as history left Woolf and her contemporaries, with mixed feelings. Half-hopeful, half-desperate, we watch the final movements of the actors—components, or body-parts, of our communal "protagonist." As Giles and Isa are left alone, emotionally compact silence covers Pointz Hall, a silence of "the night before roads were made, or houses" (*BTA* 219). This silence appears to suspend the action which, we have seen, needs to evolve into a (primordial) fight. The last word in the novel—at the point where its own "silence" should begin—is, however, a sound, the commencement of interrelating: "They spoke" (219). It is with a human voice, I note, that the novel both opens and closes. The trajectory has altered this voicing: while the beginning of *Between the Acts* parodies the conventional exchange in which what is important is silenced, the concluding intervoicing is decisively "primordial" and, presumably, meaningful. The subject of Giles and Isa's talk is not disclosed, yet we know it. We also know that it will engender another set of personal and historical agons, perhaps even "another life" (219). Rather than fading away, the last chime, we are relieved to hear, opens a space for a new play.

With its affirmation of life and relationship, on the one hand, and its lamentation of human destructiveness, on the other, the tenor of Woolf's last novel is indeed that of the fading-out tones of the gramophone, "triumphant yet valedictory" (196). The triumph here refers, we have seen, to an "erotic" persistence, the carrying-on of this lament against the horrors of history. If this final proposition of perdurance is melancholic, it is productively so. It says that, much as we may admire the sometimes emancipatory and aesthetically alluring nature of stasis, or the revelation of past historical gaps, it is only through a future-oriented human action that personal and general history keeps moving—even when this action takes form of anticipatory mourning of future catastrophes. For this reason Woolf's vision of perdurance in history is inextricable from her mature conviction that no human activity occurs in vacuum. The rooms of Pointz Hall are *rooms* only when they are inhabited; books in the library/words are *books/words* only when they have an audience (Woolf's intimate concern); the world, even when sardonically represented, is *the world* only with the human in it and the human articulating it, for the human itself is the pattern of that world. Silence, finally, is powerful and revelatory only in interaction with an influx of voices, distinct and dissonant, yet unified in a compositional whole.

Conclusion

Redescribing The World: Closing Apertures

The modernist "composer" is "rarely a crusader," Daniel Albright notes (3). Rather, she or he effects a change by probing technical boundaries, by investigating the possibilities of "aesthetic liberation" so as to foreground the potential for advancement not only in the realm of the arts, but also in material history itself. The intricate ways in which history penetrates modernist fiction, wields its form, reshapes its epistemology, and reframes the notion of the human represented in it, have stirred scholars' imagination and critical powers for almost a century. While modernist interventions in material history are profound, modernist scholars know that they are discernible only as effects, reconstellations of text by a force whose shape and meaning is deliberately left indistinct—much like the black hole whose efficiency we can gauge only through its imprints on the figuration of contiguous space. Critics have tried to address this detour effectiveness through a number of paradigms, and to add to the stock is a task both stimulating and disheartening. I have approached it with a belief that the modernist engagement with history is both most poignant and most effective when it acknowledges the rarity of historical "healing" and yet persists in its representation. I have used the term "countermourning" tentatively to describe one such writing practice: a kind of writing where the new content of historical experience is represented, enacted, and/or induced in the reader in such way that interpretative closure and the affective attitudes of acceptance and resignation (and thus also the affect-activity of consolation) are suspended. Questioning the efficacy of mourning rites as it performs them, countermourning fiction, I have argued, productively activates precisely that structural template which scholars keen on highlighting modernists' historical agency usually shun: melancholia.

While critical and cultural theories have been alert to the variants of resistant mourning, the category of "countermourning," derived from anthropology, proves to be particularly advantageous for modernist studies: it avoids straitjacketing modernist fiction into rubrics such as "normative" and "pathological," "progressive" and "regressive," "engaged" and "non-engaged," and, at the same time, takes into account historical and social vicissitudes and implications of modernist experiments, that is, the "lives" of modernist texts as literary rituals specific to human relations at a particular moment in time. It is in this spirit that I have also approached melancholia, the select modus of enunciation in countermourning fiction and the principle hermeneutic tool in this book. The marked rise of interest in affectivity, and the specific discursive dominance of the concept/condition of melancholia in the late nineteenth and early twentieth century (and, as I have suggested, wherever and whenever a particular constellation of social vicissitudes—waning of mourning practices, engagement or clash with modernization, unsettlement of givens, relegation of social losses into private sphere, and related phenomena—occurs) have served as pointers to the critical framework through which contemporary literary production and its relationship with certain transformations in the social sphere should be addressed in this book. The meaning of the concepts or categories that involve affects is always defined by the historical and cultural context their users are traversing, and so I have found *modernist* reconceptualizations of melancholia and its symptomatology particularly effective when assessing modernist fiction. Indeed, methodological approaches that derive from, and thus carry the "corrective" of, the object of study itself, not only give us a superior insight into the period-specific life of concepts—and thus their possible uses in literary production of the time—but also force us to reflect on retrospective readings that we impose on the subject.

For this reason, the critical framework operative in this book is premised on a few hermeneutic transversals that have become available in parallax but that were themselves suggested by the modernist psychoanalytic theory of melancholia. Challenging the way in which these concepts are commonly used in literary scholarship, this book, first, affirms continuities between mourning and melancholia, and posits the emergence of artwork at the precise site where the two meet. For the sake of both interpretative efficiency and conceptual clarity, I have furthermore differentiated a structure of experience/medical condition that we term "melancholia" and a symbolized behavioral posture labeled "melancholy," the latter being invoked through the varieties of public self-fashioning such as ennui, spleen, and the like. While previous aesthetic involvements with melancholia privileged the creation of allegories and emblems of melancholy and melancholic "types," modernists, this book argues, were much more interested in exploring the filiations between the melancholic structure of experience and the melancholic form of an artwork: they used the symptomatology of melancholia as a model for giving form to general history and period-specific history—its occlusions, paradoxes, transactions, and its impact on the affective functioning of the human. This kind of artistic engagement corresponds closely to the twentieth-century reconceptualization of clinical melancholia as decipherable not in symbols or emblems but precisely in the hindrances to, or modifications of, the normative/accepted functioning of the system of signs. As a consequence of contemporary reassessment of the symptom itself, the social function of such texts is complex: they perform societal correctives while acknowledging their frailty; they signal the melancholic's affective regression from, or disgust with, community, while insisting on verbalizing this state—on naming what has remained or is destined to remain psychologically and socially unnameable, so that both a new community and no-community could be envisioned; and, they forcefully import the struggles of ambivalence distinctive of the melancholic condition into their own horizon of interpretation.

To illuminate the operation of melancholia in modernist texts *Modernism and Melancholia* zooms in on the genre that, on the one hand, boasts special receptivity to extra-literary discourses, and, on the other hand, most vocally proclaims and most successfully disseminates its purported affinity with history-recording: the novel. Each in its own style and through its specific ways of focusing the narrative material, Andrei Bely's *Petersburg*, Franz Kafka's *The Castle*, and Virginia Woolf's *Between the Acts* engage the melancholic quandaries of their epoch: need for autonomy yet belonging; epiphanic search for unmediated totality; doubts about and devotion to language; issues of participation and non-participation in historical events; and, most importantly perhaps, the role of art in expressing, or working in, history. Significantly, these novels probe the symptomatology of melancholia not only to index their authors' melancholic concerns but also to challenge the inherited modes of narration and recording (including the recording of history). Their experimental countermourning, the previous pages have demonstrated, reshapes all the major aspects of the novel as a genre—its language, the space and time that it establishes, its narrative subject (an abstract or material object that functions as the coalescing point for representation), and the relationship between the narrative material and its epistemological and aesthetic boundaries (beginning, closure, absence, presence). Three vital elements of novelistic representation are particularly affected by this melancholic metabolizing of history: the character, the chronotope, and language.

In the late nineteenth and early twentieth century the representation of melancholia gradually moved from an exposition of melancholic types to the reconstitution of the protagonist as heterogeneous and thence analogous to the newly defined "melancholic" ego. Comparable to Freud's contemporary "heterogenic turn," this melancholic restructuring of character in fiction sees narrative bodies transforming into free-floating fragments, subject-object continuums, or discordant multitudes, and, at times, textual entities auto-reflexive to the point of self-cancellation. One can observe the effects of this new set of figurative strategies in the symbolic overtax of Bely's characters and their simultaneous tensional fluidity as mere particles of space; in the accentuated functionality of Kafka's characters that lays bare not any coherent psychological outlook (or any specific psychological disturbance, for that matter) but the social and psychological function of "self" as an operational or malfunctioning coalescing point for drives; and in Woolf's refiguration of character as embodiment of psychic transitivity and sign of (im)possible merger. As the previous pages have argued, such strategies of figuration have one distinct social function: by putting center-stage a fragmented, heterogeneous and emphatically auto-reflexive "melancholic self," modernist novelists also challenge what they perceive to be a misleadingly homogenous picture of the world-subject.

The same turn is observable in the novelistic chronotope that these figures inhabit, or into which they, as in the case of Bely's characters, extend. A privileged site for interaction with history and the most important symbolic container for affects, the chronotope in modernist fiction foregrounds the permeability of the inner and the outer time-space in the exact fashion in which the boundaries between the two are challenged in melancholia. As a result of this metabolic processing of interior affects and external perceptions, an emotionally accentuated, fragmented, and undecided space is created; and this space still paradoxically aspires to be a "realistic" representation of the material world (the chronotope in Bely's *Petersburg* is probably the most playful instance of such claim, while Kafka's contained limbo between the two deaths may well be its most somber articulation). As observable in all three novels under scrutiny here, the modernist chronotope often projects histories of *longue durée* and/or gestures toward a quasi-mythic totality, while simultaneously insisting on the impossibility of affirming, or even cohering, any comprehensive visions of history. To realize this double move, the modernist chronotope often depends on the stringing of (unreliable) memories and actantial iteration, both of which blur the boundaries between the past, the present, and the future, and is most frequently constellated through a drive to engage with gaps and absences in the time-space of the novel. In novels such as Woolf's *Between the Acts* these gaps serve as performative embodiments of the melancholic hole that both promises the return of lost objects and precludes their reappearance; and thus as a good analogue for some irretrievables of received history.

This reworking of the novelistic world entails feverish examination of language: the inconclusive probing of phonemes, rhythms, and sounds (Bely, Woolf); insistence on ambiguous qualifiers and quantifiers (Kafka); presentation of occlusion, linguistically and typographically (Bely, Woolf); marked use of parataxis (Bely, Kafka, Woolf); and deployment of many other narrative devices cognate with, or derived from, the symptomatology of melancholia. In terms of emulating the melancholic's language, Bely's and Kafka's verbal performances in particular present the extremes of the melancholic discursive practice: while the former performatively engages almost all markers of the associative, hyperactive speech found in "subclinical" melancholia, the latter disturbingly replicates the slothfulness and tonal monotony characteristic of more severe, stuporous forms of the condition. Both, however, operate around textual gaps: while Bely's syntax is ludically punctuated by unwarranted elisions and insertions of blank space, Kafka's lengthy sentences are semantically segmented in such ways that meaning is at once espoused and denied, disquietingly insisting on the melancholic foreclosure of the critical signifier. The same strategy is given grave historic significance in the performance of the chorus in Woolf's novel—a text about those situations, personal and historical, that challenge our command of metaphor and our ability to concatenate. I have correlated the impassioned, painfully elaborated, verbal investigation such as we find in these three novels and many other modernist texts with the melancholic patient's attitude toward language—his or her simultaneous mistrust and exaltation of language; a joint structure of feeling that presents itself as a call for (knowingly impossible) revitalization of the links between the signifier and the signified.

The last juncture is important; for such writing practice presupposes a certain amount of belief in the efficacy of mourning ritual that is literature—a belief that Bely, Kafka, and Woolf seem to have shared. It is for this reason that I have deliberately left open the question of ultimate social efficacy of the modernists' use of melancholia (noting, too, that, from an important perspective, social efficacy is unquantifiable), and have settled on a view of melancholia as not an escapist "frame of mind," but as a distinct writing-reading practice that reflects upon, constitutes, and generates experiential reality. This practice creates ripples: engaging with the unappropriables in Bely's, Kafka's, and Woolf's fiction is an experience with transforming effects on the reader, the social or personal significance of which modernist scholars rarely admit (for fear of being sentimental), but on which thinkers such as Agamben, Adorno, Benjamin, Bloch, Freud, Jameson, and Ricoeur—to mention only those often invoked in this book—all seem to agree. For one, Agamben has linked his own inquiry into aesthetic melancholia to the formation of utopias: "Only if one is capable of entering into relation with unreality and with the unappropriable as such is it possible to appropriate the real and the possible," he writes insightfully (*Stanzas* xix). The incidence of reading a text, and a "melancholic" text in particular, here appears as an exercise in possibilization: it re-describes the world and suggests new modes of being to the critic herself. I suspect that the same or similar may apply to the studies of affects in general, as these tend to establish and sustain particularly strong emotive rapports between the context, the text, and the reader. But I should like to bracket these general observations now—deserving as they are of another book—and instead, in closure, point to the specific methodological gain that an engagement with melancholia's apertures may offer to new modernist studies. Let me follow Freud and Woolf in suggesting a structural analogy here: the apertures inherent to a concept may facilitate and support openness in its context-specific applications.

The issue of contextual specificity is not incidentally invoked here. One of the dangers of proposing any, however broad, paradigm for reading modernist production is that it risks speaking to one specific set of texts and readers at the expense of others who may not share all or some of the operative parameters inscribed in the paradigm. I am very much aware of the challenges implied; I myself have recently expressed doubts in universal validity of the affiliation between modernity and modernism as such (Bahun in Wollaeger 42). One could guard a paradigm (e.g., modernist melancholia, or practice of countermourning, defined in this book in the context of European modernism) from the flood of global exceptions by simply abrogating the privilege of general validity. But this strategy only seemingly solves the problem, and it forces, in turn, the disquieting questions about purposefulness of critical endeavor itself. More useful and daring, it seems to me, is to think through the paradigm as a *weakened concept*, and thus flexible and site-specific. Thus rethought, the framework of melancholia appears to be particularly amenable to geocultural extensions and modifications. This is so because, for all the overflowing of its notional scope (or precisely because of it), melancholia most frequently announces itself as a "weakened" concept: productively besmirched by human affect, it is necessarily creolized by the cultural, social, historical, and disciplinary contexts from which it is defined. To use this "weakened" concept responsibly to analyze global modernist production, then, would imply an investigation of not only the applicability of psychoanalytic insights across the globe (an endeavor which, I suspect, always runs the risk of simplification) but also, and more productively, of what site-specific conceptualizations of conditions and affective postures related to melancholia exist in various locales, and how they square, historically and structurally, with modernist practices in these sites.

This book has already made one small step in that direction. Despite the commensurability of their "melancholic" concerns, and some degree of shared material and cultural history, Bely's, Kafka's, and Woolf's texts are presented here as exemplary in their harkening to their specific historical vicissitudes: historical melancholia of Bely's 1913/1915-1916/1922 novel, tracking the tumultuous passage from imperial Russia to the early Soviet Union, is different from the melancholic performance of Kafka's 1922 Czech-German-Jewish narrative that, amidst negotiations of national and subnational identities, probes the routes to an irretrievable "home"; and both are unlike Woolf's negotiation of the tropes of Englishness and Britishness through "mourning in advance" at the beginning of the Second World War, and her reappropriation of Freud's theory of drives for feminist concerns. And so, in *Modernism and Melancholia*, the concept of melancholia also subtly changes and accrues meanings with each locale and each writer. Yet there is something that unites these diverse performances: their authors' belief that a relay of this complex affective posture necessitates a comparable reshaping of the novel by the kind of representation that makes use of inconsistency, incoherence, over-determination, and other markers of "symbolic collapse." As I am closing this book and projecting toward future inquires in the subject, I venture to suggest that identifying such or similar writerly response to a comparable set of affects and describing it in its own terms *before* recasting it in the vocabulary of the imported conceptual scaffold may be one way to extend this investigation to other geocultural contexts and temporalities; it may also be a means to liberate oneself from the pressure of the paradigm, while still making use of it. This hermeneutic missive asks us to develop critical practices that include, as the very principle of their operation, openness to the correctives provided by the object of inquiry itself; it invites us to honor modernist texts, whenever and wherever they appear, as not only conceptually rich but also conceptually insubordinate.

Notes

Introduction

1. *Pace* Adorno, *Kierkegaard.*

2. These descriptions appear in Eco; Foster xi; Levin 292; Lukács, *The Meaning of Contemporary Realism*, 17–46; Simmel, "The Crisis of Culture," *Simmel on Culture*, 94.

3. On this topic, see Friedman, "Definitional Excursions," and the variety of essays collected in Wollaeger, esp. Mark Wollaeger, "Introduction," 3–22.

4. On the nosological difficulties in classifying and diagnosis of the condition, see Stroebe et al; Taylor and Fink 1–2, 346–370. On melancholia as a specifier for major depressive episode, see *DSM IV-TR* 419–20.

5. On a cursory look, one is led to believe that a similar dynamic abides in temporally different modernisms; but such investigation is beyond the scope of the present book.

6. See pseudo-Aristotle. For a comparable psychoanalytic discussion, see Klein, "Mourning and its Relation to Manic-Depressive States," *WMK* I: 360, and "Infantile Anxiety Situations Reflected in a Work of Art and in the Creative Impulse," *WMK* I: 210–218; Jamison, esp. 50–99 and 102–147.

7. See, among others, Bhabha; Butler; Wilson. On "resistant mourning," see Derrida; Rae; Clewell, "Mourning beyond Melancholia" and *Mourning.*

8. On "matrix approach" to modernism, see Schwartz 5, 9.

9. It is in this sense, I believe, that melancholic performance emerges as both a symptomatic representation of history and its "negative," what Adorno called a "determinate negation of a determinate society" (Adorno, *Aesthetic Theory*, 321).

Chapter 1

1. See, influentially, Lacan, "The Essence of Tragedy"; Staten; Butler; Derrida 139–164.

2. Homans, "Introduction," 23. See Young, *The Texture of Memory* and *At Memory's Edge.* Jochen and Esther Gerz designed, among other notable interventions in monumental art, the "Monument against Fascism" (Hamburg, Germany, 1986).

3. The details on the above-mentioned turn-of-the century discussions of melancholia are listed in the Bibliography. See, also, influentially, Kraepelin.

4. Freud, *Freud to Fliess*, 250. For Freud's first discussion of melancholia, however, see *Freud to Fliess*, 99.

5. The letter by a melancholic patient held in a French asylum, recorded in Roubinovitch and Toulouse 171; also qtd. in James, *The Varieties of Religious Experience*, 101; see 88–112.

6. The First World War introduced the "idea of endless war as an inevitable condition of modern life" (Fussell 74) and the October Revolution staged an exemplary modernist move—the overthrow of the old and the enthronement of the new (Anderson 96–113).

7. *Pace* Stauth and Turner in Sheppard, "Modernism and Modernity," 17.

8. On Freud as "successful mourner," see Capps; Homans, *The Ability to Mourn*.

9. As invoked by Virginia Woolf, *Three Guineas*, 85.

10. Freud's sons Ernst and Martin were recruited at the onset of the war and for the two years the family was, as testified by Freud, in a state of mourning-in-advance (Abraham and Freud 211). For Freud's reactions to the First World War, see, also, Jones II: 168–206. For details of the Freud-Jung break-up, see Freud and Jung 529–37.

11. Jones 285. For a more general account, see, also, Freud, Ferenczi, Abraham, Simmel, and Jones; and *SE* XVII: 205–216.

12. On filiations between Freud's thought on mourning and anthropological assessment of mourning practices, in particular, Robert Hertz's studies of attitudes toward death, see Laplanche and Pontalis 485.

13. See, among others, Butler; Clewell, "Mourning beyond Melancholia;" Derrida; Woodward.

14. Freud is indebted to Karl Abraham for the latter argument. See Karl Abraham, "A Short Study of the Development of the Libido, Viewed in the Light of Mental Disorders" in *Selected Papers of Karl Abraham*, esp. 436-38.

15. Because it enables the investigation of transgenerational loss, and of the possibility of a silenced past being spoken through a melancholic counter-narrative, this particular aspect of Freud's thought has proved productive in subsequent melancholia studies and, in particular, in readings of postcolonial melancholia; see, as examples of the variety of the spectrum, Nicolas Abraham and Maria Torok; Baucom, Gilroy; Eng and Kazanjian.

16. In his essay on Beckett's *Endgame*, Adorno has made a similar claim in relation to modernist art as such: that disgust, or nausea, has been the most productive force in the arts since Baudelaire ("Trying to Understand *Endgame*," 121). Incidentally, Adorno also relates this nausea to "tedium of spirit with itself" (121), paraphrasing John Climacus's well-known description of *acedia* (cf. Climacus 162).

17. Two equally probable interpretations arise from Freud's recasting of melancholia as universally formative: a) melancholia gets subsumed under mourning: the qualities previously described as distinctive of melancholia (incorporation and the inner battles of the ego) actually pertain to every mourning-process; b) mourning gets subsumed under melancholia: melancholia is constitutional, and mourning is merely its psychologically competent handling—that is, a series of adequate mourning-rites. For the first interpretative focus, see Derrida; Laplanche 234–59. For the second interpretative stream, see Kristeva, *Black Sun*. For a clinical compromise, see Baker.

18. Such reading is almost a staple in Joyce studies. For one of the more comprehensive studies of Joyce's view of history in the context of this phrase, see Spoo.

19. This association is announced a few pages earlier; see Joyce 32.

20. Some valuable research on these comparative links exists. On Kierkegaard and Freud, see, in particular, Nordentoft, esp. 254–272; on Kierkegaard and Joyce, see Goldman (Arnold), and, more recently, Lisi.

21. Nordentoft; Ferguson. On significance of melancholia as personal experience, see Kierkegaard, *The Point of View for My Work as an Author, KW* XXII: 79–83.

22. Thence Kierkegaard's circumlocutory definition of the self reads as follows: "The self is a relation that relates itself to itself or is the relation's relating itself to itself in the relation; the self is not the relation but it is the relation's relating itself to itself" (*KW* XIX: 13).

23. On *acedia*, see Climacus 162–64 (Gradus XIII, cols. 857–64 in Migne). Johannes Climacus is one of Kierkegaard's most important pseudo-selves, the "author" of *Philosophical Fragments* and its companion piece, *The Concluding Unscientific Postscript*, as well as of *Johannes Climacus, or De omnibus dubitandum est*.

24. For Benjamin's negative evaluation of Kierkegaard's thought, see *SW* II: 703–705. For Kierkegaard's influence on Benjamin, however, see Nägele.

25. See, also, Bersani 2. *Pace* Agamben, *The Man without Content*, 105–6.

26. This process is similar to the dynamics of "altering and disguising" in creative writing. Cf. "Creative Writers and Day-dreaming," *SE* IX: 143–153; *Moses and Monotheism, SE* XXIII: 1–138, esp. 70–72.

27. See, also, *Birth of Clinic*, 91-92, 93-100, and, on the discursive profiling of the melancholic symptom, 124.

28. Also juxtaposed, with a different purpose and conclusions, in Agamben, *The Man without Content*, 108; see, also, Agamben, *Stanzas*, 11–5.

29. Such was, at least, the case of the late eighteenth-century novel, according to Habermas in *The Structural Transformation of the Public Sphere*.

30. Lukács, *The Theory of the Novel*, 60. Basing his argumentation in *The Theory of the Novel* on the difference between the state of immanence ("undivided totality"/ "integration"/ "homogeneity") and transcendence (various grades of "separation"/ "division"), Lukács locates the provenance of the genre of the novel in the epic. Unlike the epic, however, where one may intimate a link to the "concrete totality" of life, the novel, Lukács claims, is doubly estranged (separated) from the presumed totality of life. This secondary separation allows the novel to structure itself as the form of "transcendental homelessness," galvanized by dual reflexivity. The conceptual language employed by Lukács in *The Theory of the Novel* bears the traces of the modernist melancholic apprehension of history we have come to appreciate in Kierkegaard and Benjamin, and his "historico-philosophical" theory appears as an interlocutor for a wide range of psychoanalytic tenets revolving around the concept of melancholia. Little wonder, then, that Lukács's Preface written in 1964 denounces *The Theory of the Novel* as a product of his youthful "'Kierkegaardisation' of the Hegelian dialectic of history" (18).

31. Sometimes they transplant the biographical search for home observable in realist fiction into the communal experience of homelessness, or, as Lukács would later allege, into "impersonal" homelessness (*The Meaning of Contemporary Realism*, 1958).

32. "Fusées," no. 15, *Oeuvres complètes*, 630; my translation. Also quoted, but with a different purpose, in Holland xi.

33. Naturally, the process outlined above implies creative distribution rather than direct transposition of the material world, in both Bakhtin's theory and my reading thereof. The

chronotope of a certain work can concern spaces and times that are not necessarily linked to the present of writing, or, else, those which sport temporality or spatiality that is impossible in "actual reality." For one eloquent modernist example, see Vladislav Vančura's *Marketa, The Daughter of Lazar* (1931).

34. This change in structure of experience found expression in transformative moments of scientific discourse such as Einstein's 1905 "relativity theory," Heisenberg's 1927 "principle of indeterminacy," and Simmel's analysis of the mental life of city dwellers (1903) and money economy (1900; 1907). For a comprehensive discussion of these issues, see Kern.

35. The latter is most influentially embodied in Henri Bergson's discussion in *Creative Evolution* (see, esp., 4-5).

36. It is coming to terms with holidays and anniversaries—those axial moments in personal history that reinforce the continuities between past and present—that enables the subject's future operation.

37. See Benjamin, "N," 61, as discussed in Bahun, "The Burden of the Past," 106-107.

38. The subtitle of this section is a paraphrase of the dictum in Heidegger 94.

39. *The Modernist Papers* 8. See, also, in an earlier account, Genette 201–18.

40. *Black Sun* 43–44. Kristeva's discussion is reliant on Klein I: 220–221; Segal, "Notes on Symbol Formation," 391-97; and Abraham and Torok, *The Shell and the Kernel*, 127–28. On the difference between *Verneinung* and *Verleugnung*, see Freud, "Negation," *SE* XIX: 235-9.

41. *Petersburg* 52; *Peterburg* 77. Cf., also, John Elsworth's translation of the 1916 text in Bely, *Petersburg 1916* 102.

42. *The Sense and Non-sense of Revolt* 60. See, also, Segal, *Psychoanalysis, Literature, and War*, 17–48, 123–32, 133–56.

Chapter 2

1. *Na perevale I-III: Krizis zhizni, Krizis mysli, Krizis kul′tury* III: 74. Appropriating the title of Georg Simmel's 1916 article "The Crisis of Culture" ("Die Krisis der Kultur"), Bely's book-length essay *Krizis kul′tury* is both an homage to and a polemic with Simmel's influential discussions on the relationship between art and life. According to Simmel, artistic and scientific forms, or what we call culture, express life and their form is shaped by life, but they over time become obsolete, indeed "opposed" to life. In the early twentieth century, he writes, the individual's mental life has undergone dramatic changes and these necessitated new forms of expression. Modernist avant-garde experiments (Simmel has in mind futurism and expressionism) display "a passionate desire for the expression of life, for which traditional forms are inadequate, but for which no new forms have been devised, and which therefore seeks pure expression in a negation of form, or in forms that are almost provocatively abstruse" (*Simmel on Culture* 94). Bely was an avowed admirer of Simmel's thought and the two appeared together in the 1910 Russian edition of *Logos*, to which Simmel contributed the essay "Zur Metaphysik des Todes" ("Toward a Metaphysics of Death," translated into Russian as "K voprosu o metafizike smerti"), and Bely contributed an account of Potebnia's thought on language, discussed below.

2. On display in The Museum of Andrei Bely, 53–55 Arbat Street, Moscow. The chart might have been intended to accompany, or shed light on, Bely's coextensively written *History of the Evolution of the Self-knowing Spirit* (*Istoriia stanovleniia samosoznaiushchei dushi*, unpublished).

3. Boris Pasternak, Boris Pilnyak, and Gregory Sanikov, in their Obituary in *Izvestiia* (Jan 9, 1934), as quoted in Malmstad, "Preface," 9. For the listing of Bely's opus, see Malmstad 357–359.

4. For the publication history of *Petersburg*, see Dolgopolov, "Roman A. Belogo *Peterburg*," esp. 569–583. Bely's unrealized screenplay, *Peterburg: Kinostsenarii po romanu, chasti 1–5* (1918), is hosted in Otdel rukopisei Gosudarstvennoi biblioteki imeni V. I. Lenina 516/3/37, 43—verso 44; cf. Tsivian 149–53. Bely's play *The Death of the Senator: Petersburg* (1925) premiered on the stage of MKHAT-2 on September 14, 1925. I have chosen the 1922 Berlin edition as the primary text, but I refer to the 1913, 1916, and 1928 editions when they provide additional insights.

5. On the role of embodied essences in Bely's work, see Langen 7–24. On the doctrine of Divine Wisdom, see Cioran, *Vladimir Solov´ev and the Knighthood of Divine Sophia*. On the influence of onomatodoxy on Russian thought on language, see Seifrid 82–129. For Bely's significant engagement with anthroposophy, see his letter of May 7, 1912, Rossiiskii gosudarstvennyi arkhiv literatury i iskusstva 53/1/100; Malmstad, "Andrei Bely i antroposofiia." Consider, however, Shklovsky's rather plausible claim that Bely's own "craftsmanship . . . devoured anthroposophy" in his text (174).

6. For Bely's account of symbolization as a shaping childhood experience, see Bely, *Na rubezhe dvukh stoletii* 115.

7. On socio-ethical aspects of symbolism, see Bely, "The Emblematics of Meaning," 111–97.

8. Maguire and Malmstad establish that the story spans September 30 to October 9, 1905 ("Translator's Introduction," *Petersburg* xiv). For the historical information on the period, see Riasanovsky 368–422, and, more comprehensively, Ascher.

9. For scholarship on "*mozgovaia igra*," see Alexandrov 109–18.

10. I borrow the term "melancholy of history" from Peter Fritzsche's discussion of the social mood after the French Revolution. See Fritzsche, esp. Chapter 3.

11. The 1916 text reads "*bezotchetnost' toski*"—inexplicable instinct of anguish; "unaccountable longing" (*Petersburg 1916* 120).

12. For the student's suicide note, see Lavretskii, also quoted in Steinberg 820. On these social postures more generally, see Steinberg 821–23.

13. For a contemporary assessment of displaced laughter, see Logvinovich 107–14; see, also, Steinberg 825.

14. For an alternative reading, see Emery 86. For Bely's anthroposophical belief in the coming of a "saturnine era," see letter to Blok of May 19/ June 1, 1912 in Bely-Blok 465.

15. For a survey of scholarship concerning Nikolai and the senator's shared identity, see Emery 83–84.

16. Berrios, *The History of Mental Symptoms*, 305. See, Cotard, "Du délire hypocondriaque dans une forme grave de mélancolie anxieuse," 168–74; "Du délire des négations," 152–70 and 282–96.

17. See Morrissey 312–45.

18. For a recent clinical assessment of the Cotard Syndrome, see Hansen and Bolwig.

19. See, also, Matich 285. Matich seems to imply, but never explicitly mentions, the link between incorporative phantasies and melancholia.

20. The discussion of the relationship between what Bely's contemporaries saw as one of the key symptoms of melancholia—namely, displaced laughter—and Bely's comic strategies,

unfortunately, has to be omitted here due to the limitations of space. The reader is, however, invited to reflect on the complex status of the comic in Bely's text in this light, too.

21. On these characteristics of melancholic language, see P. Hardy, R. Jouvent, and D. Widlöcher; Widlöcher, *Le Ralentissement dépressif*; Widlöcher, *Les Logiques de la dépression*. Bely assigned esoteric and affective meanings to different colors as early as in his 1903 article "Sacred Colors." On Bely's theories and use of colors, see Cioran, "A Prism for the Absolute: The Symbolist Colors of Andrey Bely."

22. Contrary to early interpreters who considered Bely's excisions in the 1922 text random and aimless, I regard all omissions and their traces in the text as a deliberate narrative strategy to foreground both melancholic and comic fissures of the textual idiom.

23. In the 1916 edition, the blank space is gradated. On Bely's typographical experimentation, see Janecek 26–67.

24. In the 1913 and 1916 versions, the difference consists of the omission of a word, apparently with the same intention; cf. *Peterburg* 77, 114.

25. On the foundation of St. Petersburg, see Riasanovsky 213–42. On the cultural symbolism of the city, see, influentially, Lotman, "The Symbolism of St. Petersburg."

26. For these and many other topographical incongruities, see Dolgopolov, "Obraz goroda v romane Andreia Belogo *Peterburg*."

27. On these chimeric properties of the city and its dwellers, see Lotman, "The Symbolism of St. Petersburg," esp. 197.

Chapter 3

1. On March 26 and 28, 1911, respectively; see Kafka, *Diaries 1910-1923*, 45–49.

2. On the genesis of *The Castle*, see Göhler 31–33.

3. See Max Brod, "Some Remarks . . ." 250–4; Göhler 32–33. On Kierkegaard, see Kafka, *Briefe* 236, 333f.

4. Kafka's request to have all his unpublished writings destroyed has troubled scholars since the first publication of *The Trial* in 1925, featuring Brod's editorial comment that he saved the text in defiance of his friend's explicit wish. Whatever the motivation for this peculiar demand might be—and critics have speculated ardently on this matter—this request should be interpreted in conjunction with Kafka's equally important decision to leave his novels unfinished. Rather than being taken as evidence of the writer's lack of confidence or skill, these decisions could be interpreted as two sides of one self-conscious artistic gesture, as parenthetically suggested above. On listings, editions, and availability of Kafka's opus, see Durrani 206–25.

5. *Das Schloß* 250; *Castle* 205. For K.'s likening of his own existence to that of the Castle, see *Castle* 217.

6. On various editions of Kafka's *The Castle*, see Durrani 209–214; Dowden 8–13.

7. For the above-mentioned interpretations, see Kracauer; Brod, "Nachwort zur ersten Ausgabe" 481–2; Emrich; Deleuze and Guattari; Corngold, *The Necessity of Form*. The text's obstinate refusal to be "finalized" or "completed" in writing and interpretation may also account for its weak integration in any of the socio-symbolic and political systems that have tried to appropriate it. While Kafka's fiction has admittedly turned into a sought cultural commodity, its status as commodity appears still to rely precisely on its opposition to the official culture. Cf. Adorno, "Notes on Kafka," 243–71.

8. *Lambent Traces* xi. On Kafka's cultural background, see Spector.

9. *Diaries* 301. *"Nazdar"* means "cheers" in Czech.

10. See Němcová. These parallels have been noticed, among others, by Brod ("Some Remarks..." 252–54) and Zimmermann (181–92). Another set of illuminating intertextual connections (again, *à rebours*) could be established between Němcová's following novel *In the Castle and in the Village by the Castle* (*V zámku a v podzámčí*, 1858) and Kafka's *The Castle*. This comparative inquiry is, unfortunately, beyond the scope of the present chapter.

11. On these doubts, see, among others, Suchoff 136–77; and Spector 160–94.

12. *Castle* 12. The verb "*(sich) vermessen*" denotes reassessing, mismeasuring, audacity, and other meanings.

13. Kafka's writing of *The Castle* coincided with the publication of Max Brod's *Heidentum, Christentum, Judentum: Ein Bekenntnisbuch* and Kafka and Brod's intense debate about Greek thought, paganism, and questions of cultural identity and segregation. See Kafka Brod op. cit. and Kafka, *Briefe* 279f.

14. Boa, "The Castle," 63. For the context, see Masaryk x, 2–23.

15. What "the proper stuff of fiction" may be is, of course, the question Woolf posed in her 1919 essay "Modern Fiction" (*Common Reader* 150). See, also, Kafka, *Letters to Milena*, 8–15.

16. The distortion of realistic coordinates of space and time in Kafka's fiction has received much critical attention. See, for one, Beicken.

17. Prelovšek 153. Josip Plečnik's work has received much critical attention recently, and he is hailed as both the most unusual among modernist architects and the precursor of postmodern architecture. Prelovšek's is, however, still the most comprehensive study of Plečnik's work available in English.

18. For an extensive discussion of this issue, see Berglund, esp. 208–10.

19. See, for one insightful discussion, Doležel, "Kafka's Fictional World."

20. See, influentially, W. G. Sebald 22–34.

21. See Blanchot, "Reading Kafka" and "Literature and the Right to Death" in *The Work of Fire*, 10–26 and 300–44, respectively.

22. See, also, Adorno, *Negative Dialectics*, 362.

23. The subheading is a quotation from *Castle* 23.

24. On Kafka's engagement with Kierkegaard, see Bunder I: 523–28. See, also, Sheppard, "Kafka, Kierkegaard, and the K.'s."

25. See David; Sheppard, "Kafka, Kierkegaard, and the K.'s."

26. This is not to say that Kierkegaard and Kafka failed to discursively deliberate on this issue—even obsessively so.

27. For bibliographic information on the debate whether any change in K.'s behaviour occurs in the course of the novel, and, if so, when exactly it occurs, see Bunder II: 463.

28. For Kafka's personal concern with actantial possibilities in 1921-1922, see, for example, *Letters to Milena* 203.

29. Cf. Sheppard, *On Kafka's Castle: A Study*; *pace* Philippi.

30. For a complementary discussion, see Durusoy.

31. Kafka's use of the adjective "*trübselig*," translated as "melancholy" by Mark Harman, deserves a parenthetical explanation. Traditionally, and in particular in the discursive use of the German Romanticists, *trübselig* denotes an opaque, despondent, lonesome soul, and is frequently affiliated with the elevation of such subjecthood as yearning for the sublime.

It is only in an extended, and largely discursive, sense that this adjective refers to a sufferer from melancholia, and it is indicative that Freud did not use this descriptive a single time in either "Mourning and Melancholia" or *The Ego and the Id*, his two major discussions of melancholia. The difference invoked here approximates the distinction between "melancholy" and "melancholia" (in English), which I have expounded on earlier. In this context, and with an ear open to the ironic undercurrents of this passage, Kafka's use of *trübselig* is strategic, and it operates in a comparable fashion to Bely's invocation of the discourse of melancholy in *Petersburg*.

32. For a different but complementary reading, see Boa, *"The Castle,"* 61–79.

33. Cf. Blickle 28; more generally, see, Blickle and Palfreyman. For a discussion of the features of the *Heimat* aesthetics in Kafka's novel, see Boa, *"The Castle"*, 64–65.

34. See *Diaries* 212–13, 244, 300; Corngold, *Necessity of Form*, esp. 228–49.

35. Bloch III: 1375–76; translation modified. The last clause is also the motto of Boa, *"The Castle."*

Chapter 4

1. *Letters* V: 444–45. The Shakespeare reference is from *Macbeth*, III. i. 92–95.

2. For the listing of Woolf's writings, see Kirkpatrick and Clarke.

3. To sample these critical attacks, see Lewis (Wyndham) 158–77; and Leavis.

4. For a more elaborate discussion of Woolf's reconceptualization of the reading and writing practices, see Bahun "The Burden of the Past."

5. *Anon* 1-2. For the text and its context, see Silver.

6. Leaska, "Afterword," *PH* 451; Eberly; Esty; Beer, "The Island and the Aeroplane"; Cuddy-Keane; Ames, "Carnivalesque Comedy in Virginia Woolf's *Between the Acts*"; Froula 289; Pridmore-Brown; Moore 147.

7. For an insightful discussion of Woolf's canine tropes, see Goldman (Jane).

8. For a different genealogy of La Trobe's pageant play, see Esty 247–48. On Woolf and Brecht, see Wiley.

9. Cf. *Diary* V: 15 and the stage setting for the first act of Henrik Ibsen's *Hedda Gabler* (1890).

10. For the argument that, in *Between the Acts*, the writer moves from a Kleinian (matri-centric) to a Freudian (androcentric, heterosexual) analysis of society, see Abel 108–30.

11. On the vicissitudes and modes of Woolf's reading of Freud, see Bahun, "Virginia Woolf and Psychoanalytic Theory," 92–109.

12. Virginia Woolf, Holograph Reading Notes, vol. 21, Berg Collection, New York Public Library.

13. Cf. William Shakespeare, "Troilus and Cressida," Act 5, Scene 2: "The bonds of heaven are slipp'd, dissolved, and loosed;/And with another knot, five-finger-tied,/The fractions of her faith, orts of her love,/The fragments, scraps the bits and greasy relics/Of her o'er-eaten faith, are bound to Diomed." Shakespeare, *Troilus and Cressida*, V. ii. 154–58.

14. According to Baucom, the constructions of "Englishness" has been consistently related to residing in, or longing for, magic, "auratic" locales, real or imaginary. He terms these sites "redemptive locales" (31) and sees the attachment to them continuing to influence the construction of Englishness in the post-imperial era, even though the engagement with another category, race, came to dominantly define "post-imperial melancholy."

15. *Diary* V: 89. Woolf commonly used the term "personal intensity," or "intensity," to denote a wide cluster of diverse psychological traits, dynamics, affects, and reactions to reality that comprise an individual's mindscape and behavior, as well as the impressionistic picture of an individual that the writer configures on the basis of these variegated data (for example, colors and tonalities associated with a certain character).

16. See Bahun, "Broken Music, Broken History." As in music, it is the emphasis on repeated measure that holds this unruly whole together. For example, repetition of and variation on the word "cradle" evokes the mythic and concrete circularity of life in key moments in the text, whereas consistent reproduction of words from the pageant in the "world of the characters" signals the intimate association between the structure of theater play and the dynamics of human life. Cf., also, Hillis Miller 203.

17. On the role of drawing room in Woolf's work, see, insightfully, DiBattista 41–63, esp. 62–63.

18. Parenthetically, the game of soccer originated in Middle Ages England and gained its popularity in the Elizabethan Age. The rules of the game were, however, different from those of the present-day sport. The game was played with a stone that was kicked throughout the whole town to the goal, customarily the very "gate" of the town. The game played by very young boys sometimes resembles this "original game." The first twenty minutes of the pageant that precede the scene in question deal with the history of England from the "barbaric period" to the Elizabethan Age.

19. Cf., with different conclusions, Beer 99–123, esp. 102.

20. *BTA* 76. On the multiple functions of the gramophone in *Between the Acts*, see Pridmore-Brown; Scott 97–113, esp. 104–13.

21. Incidentally, Woolf met Klein while she was writing *Between the Acts*; see *Diary* V: 208.

22. Cf. Kristeva 1989: 217.

23. Beckett 418. Cf. Adorno on Beckett, See, also, Adorno, *Negative Dialectics*, 381ff.

24. Cf. Abraham and Torok, *The Woolf Man's Magic Word*, 77–81. In de-italicizing the pageant portions of the text I follow Mark Hussey's editorial decision in the new edition of *Between the Acts*. See Hussey.

25. In a modified form and different context, parts of the present discussion appear in Bahun, "Broken Music."

Bibliography

Abel, Elizabeth. *Virginia Woolf and the Fictions of Psychoanalysis*. Chicago: The University of Chicago Press, 1989.

Abraham, Karl. *Selected Papers of Karl Abraham, M.D.* Trans. Douglas Bryan and Alix Strachey. New York: Brunner/Mazel Publishers, 1927.

Abraham, Karl, and Sigmund Freud, *A Psycho-Analytic Dialogue: the Letters of Sigmund Freud and Karl Abraham, 1907-1926*. Ed. Hilda C. Abraham and Ernst L. Freud. Trans. Bernard Marsh and Hilda C. Abraham. New York: Basic Books, Inc., 1965.

Abraham, Nicolas, and Maria Torok. *The Shell and the Kernel*. Trans. Nicholas Rand. Chicago: The University of Chicago Press, 1994.

_____ *The Woolf Man's Magic Word: A Cryptonymy*. Trans. Nicholas Rand. Foreword Jacques Derrida. Minneapolis: University of Minnesota Press, 1986.

Adorno, Theodor W. *Aesthetic Theory*. Trans. C. Lenhardt. London: Routledge and Kegan Paul, 1984.

_____. *Kierkegaard: Konstruktion des Ästhetischen*. Tübingen: Mohr, 1933.

_____. *Negative Dialectics*. New York: The Seabury Press, 1973.

_____. "Notes on Kafka." *Prisms*. Trans. Samuel M. Weber. Cambridge: The MIT Press, 1983. 243-71.

_____. *Notes to Literature*. Trans. Shierry Weber Nicholson. 2 vols. New York: Columbia University Press, 1991-1992.

_____. "Trying to Understand *Endgame*." *New German Critique* 25 (1982): 119-50.

_____. "Wagner's Relevance for Today." *Essays on Music*. Sel., intro., com. Richard Leppert. Trans. Susan H. Gillespie. Berkeley: University of California Press, 2002. 584-602.

Agamben, Giorgio. *The Man without Content*. Trans. Georgia Albert. Stanford: Stanford University Press, 1999.

_____. *Stanzas: Word and Phantasm in Western Culture*. Trans. Ronald L. Martinez. Minneapolis and London: University of Minnesota Press, 1993.

Albright, Daniel. "Introduction." *Modernism and Music: An Anthology of Sources*. Chicago: The University of Chicago Press, 2004.

Alexandrov, Vladimir E. *Andrei Bely: The Major Symbolist Fiction*. Cambridge, Mass.: Harvard University Press, 1985.

Ames, Christopher. "Carnivalesque Comedy in Virginia Woolf's *Between the Acts*." *Twentieth Century Literature* 44/4 (1998): 394–408.

Anders, Günther. *Franz Kafka: Pro und Contra*. Munich: Beck, 1951.

Anderson, Perry. "Modernity and Revolution." *New Left Review* 144 (1984): 96–113.

Arendt, Hannah. "Franz Kafka: A Revaluation." *Essays in Understanding 1930-1954*. Ed. Jerome Kohn. New York: Harcourt Brace, 1994. 69–80.

_____. "The Jew as Pariah. A Hidden Tradition." *Jewish Social Studies* 6/2 (1944): 99–122.

Ariès, Philippe. *The Hour of Our Death*. Trans. Helen Weaver. New York: Knopf/Random House, 1981.

_____. *Western Attitudes toward Death: From the Middle Ages to the Present*. Trans. Patricia M. Ranum. Baltimore: The Johns Hopkins University Press, 1975.

Aristotle [pseudo-Aristotle]. "Problema XXX. 1." *Problems II: books XXII—XXXVIII and Rhetorica ad Alexandrum*. London: William Heinmann Ltd., 1957. 10–12.

Ascher, Abraham. *The Revolution of 1905: A Short History*. Stanford: Stanford University Press, 2004.

Auerbach, Erich. *Mimesis: The Representation of Reality in Western Literature*. Fiftieth anniversary edition. Trans. Willard Trask. Princeton: Princeton University Press, 2003.

Bahun, Sanja. "The Balkans Uncovered: Toward *histoire croisée* of Modernism." Wollaeger 25–47.

_____. "The Burden of the Past, the Dialectics of the Present: Notes on Virginia Woolf's and Walter Benjamin's Philosophies of History." *Modernist Cultures* 3/2 (July 2008): 100–15.

_____. "Broken Music, Broken History: Sound and Silence in Virginia Woolf's *Between the Acts*." *Virginia Woolf and Music*. Ed. Adriana Varga. Bloomington: Indiana UP, 2014; forthcoming.

_____. "'Full Fathom Five Thy Father Lies:' Freud, Modernists, and History." *Exit 9: Reading Scars* 6 (2004): 3–22.

_____. "Virginia Woolf and Psychoanalytic Theory." *Virginia Woolf in Context*. Eds. Jane Goldman and Bryony Randall. Cambridge University Press, 2013. 92–109.

Bahun-Radunović, Sanja, and Marinos Pourgouris. Eds. *The Avant-garde and the Margin: New Territories of Modernism*. New Castle: Cambridge Scholars Press, 2006.

Bakhtin, Mikhail. *The Dialogic Imagination*. Ed. Michael Holquist. Trans. Caryl Emerson and Michael Holquist. Austin: University of Texas Press, 1981.

_____. *Problems of Dostoevsky's Poetics*. Ed. and trans. Caryl Emerson. Minneapolis: University of Minnesota Press, 1984.

_____. *Speech Genres and Other Late Essays*. Austin: University of Texas Press, 1986.

Baker, J. E. "Mourning and the Transformation of Object Relationships: Evidence for the Persistence of Internal Attachments." *Psychoanalytic Psychology* 18/1 (2001): 55–73.

Banfield, Ann. "Remembrance and Tense Past." *The Cambridge Companion to the Modernist Novel*. Ed. Morag Shiach. Cambridge: Cambridge University Press, 2007. 48–62.

Barta, Peter I. *Bely, Joyce, and Döblin: Peripatetics in the City Novel*. Gainesville: University Press of Florida, 1996.

Baucom, Ian. *Out of Place: Englishness, Empire and the Locations of Identity*. Princeton: Princeton University Press, 1999.

Baudelaire, Charles. *Oeuvres complètes*. Ed. M. Ruff. Paris: Seuil, 1968.

———. *The Painter of Modern Life and Other Essays*. Ed. and trans. Jonathan Mayne. London: Phaidon Press, 1964.

Beckett, Samuel. *Molloy; Malone Dies; The Unnamable*. London: Calder, 1959.

Beebe, Maurice. "What Modernism Was." *Journal of Modern Literature* 3 (1974): 1065–84.

Beer, Gillian. *Arguing with the Past: Essays in Narrative from Woolf to Sidney*. New York: Routledge, 1989.

———. "The Island and the Aeroplane: The Case of Virginia Woolf." *Nation and Narration*. Ed. Homi K. Bhabha. London and New York: Routledge, 1990. 265–90.

———. "Virginia Woolf and Pre-History." *Virginia Woolf: A Centenary Perspective*. Ed. Eric Warners. London: Macmillan, 1984. 99–123.

Beicken, Peter. *Franz Kafka. Eine kritische Einführung in die Forschung*. Frankfurt: Athenäum Fischer, 1974.

Bely, Andrei. *Andrei Bely i Aleksandr Blok: Perepiska 1903-1919*. Ed. A. V. Lavrov. Moscow: Progress-Pleiada, 2001.

———. *The Death of the Senator: Petersburg. (Gibel′ senatora (Peterburg): istoricheskaiia drama)*. Ed. John Malmstad. Berkeley: Berkeley Slavic Specialties, 1986.

———. "The Emblematics of Meaning." *Selected Essays of Andrei Bely* 111–97. Originally published as "Emblematika smysla" (1909). *Simvolizm*. Moscow: Musaget, 1910. 49–143.

———. "Formy iskusstva." *Mir iskusstva* 12 (1902): 343–61.

———. *Glossaloliia. Poema o zvuke*. Berlin: Epokha, n.d. [1922].

———. "The Magic of Words." *Selected Essays of Andrei Bely*. Trans. Steven Cassedy. Berkeley: University of California Press, 1985. 93–110. Originally published as: "Magiia slov" (1909). *Simvolizm*. Moscow: Musaget, 1910. 429–48. Reprinted in *Slavische Propyläen* 62. Munich: Wilhelm Fink, 1969.

———. *Masterstvo Gogolia*. Moscow: Khudozhestvennaia literatura, 1934.

———. "Mysl′ i iazyk. (Filosofiia iazyka A. A. Potebni)." *Logos*. Russian Edition. 1/2 (1910): 240–58.

———. *Na perevale I-III: Krizis zhizni, Krizis mysli, Krizis kul′tury*. 3 vols. Petersburg: Alkonost, 1918–1920.

———. *Na rubezhe dvukh stoletii*. Moscow-Leningrad: Zemlia i fabrika," 1930.

———. "Ob itogakh razvitiia novogo russkogo iskusstva." *V mire iskusstv* 17–18 (1907). Reprinted in Bely, *Arabeski*. Moscow: Musaget, 1911. 256–62.

———. *Peterburg: Kinostsenarii po romanu, chasti 1–5 (Peterburg: A Film Script from the Novel*, 1918). Otdel rukopisei Gosudarstvennoi biblioteki imeni V. I. Lenina [Moscow: The Manuscript Department of the Lenin State Library]. Fond 516, cardboard 3, unit of archival preservation 37. 43-verso 44.

———. *Peterburg: Roman v vos′mi glavah s prologom i epilogom [Petersburg: the novel in eight chapters with a prologue and an epilogue]*. Ed. D. S. Lihachev. Literaturnye pamyatniki. Moscow: Nauka, 1981.

———. *Petersburg*. Trans. John Elsworth. London: Pushkin Press, 2009.

———. *Petersburg*. Trans. Robert A Maguire and John Malmstad. Bloomington: Indiana University Press, 1978.

———. *Pochemu ia stal simvolistom i pochemu ia ne perestal im byt′ vo vsekh fazakh moego ideinogo i khudozhestvennogo razvitiia*. Ann Arbor: University of Michigan, 1982.

_____. "Shtempelevannaia kalosha." Reprinted in Bely, *Arabeski*. Moscow: Musaget, 1911. 342–46. Originally published in *Vesy* 5 (1907).

Benjamin, Jessica. *Shadow of the Other: Intersubjectivity and Gender in Psychoanalysis*. London: Routledge, 1997.

Benjamin, Walter. *The Arcades Project*. Ed. Rolf Tiedemann. Trans. Howard Eiland and Kevin McLaughlin. Cambridge, MA: Harvard University Press, 1999.

_____. *Charles Baudelaire: A Lyric Poet in the Era of High Capitalism*. Trans. Harry Zohn. London: Verso, 1973.

_____. "N [Re the Theory of Knowledge, Theory of Progress]." *Benjamin: Philosophy, Aesthetics, History*. Ed. Gary Smith. Chicago: University of Chicago Press, 1989. 43–82.

_____. *Selected Writings*. 4 vols. Cambridge, Mass. and London: Harvard University Press, 1996-2003.

Benjamin, Walter, and Gershom Scholem. *The Correspondence of Walter Benjamin and Gershom Scholem, 1932-1940*. Trans. Anson Rabinbach and Gary Smith. Cambridge, Mass.: Harvard University Press, 1992.

Benziman, Galia. " 'Dispersed Are We': Mirroring and National Identity in Virginia Woolf's *Between the Acts*." *Journal of Narrative Theory* 36/1 (2006): 53–71.

Berdyaev, Nikolaj. "Astral'nyi roman: Razmyshlenie po povodu romana A. Belogo *Peterburg*," *Andrei Belyi—Pro et Contra: lichnost' i tvorchestvo Andreia Belogo v otsenkakh i tolkovaniiakh sovremennikov: antologiia*. Ed. Aleksandr Lavrov. Saint Petersburg: Izd-vo Russkogo Khristianskogo gumanitarnogo instituta, 2004. 411–18.

Berglund, Bruce R. "Demokratický Hrad jako posvátný prostor (Náboženství a ideály o obnově Pražského hradu." *Souvislosti* 3 (2007): 208–21.

Bergson, Henri. *Creative Evolution*. Trans. Arthur Mitchell. Mineola, NY: Dover Publications, 1998.

Berman, Marshall. *All That Is Solid Melts into Air: The Experience of Modernity*. New York: Simon and Schuster, 1982.

Berman, Jessica. *Modernist Fiction, Cosmopolitanism, and the Politics of Community*. Cambridge: Cambridge University Press, 2001.

Berrios, German E. *The History of Mental Symptoms: Descriptive Psychopathology since the Nineteenth Century*. Cambridge: Cambridge University Press, 1996.

Berrios, German E. and R. Luque. "Cotard Syndrome: Analysis of 100 Cases." *Acta. Pychiatr. Scand.* 91 (1995): 185–88.

Bersani, Leo. *Baudelaire and Freud*. Berkeley, Los Angeles, London: University of California Press, 1977.

Bhabha, Homi. "Postcolonial Authority and Postmodern Guilt." *Cultural Studies: A Reader*. Eds Lawrence Grossberg, Cary Nelson, and Paula A. Treichler. Stanford: Stanford University Press, 1993. 56–68.

Bion, Wilfred Ruprecht. *Elements of Psycho-Analysis*. London: Heinemann, 1963.

Blanchot, Maurice. *The Work of Fire*. Trans. Charlotte Mandell. Stanford: Stanford University Press, 1995.

Blickle, Elizabeth and Rachel Palfreyman. *Heimat: A German Dream*. Oxford: Oxford University Press, 2000.

Blickle, Peter. *Heimat: A Critical Theory of the German Idea of Homeland*. Rochester: Camden House, 2002.

Bloch, Ernst. *The Principle of Hope*. 3 vols. Trans. Neville Plaice, Stephen Plaice, and Paul Knight. Oxford: Blackwell, 1986.

Bloom, Harold, ed. *Modern Critical Interpretations: Franz Kafka's "The Castle."* New York, New Haven, and Philadelphia: Chelsea House Publishers, 1988.

Boa, Elizabeth. *"The Castle." The Cambridge Companion to Kafka*. Ed. by Julian Preece. Cambridge: Cambridge University Press, 2002. 61–80.

———. *Kafka: Gender, Class, and Race in the Letters and Fictions*. Oxford: Clarendon, 1996.

Bowlby, Rachel. *Virginia Woolf: Feminist Destinations*. Oxford: Basil Blackwell, 1988.

Breton, André. *Nadja. Oeuvres Complètes*. 4 vols. Paris: Gallimard, 1988. I: 643–753.

Britton, Ronald. *Belief and Imagination: Explorations in Psychoanalysis*. London: Routledge, 1998.

Broch, Hermann. "James Joyce und die Gegenwart." *Schriften zur Lietartur I*. Ed. Paul Michael Lützeler. Frankfurt am Main: Suhrkamp, 1975. 63–95.

Brod, Max. *Heidentum, Christentum, Judentum: Ein Bekenntnisbuch*. 2 vols. Munich: Wolff, 1921.

———. "Nachwort zur ersten Ausgabe." Franz Kafka, *Das Schloss: Roman*. Frankfurt am Main: S. Fischer Verlag, 1951. 481–92.

———. "Some Remarks on Kafka's *The Castle.*" *Franz Kafka: A Biography*. Cambridge, MA: De Capo Press, 1995. 250–54.

Brush, Edward N. "An Analysis of One Hundred Cases of Acute Melancholia." *British Medical Journal* (25 September 1897): ii: 777–79.

Buckler, Julie A. *Mapping St. Petersburg: Imperial Text and Cityshape*. Princeton: Princeton University Press, 2005.

Bunder, Hartmut. Ed. *Kafka-Handbuch in zwei Bänden*. 2 vols. Stuttgart: Kröner, 1979.

Bürger, Peter. *Theorie der Avantgarde*. Frankfurt: Suhrkamp, 1974.

Burton, Robert. *The Anatomy of Melancholy*. London: George Bell and Sons, 1896.

Butler, Judith. *The Psychic Life of Power: Theories in Subjection*. Stanford: Stanford University Press, 1997.

Calinescu, Matei. *Faces of Modernity: Avant-garde, Decadence, Kitsch*. Bloomington: Indiana University Press, 1977.

Capps, Donald. *Men, Religion, and Melancholia: James, Otto, Jung, and Erikson*. New Haven: Yale University Press, 1997.

Cassedy, Steven. "Bely's Theory of Symbolism as a Formal Iconics of Meaning." Malmstad (Ed.). 285–312.

Caughie, Pamela, ed. *Virginia Woolf in the Age of Mechanical Reproduction*. New York: Garland Publishing, 2000.

Certeau, Michel de. *The Practice of Everyday Life*. Trans. Steven Rendall. Berkeley: University of California Press, 1984.

Cioran, Samuel D. *The Apocalyptic Symbolism of Andrei Belyj*. The Hague: Mouton Press, 1973.

———. "A Prism for the Absolute: The Symbolist Colors of Andrey Bely." *Andrey Bely: A Critical Review*. Ed. Gerald Janecek. Lexington: University Press of Kentucky, 1978. 103–14.

———. *Vladimir Solov'ev and the Knighthood of Divine Sophia*. Waterloo, ON: Wilfrid Laurier Press, 1977.

Clarke, Stuart N. "The Horse with a Green Tail." *Virginia Woolf Miscellany* 34 (Spring 1990): 3–4.

Clewell, Tammy. "Mourning beyond Melancholia." *Journal of American Psychoanalytic Association* 52/1 (2002): 43–67.

_____. *Mourning, Modernism, Postmodernism.* New York: Palgrave Macmillan, 2009.

Climacus, John. *The Ladder of Divine Ascent.* Trans. Colm Luibheid and Norman Russell. New York: Paulist Press, 1982. The Greek text is published in Jacques-Paul Migne, *Patrologiae Graecae.* Vol. 88: Cosmas Indicopleustes, Constantine the Deacon, Joannes Climacus, Agathias Myrinæ, Gregory of Antioch, Joannes Jejunator, Patriarch of Constantinople. Paris: J.-P. Migne, 1857-58. 631-1164.

Cohn, Dorrit. "K. Enters *The Castle*—On the Change of Person in Kafka's Manuscript." *Euphorion* 62 (1968): 28–45

Corngold, Stanley. *Franz Kafka: The Necessity of Form.* Ithaca: Cornell University Press, 1988.

_____. *Lambent Traces: Franz Kafka.* Princeton: Princeton University Press, 2004.

Cotard, Jules. "Du délire hypocondriaque dans une forme grave de mélancolie anxieuse." *Ann. Méd. Psychol.* 4 (Paris, 1880): 168–74.

_____. "Du délire des négations." *Arch. Neurol.* 4 (Paris, 1882): 152–70.

Counts, David R. and Dorothy A. Counts. *Coping with the Final Tragedy: Cultural Variation in Dying and Grieving.* Amityville, NY: Baywood, 1991.

Crone, Anna Lisa and Jennifer Jean Day. *My Petersburg/Myself: Mental Architecture and Imaginative Space in Modern Russian Letters.* Bloomington: Slavica Publishers/Indiana University Press, 2004.

Cuddy-Keane, Melba. "The Politics of Comic Modes in Virginia Woolf's *Between the Acts*." *PMLA* lo5 (March 1990): 273–85.

David, Claude. "Die Geschichte Abrahams: Zu Kafkas Auseinandersetzung mit Kierkegaard." *Bild und Gedanke: Festschrift für Gerhart Baumann zum 60. Geburtstag.* Ed. Günter Schnitzler et al. M unich: Fink, 1980. 79–90.

De Man, Paul. "Reading (Proust)." *Allegories of Reading: Figural Language in Rousseau, Nietzsche, Rilke, and Proust.* New Haven and London: Yale University Press, 1979. 57–78.

DeKoven, Marianne. "'Why James Joyce Was Accepted and I Was Not': Modernist Fiction and Gertrude Stein's Narrative." *Studies in the Literary Imagination* 25/2 (1992): 23–30.

Deleuze, Gilles and Félix Guattari. *Kafka: toward a Minor Literature.* Trans. Dana Polan. Minneapolis: University of Minnesota Press, 1986.

Derrida, Jacques. "By Force of Mourning." *Work of Mourning.* Trans. Pascale-Anne Brault and Michael Naas. Chicago: The University of Chicago Press, 2003; 139–64.

Diagnostic and Statistical Manual of Mental Disorders, IV edition-TR. Washington, D.C.: American Psychiatric Association, 2000.

DiBattista, Maria. *Imagining Virginia Woolf: An Experiment in Critical Biography.* Princeton: Princeton University Press, 2009.

Doležel, Lubomír. "Kafka's Fictional World." *Canadian Review of Comparative Literature* 11/1 (March 1984): 61–83.

_____. "The Visible and Invisible Petersburg." *Russian Literature* 7 (1979): 465–90.

Dolgopolov, Leonid K. "Obraz goroda v romane Andreia Belogo *Peterburg*." *Izvestiia Akademii Nauk. Seriia literatury i iazyka* 34/1 (1975).

_____. "Roman A. Belogo *Peterburg*." *Peterburg*. 525–623.

Dowden, Stephen D. *Kafka's Castle and the Critical Imagination*. Columbia, SC: Camden House, 1995.

Dumas, Georges. *Les états intellectuels dans la mélancolie*. Paris: Félix Alcan, 1895.

Durrani, Osman. "Editions, Translations, Adaptations." *The Cambridge Companion to Kafka*. Ed. Julian Preece. Cambridge: Cambridge University Press, 2002. 206–25.

Durusoy, Gertrud. *L'incidence de la litterature et de la langue tcheques sur les nouvelles de Franz Kafka*. Berne: Peter Lang, 1981.

Eberly, David. "Face-to-Face: Trauma and Audience in *Between the Acts*." *Virginia Woolf and Trauma: Embodied Texts*. Ed. Suzette Henke and David Eberly. New York: Pace University Press, 2008. 205–22.

Eco, Umberto. *The Open Work*. Trans. Anna Cancogni. Cambridge, Mass.: Harvard University Press, 1989.

Ellenberger, Henri F. *The Discovery of the Unconscious: The History and Evolution of Dynamic Psychiatry*. New York: Basic Books, 1970.

Elsworth, J. D. *Andrei Bely: a Critical Study of the Novels*. Cambridge: Cambridge University Press, 1983.

_____. "Andrei Bely's Theory of Symbolism." *Forum for Modern Language Studies* 11/4 (1975): 305–33.

Emery, Jacob. "Kinship and Figure in Andrey Bely's *Petersburg*." *PMLA* 123/1 (January 2008): 76–91.

Emrich, Wilhelm. *Franz Kafka: A Critical Study of His Writings*. Trans. S. Z. Buehne. New York: Ungar, 1984.

Eng, David, and David Kazanjian, eds. *Loss: The Politics of Mourning*. Berkeley: University of California Press, 2003.

Erlich, Victor. *Russian Formalism: History-Doctrine*. The Hague: Mouton, 1969.

Esty, Joshua. "Amnesia in the Fields: Late Modernism, Late Imperialism, and the English Pageant-Play." *ELH: English Literary History* 69 (2002): 245–76.

Eysteinsson, Astradur. *The Concept of Modernism*. Ithaca: Cornell University Press, 1990.

Ferguson, Harvie. *Melancholy and the Critique of Modernity: Søren Kierkegaard's Religious Psychology*. London and New York: Routledge, 1995.

Flatley, Jonathan. *Affective Mapping: Melancholia and the Politics of Modernism*. Cambridge, Mass.: Harvard University Press, 2008.

Fletcher, John, and Malcolm Bradbury. "The Introverted Novel." *Modernism 1890-1930*. Eds. Malcolm Bradbury and James McFarlane. Harmondsworth, London and New York: Penguin Books, 1991 [1976]. 394–415.

Ford, Ford Madox. *The Good Soldier: A Tale of Passion*. New York: Vintage Books, 1989.

Forter, Greg. "Against Melancholia: Contemporary Mourning Theory, Fitzgerald's *The Great Gatsby*, and the Politics of Unfinished Grief." *differences: A Journal of Feminist Cultural Studies* 14/2 (2003): 134–70.

Foster, Hal. "Postmodernism: A Preface." *The Anti-Aesthetic: Essays on Postmodern Culture*. Ed. Hal Foster. Port Townsend, Wash.: Bay Press, 1983. ix–xvi.

Foucault, Michel. *The Birth of the Clinic: An Archaeology of Medical Perception*. New York: Vintage/Random House, 1994.

_____. *The Order of Things: An Archeology of the Human Sciences*. New York: Vintage Books, 1973.

Fox, Stephen D. "The Fish Pond as Symbolic Center in *Between the Acts*." *Modern Fiction Studies* 18 (1972): 467–73.

Frank, Joseph. "Spatial Form in Modern Literature." *The Widening Gyre: Crisis and Mastery in Modern Literature*. Bloomington: Indiana University Press, 1963. 3–62.

Freud, Sigmund. *The Complete Letters of Sigmund Freud to Wilhelm Fliess: 1887-1904*. Trans. and ed. Jeffrey Moussaieff Masson. Cambridge, Mass.: Harvard University Press, 1985.

_____. *Letters of Sigmund Freud*. Ed. Ernst Freud. Trans. T. Stern and J. Stern. New York: Basic Books, 1960.

_____. "Memorandum on the Electrical Treatment of War Neurotics." *The International Journal of Psycho-Analysis* 37 (1956): 16–18.

_____. *The Standard Edition of the Complete Works of Sigmund Freud*. Ed. James Strachey. London: Hogarth Press, 1957; New York: W. W. Norton, 1961.

-"Analysis Terminable and Interminable." *SE* XXIII: 211–53.

-*Beyond the Pleasure Principle*. *SE* XVIII: 7–64.

-*Civilization and its Discontents*. *SE* XXI: 64–145.

-"A Connection between a Symbol and a Symptom." *SE* XIV: 339–40.

-"Creative Writers and Day-dreaming." *SE* IX: 143–53.

-*The Ego and the Id*. *SE* XIX: 3–66.

-*Group Psychology and the Analysis of the Ego*. *SE* XVIII: 67–143.

-*From the History of an Infantile Neurosis*. *SE* XVII: 7–122.

-"Inhibitions, Symptoms and Anxiety." *SE* XX: 77–174.

-"Instincts and Their Vicissitudes." *SE* XIV: 117–40.

-*The Interpretation of Dreams*. *SE* IV; V: 339–625.

-"Mourning and Melancholia." *SE* XIV: 237–58.

-*Moses and Monotheism*. *SE* XXIII: 1–138

-"Negation." *SE* XIX: 235–39.

-"On Transience." *SE* XIV: 303–8.

-*Psycho-Analytic Notes on an Autobiographical Account of a Case of Paranoia (Dementia Paranoides)*. *SE* XII: 3–82.

- *Studies on Hysteria*. With Joseph Breuer. *SE* II.

-"Thoughts for the Times on War and Death." *SE* XIV: 273–300.

-*Totem and Taboo: Some Points of Agreement between the Mental Lives of Savages and Neurotics*. *SE* XIII: 1–161.

Freud, Sigmund, and Carl Gustav Jung. *The Freud/Jung Letters: the Correspondence between Sigmund Freud and C. G. Jung*. Ed. William McGuire. Trans. Ralph Manheim and R. F. C. Hull. Princeton: Princeton University Press, 1974.

Freud, Sigmund, Sándor Ferenczi, Karl Abraham, Ernst Simmel, and Ernest Jones, *Psycho-Analysis and the War Neuroses*. London: The International Psychoanalytical Press, 1921.

Friedman, Susan Stanford. "Definitional Excursions: The Meanings of Modern, Modernity, Modernism." *Modernism/Modernity* 8/3 (2001): 493–513.

_____. "Periodizing Modernism: Postcolonial Modernities and the Space/Time Borders of Modernist Studies," *Modernism/Modernity* 13/3 (September 2006) 425–443.

Fritzsche, Peter. *Stranded in the Present: Modern Time and the Melancholy of History*. Cambridge, Mass.: Harvard University Press, 2004.

Froula, Christina. *Virginia Wolf and the Bloomsbury Avant-garde: War, Civilization, Modernity*. New York: Columbia University Press, 2007.

Fussell, Paul. *The Great War and Modern Memory*. Oxford: Oxford University Press, 1975.

Galison, Peter. *Einstein's Clocks, Poincarés Maps*. New York: W. W. Norton & Co, 2003.

Garber, Frederick. "Time and the City in Rilke's *Malte Laurids Brigge*." *Contemporary Literature* 11/3 (Summer 1970): 324–339.

Garff, Joakim. *"Den Søvnløse:" Kierkegaard læst æstetisk/biografisk*. København: C. A. Reitzels Forlag, 1995.

Gay, Peter. *Freud: A Life for Our Time*. New York: Norton, 1988.

———. *Weimar Culture: The Outsider as Insider*. Westport: Greenwood Press, 1968.

Genette, Gérard. *Mimologics*. Trans. Thais E. Morgan. Lincoln and London: University of Nebraska Press, 1995.

Gennep, Arnold van. *The Rites of Passage*. Trans. Monika B. Vizedom and Gabrielle L. Caffee. London: Routledge, 2004 [1909].

Gilman, Sander. *Franz Kafka: The Jewish Patient*. New York and London: Routledge, 1995.

Gilroy, Paul. *After Empire: Melancholia or Convivial Culture? Multiculture or Postcolonial Melancholia*. London: Routledge, 2004. Reprint: *Postcolonial Melancholia*. New York: Columbia University Press, 2005.

Göhler, Hulda. *Franz Kafka, Das Schloß: "Ansturm gegen die Grenze:" Entwurf einer Deutung*. Bonn: Bouvier Verlag Herbert Grundmann, 1982.

Goldman, Arnold. *The Joyce Paradox: Form and Freedom in His Fiction*. Evanston, IL: Northwestern University Press, 1966.

Goldman, Jane. "'Ce chien est à moi': Virginia Woolf and the Signifying Dog." *Woolf Studies Annual* 13 (2007): 49–86.

Goodwin, Frederick K., and Kay Redfield Jamison. *Manic-Depressive Illness: Bipolar Disorders and Recurrent Depression*. Oxford: Oxford University Press, 1990.

Gorer, Geoffrey. *Death, Grief, and Mourning*. Garden City, NY: Doubleday, 1965.

Gray, Ronald. "*The Castle*: To Deny Whatever is Affirmed." *Modern Critical Interpretations: Franz Kafka's The Castle*. 51–80.

Green, André. "The Dead Mother." *Life Narcissism Death Narcissism*. Trans. Andrew Weller. London and New York: 2001. 170–200.

Habermas, Jürgen. "Modernity versus Postmodernity." *New German Critique* 22 (1981): 3–14.

———. "Moral Development and Ego Identity." *Communication and the Evolution of Society*. Trans. Thomas McCarthy. Boston: Beacon Press, 1979. 69–94.

———. *The Structural Transformation of the Public Sphere: An Inquiry into a Category of Bourgeois Society*. Trans. Thomas Burger. Cambridge, MA: The MIT Press, 1989.

Haimson, Leopold. "Lenin's Revolutionary Career Revisited: Some Observations on Recent Discussions." *Kritika: Explorations in Russian and Eurasian History* 5/1 (Winter 2004): 55–80.

Hansen, E. S., and T. G. Bolwig. "Cotard Syndrome: An Important Manifestation of Melancholia." *Nordic Journal of Psychiatry* 52 (1998): 459–64.

Hansen-Löve, Aage A. *Der russische Symbolismus: System und Entfaltung der poetischen Motive*. I. Band: *Diabolischer Symbolismus (Russian Symbolism. System and Development of Poetic Motifs.* Vol. I: *Diabolic Symbolism*). Vienna: Verlag der Osterreichischen Akademie der Wissenschaften, 1989.

Hardy, P., R. Jouvent, and D. Widlöcher. "Speech and Psychopathology." *Language and Speech* 28/1 (1985): 57–79.

Harman, Mark. "Making Everything 'a little uncanny': Kafka's Deletions in the Manuscript of *Das Schloß* and What They Can Tell Us About His Writing Process." *A Companion to the Works of Franz Kafka.* Ed. James Rolleston. Rochester: Camden House, 2002. 325–46.

Harrison, Thomas. *Greeks and Barbarians.* New York: Routledge, 2002.

Hausmann, Frank-Rutger. "Doppelung und Spaltung in Luigi Pirandellos *Il fu Mattia Pascal*." *Italienische Studien* 2 (1979): 67–90.

Heidegger, Martin. *On the Way to Language.* Trans. Peter D. Hertz. San Francisco: Harper & Row Publishers, 1971.

Hertz, Robert. "A Contribution to the Study of the Collective Representation of Death." *Death and the Right Hand.* Trans. Rodney and Claudia Needham. Aberdeen: Cohen and West, 1960. 27–86.

Hillis Miller, Joseph. *Fiction and Repetition: Seven English Novels* (Cambridge, MA: Harvard University Press, 1982)

Hippocrates. *Oeuvres complètes d'Hippocrate.* Ed. E. Littré. 10 vols. Paris: Baillière, 1839-61. Reprint. Amsterdam 1973-82. <www.bium.univ-paris5.fr> *(17 April 2005).*

Hoff, Molly, and Melba Cuddy-Keane. Forum. "Virginia Woolf and the Greek Chorus." *PMLA* 106/1 (January 1991): 122–124

Holland, Eugene W. *Baudelaire and Schizoanalysis: The Sociopoetics of Modernism.* Cambridge: Cambridge University Press, 1993.

Homans, Peter, *The Ability to Mourn: Disillusionment and the Social Origins of Psychoanalysis.* Chicago: University of Chicago Press, 1989.

———. "Introduction." *Symbolic Loss: The Ambiguity of Mourning and Memory at Century's End.* Ed. Peter Homans. Charlottesville and London: University Press of Virginia, 2000. 1–40.

Hsieh, Lili. "The Other Side of the Picture: The Politics of Affect in Virginia Woolf's *Three Guineas*." *Journal of Narrative Theory* 36/1 (2006): 20–52.

Hussey, Mark. Ed. Virginia Woolf. *Between the Acts.* Cambridge: Cambridge University Press, 2011.

The ICD-10 Classification of Mental and Behavioural Disorders. Geneva: World Health Organization, 1992. <www.mentalhealth.com/icd/p22-md02.html> (December 20, 2005).

Ivanov-Razumnik, R. J. *Aleksandr Blok, Andrei Bely.* Petersburg: Alkonost, 1919; rev. and expand. Petersburg: Kolos, 1927.

James, William. "On Some Omissions of Introspective Psychology." *Mind* 9/33 (Jan 1884): 1–26.

———. *The Varieties of Religious Experience: A Study in Human Nature.* Radford, VA: Wilder Publications, 2007 [1901].

Jameson, Fredric. *The Modernist Papers.* London: Verso, 2007.

———. "Reflections in Conclusion." *Aesthetics and Politics: Theodor Adorno, Walter Benjamin, Ernst Bloch, Bertolt Brecht, Georg Lukács.* Ed. Fredric Jameson. London: New Left Books, 1977. 196–213.

Jamison, Kay Redfield. *Touched with Fire: Manic-Depressive Illness and The Artistic Temperament*. New York: Free Press/Simon and Schuster, 1993.

Janecek, Gerald. *The Look of Russian Literature: Avant-garde Visual Experiments, 1900-1930*. Princeton: Princeton University Press, 1984.

Jay, Mike and Michael Neve, Eds. *1900: A Fin-de-Siècle Reader*. London: Penguin Books, 1999.

Jelavich, Peter. "National Socialism, Art and Power in the 1930s." *Past & Present* 164 (Aug 1999): 244-65.

Johnson, Barbara. *Défigurations du langage poétique: la seconde revolution Baudelairienne*. Paris: Flammarion, 1979.

Johnston, Judith L. "The Remedial Flaw: Revisioning Cultural History in *Between the Acts*." *Virginia Woolf and Bloomsbury: A Centennial Celebration*. Ed. Jane Marcus. London: Macmillan, 1987. 253-77.

Jones, Ernest. *The Life and Work of Sigmund Freud*. 3 vols. New York: Basic Books, 1953-57.

Jonte-Pace, Diane. *Speaking the Unspeakable: Religion, Misogyny, and the Uncanny Mother in Freud's Cultural Texts*. Berkeley, Los Angeles, and London: University of California Press, 2001.

Joyce, James. *Ulysses: the 1922 Text*. Oxford: Oxford University Press, 1993.

Kafka, Franz. *Briefe 1902-1924*. Ed. Max Brod. New York: Schocken, 1958.

_____. *The Castle: a New Translation, Based on the Restored Text*. Trans. Mark Harman. New York: Schocken Books, 1998.

_____. *Das Schloß: Apparatband*. Ed. Malcolm Pasley. [The Critical Edition, volume 2]. Frankfurt am Main: S. Fischer, 1982.

_____. *Das Schloß. Roman in der Fassung der Handschrift*. [The Critical Edition, volume 1]. Ed. Malcolm Pasley. Frankfurt am Main: Fischer Taschenbuch, 2008 [1982].

_____. *The Diaries, 1910-1923*. Ed. Max Brod. New York: Schocken Books, 1976.

_____. *Letters to Milena*. Trans. Philip Boehm. New York: Schocken, 1990.

_____. *Nachgelassene Schriften und Fragmente II*. Ed. Jost Schillemeit. Frankfurt am Main: S. Fischer, 1992.

Kahane, Claire. "Of Snakes, Toads, and Duckweed: Traumatic Acts and Historical Actions in *Between the Acts*." *Virginia Woolf and Trauma: Embodied Texts*. 223-246.

Kern, Stephen. *The Culture of Time and Space, 1880-1918*. Cambridge, Mass.: Harvard University Press, 1983.

Keys, Roger. *The Reluctant Modernist: Andrei Belyi and the Development of Russian Fiction, 1902-1914*. Oxford and New York: Clarendon Press, 1996

Kierkegaard, Søren. *Søren Kierkegaard's Journals and Papers*. Ed. and trans. Howard V. Hong and Edna H. Hong, 7 vols. Bloomington and London: Indiana University Press, 1967-78.

_____. *Kierkegaard's Writings*. 26 vols. Ed. and trans. Edna H. Hong and Howard V. Hong. Princeton: Princeton University Press, 1980-2000.

Kirkpatrick, B. J., and Stuart N. Clarke. Eds. *A Bibliography of Virginia Woolf*. Fourth edition. Oxford: Oxford University Press, 1998.

Klein, Denis. *The Jewish Origins of the Psychoanalytic Movement*. Chicago: The University of Chicago Press, 1985.

Klein, Melanie. *The Writings of Melanie Klein*. 4 vols. Ed. Roger Money-Kyrle, Betty Joseph, Edna O'Shaughnessy, and Hanna Segal. New York: Free Press, 1975.

Klibansky, Raymond, Erwin Panofsky, and Fritz Saxl. *Saturn and Melancholy: Studies in the History of Natural Philosophy, Religion, and Art.* London: Thomas Nelson and Sons, 1964.

Kracauer, Siegfried. "*Das Schloss*: Zu Franz Kafkas Nachlaßroman." *Frankfurter Zeitung* (November 28, 1926); reprint. *Franz Kafka: Kritik und Rezeption 1924-1938.* Eds. Jürgen Born, Elke Koch, Herbert Mülfeit, and Mercedes Treckman. Frankfurt am Main: S. Fischer, 1983.

Kraepelin, Emil. *Psychiatrie. Ein Lehrbuch für Studierende und Ärzte. Fünfte, vollständig umgearbeitete Auflage.* Leipzig: Barth Verlag, 1896.

Kristeva, Julia. *Black Sun: Depression and Melancholia.* New York: Columbia University Press, 1989.

_____. *The Sense and Non-sense of Revolt: The Powers and Limits of Psychoanalysis.* Trans. Jeanine Herman. New York: Columbia University Press, 2000.

Kuleshova, Ekatarina. "O vliianii Vladimira Solov´eva na Bloka i Belogo." *Polifoniia idei i simvolov: Stat'i o Belom, Bloke, Briusove i Sologube.* Toronto: Sovremennik, 1981. 7–15.

Lacan, Jacques. "The Essence of Tragedy: A Commentary on Sophocles' *Antigone*," *The Ethics of Psychoanalysis (1959-1960): The Seminar of Jacques Lacan Book VII.* Trans. Dennis Porter. London: Routledge, 1992. 243–87.

_____. *The Seminar of Jacques Lacan I: Freud's Writings on Technique.* Trans. John Forrester. Ed. Jacques-Alain Miller. New York: W. W. Norton, 1991.

Lambotte, Marie-Claude. *Le discours mélancolique: De la phénoménologie à la métapsychologie.* Paris: Anthropos, 2003.

_____. "L'objet du mélancolique." *Essaim* 20/1 (2008): 7–19.

Landis, C., and J. D. Page, *Modern Society and Mental Disease.* New York: Farrar & Rinehart Inc., 1938.

Lange, Wolfgang. "Über Kafkas Kierkegaard-Lekture und einige damit zusammenhangende Gegenstände." *Deutsche Vierteljahresschrift für Literaturewissenschaft und Geistesgeschichte* 60 (1986): 286–308.

Langen, Timothy. *The Stony Dance: Unity and Gesture in Andrey Bely's Petersburg.* Evanston, IL: Northwestern University Press, 2005.

Laplanche, Jean. "Time and the Other." *Essays on Otherness.* Ed. J. Fletcher. Trans. L. Thurston. London: Routledge, 1999. 234–59.

Laplanche, Jean and Jean-Bertrand Pontalis. *The Language of Psycho-Analysis.* Trans. Donald Nicholson-Smith. New York: W. W. Norton, 1973.

Lavretskii, V. "Tragediia sovremennoi molodezhi." *Rech'* (30 September 1910): 2.

Leavis, F. R. "After *To the Lighthouse*: *Between the Acts* by Virginia Woolf, reviewed by F. R. Leavis." *Scrutiny* 10 (1942). Reprinted in Frank Raymond Leavis (ed.), *A Selection from Scrutiny.* 2 vols. Cambridge: Cambridge University Press, 1968. I: 97–100.

Lenin, Vladimir Ilich, *Essential Works of Lenin: "What Is To Be Done?" and Other Writings.* Ed. Henry M. Christman. New York: Courier Dover Publications, 1987.

Lepenies, Wolf. *Melancholy and Society.* Trans. Jeremy Gaines and Doris Jones. Cambridge, MA: Harvard University Press, 1992.

Le Rider, Jacques. *Modernity and Crisis of Identity: Culture and Society in Fin-de-Siècle Vienna.* Trans. Rosemary Morris. New York: Continuum, 1993.

LeRoy, Gaylord and Ursula Beitz, "The Marxist Approach to Modernism." *Journal of Modern Literature* 3 (1973): 1158–74.

Levenson, Michael. *A Genealogy of Modernism: A Study of English Literary Doctrine 1908-1922*. Cambridge: Cambridge University Press, 1986.

_____. "Introduction." *The Cambridge Companion to Modernism*. Cambridge: Cambridge University Press, 2001. 1–8.

_____. *Modernism and the Fate of Individuality: Character and Novelistic Form from Conrad to Woolf*. Cambridge and New York: Cambridge University Press, 1991.

Levin, Harry. "What Was Modernism?" *Refractions: Essays in Comparative Literature*. New York: Oxford University Press, 1965. 271–95.

Lewis, Pericles. *Modernism, Nationalism, and the Novel*. Cambridge: Cambridge University Press, 2000.

Lewis, Wyndham. *Men without Art*. London: Cassell and Co., 1934.

Lisi, Leonardo. *Marginal Modernity: The Aesthetics of Dependency from Kierkegaard to Joyce*. Fordham University Press, 2012.

Ljunggren, Magnus. *The Dream of Rebirth: A Study of Andrej Belyj's Novel "Peterburg."* Stockholm: Stockholm Studies in Russian Literature 15, 1982.

Lodge, David. *The Modes of Modern Writing: Metaphor, Metonymy, and the Typology of Modern Literature*. London, Melbourne, and Auckland: Edward Arnold, A Division of Hodder & Stoughton, 1977.

Logvinovich, L. "Smekh i pechal." *Zhizn'dlia vsekh* 1 (January 1912): 107–14.

Lotman, Yuri. "Poeticheskoe kosnoiazychie Andreia Belogo." *Andrei Bely: Problemy tvorchestva*. Eds Stanislav Lesnevskii and Aleksandr Alekseevich Mikhailov. Moscow: Sovetskii pisatel´, 1988. 437–443.

_____. "The Symbolism of St. Petersburg." *Universe of the Mind: A Semiotic Theory of Culture*. Trans. Ann Shukman. Bloomington and Indianapolis: Indiana University Press, 1990. 191–202.

Lukács, Georg. "Expressionism: Its Significance and Decline." *Essays on Realism*. Ed. Rodney Livingstone. Trans. David Fernbach. Cambridge, MA: The MIT Press, 1983. 76–113.

_____. *The Meaning of Contemporary Realism*. Trans. John and Necke Mander. London: Merlin Press, 1963.

_____. *The Theory of the Novel: A Historico-Philosophical Essay on the Forms of Great Epic Literature*. Trans. Anna Bostock. Cambridge, MA: The MIT Press, 1971.

Luti, Giorgio. "Il monologo interiore in Pirandello e Svevo." *Il romanzo di Pirandello e Svevo*. Ed. Lauretta Enzo. Florence: Vallecchi Press, 1984. 144–166.

Lutz, Catherine S., and Lila Abu-Lughod. "Introduction: Emotion, Discourse, and the Politics of Everyday Life." *Language and the Politics of Emotion*. Ed. Catherine S. Lutz and Lila Abu-Lughod. Cambridge: Cambridge University Press, 1990. 1–23.

Mach, Ernst. *The Analysis of Sensations and the Relation of the Physical to the Psychical*. Trans. C. M. Williams and Sydney Waterlow. London: Routledge/Thoemmes Press, 1996.

Maksimov, Dmitry. "Seeing and Hearing Andrey Bely: Sketches from Afar." *Malmstad* (Ed.). 336–356.

Mallarmé, Stéphane. "Crise de vers." *Oeuvres Complètes* (Pléiade). Ed. Henri Mondor and G. Jean-Aubry. Paris: Gallimard, 1979. 360–68.

Malmstad, John E. "Andrei Bely i antroposofiia." *Minuvshee* 8 (1989): 409–71.

_____. "Preface." *Andrey Bely: Spirit of Symbolism*. Ed. John Malmstad. Ithaca: Cornell University Press, 1987.

Marcus, Jane. *Virginia Woolf and the Languages of Patriarchy*. Bloomington: Indiana University Press, 1987.

Martínez-Hernáez, Angel. *What's Behind the Symptom? On Psychiatric Observation and Anthropological Understanding*. Amsterdam: Harwood Academic Publishers, 2000.

Masaryk, Thomas G. "The Slavs after the War." *The Slavonic Review* 1/1 (June 1922): x; 2–23.

Matich, Olga. "Poetics of Disgust: To Eat and Die in Andrei Belyi's *Petersburg*." *Slavic Review* 68/2 (2009): 282–308.

McCarthy, Vincent A. *The Phenomenology of Moods in Kierkegaard*. The Hague: Martinus Nijhoff, 1978.

McCole, John. *Walter Benjamin and the Antinomies of Tradition*. Ithaca: Cornell University Press, 1993.

Meghnagi, David. Ed. *Freud and Judaism*. London: Karnac Books, 1993.

Mitchell, Silas Weir. "An Analysis of Three Thousand Cases of Melancholia." *The Journal of Nervous and Mental Disorders* 24 (1897): 738–46.

Mitscherlich, Alexander and Marguerite Mitscherlich. *The Inability to Mourn: Principles of Collective Behavior*. New York: Grove Press, 1984.

Moore, Madeline. *The Short Season Between Two Silences: The Mystical and the Political in the Novels of Virginia Woolf*. Boston: George Allen & Unwin, 1984.

Morrissey, Susan K. *Suicide and the Body Politic in Imperial Russia*. Cambridge: Cambridge University Press, 2007.

Muller, John P. *Beyond the Psychoanalytic Dyad: Developmental Semiotics in Freud, Peirce, and Lacan*. New York and London: Routledge, 1996.

Nägele, Rainer. "Trembling Contours: Kierkegaard—Benjamin—Brecht." *Walter Benjamin and History*. Ed. Andrew E. Benjamin. London: Continuum, 2005. 102–17.

Němcová, Božena. *The Grandmother*. Trans. Františka Gregorová. Prague: One Third Publishers, 2006.

Newmark, Kevin. "Translators, Inc.: Kierkegaard, Benjamin, Mallarmé & Co." *parallax* 14, Special Issue: Translator's Ink (January-March, 2000): 39–55.

Nietzsche, Friedrich. *The Birth of Tragedy*. Trans. Francis Golffing. Garden City, NY: Doubleday, 1956.

——. "On Truth and Lying in an Extra-Moral Sense." *Friedrich Nietzsche on Rhetoric and Language*. Ed. and trans. Sander L. Gilman, Carole Blair, and David J. Parent. Oxford: Oxford University Press, 1989. 246–57.

Nordentoft, Kresten. *Kierkegaard's Psychology*. Trans. Bruce H. Kirmmse. Pittsburgh: Duquesne University Press, 1978.

North, Michael. *Reading 1922: A Return to the Scene of the Modern*. New York: Oxford University Press, 1999.

Ortega y Gasset, José. *The Dehumanization of Art and Other Essays of Art, Culture, and Literature*. Trans. Helene Weyl. Princeton: Princeton University Press, 1972.

Oxford English Dictionary Online. <www.dictionary.oed.com>.

Parker, G., D. Hadzi-Pavlovic, and M. P. Austin. "Sub-typing Depression I: Is Psychomotor Disturbance Necessary and Sufficient to the Definition of Melancholia?" *Psychological Medicine* 25 (1995): 815–23.

Pensky, Max. *Melancholy Dialectics: Walter Benjamin and the Play of Mourning*. Amherst: University of Massachusetts Press, 2001.

Philippi, Klaus-Peter. *Reflexion und Wirklichkeit: Unterzuchungen zu Kafkas Roman "Das Schloß."* Tubingen: Max Niemeyer Verlag, 1966.

Pinkney, Tony. "Modernism and Cultural Theory." Raymond Williams. *The Politics of Modernism: Against the New Conformists.* London: Verso, 1989. 1–29.

Pons, L., J. L. Nurnberger, Jr., and D. L. Murphy. "Mood-Independent Aberrancies in Associative Processes in Bipolar Affective Disorder: An Apparent Stabilizing Effect of Lithium." *Psychiatry Research* 14 (1985): 315–22.

Potebnia, Aleksandr Afanas´evich. *Iz lektsii po teorii slovesnosti.* Khar´kov: Parovaia tip. i litografiia M. Zil´berberg, 1894.

Poulet, Georges. *Proustian Space.* Baltimore: The Johns Hopkins University Press, 1977.

Prelovšek, Damijan. *Jože Plečnik, 1872-1957: Architecture Perennis.* Trans. Patricia Crampton and Eileen Martin. New Haven: Yale University Press, 1997.

Pridmore-Brown, Michele. "1939-40: Of Virginia Woolf, Gramophones, and Fascism." *PMLA* 113/3 (May 1998): 408–21.

Proust, Françoise. *L'Histoire à contretemps: Le temps historique chez Walter Benjamin.* Paris: Cerf, 1994.

———. "Melancolia illa heroica." *Furor* 19-20 (1990): 85–109.

Proust, Marcel. *In Search of Lost Time.* 6 vols. Trans. Andreas Mayor and Terence Kilmartin; revised D. J. Enright. New York: Random House, 1999.

Quiñones, Ricardo J. *Mapping Literary Modernism: Time and Development.* Princeton: Princeton University Press, 1985.

Rae, Patricia. *Modernism and Mourning.* Lewisburg, PA: Bucknell University Press, 2007.

Rainey, Lawrence. "The Cultural Economy of Modernism." *The Cambridge Companion to Modernism.* 33–69.

Ramazani, Jahan. *Poetry of Mourning: The Modern Elegy from Hardy to Heaney.* Chicago: University of Chicago Press, 1994.

Riasanovsky, Nicholas Valentine. *A History of Russia.* 7th edition. New York and Oxford: Oxford University Press, 2005.

Ricoeur, Paul. *Time and Narrative.* 3 vols. Trans. Kathleen McLaughlin and David Pellauer. Chicago: The University of Chicago Press, 1984-1988.

Rilke, Rainer Maria. *Gesammelte Briefe in Sechs Bänden.* Eds Ruth Sieber-Rilke and Carl Sieber. 6 vols. Leipzig, 1939-1940.

Robertson, Ritchie. *Kafka: Judaism, Politics, and Literature.* Oxford: Clarendon, 1985.

Roccatagliata, Giuseppe. *A History of Ancient Psychiatry.* Westport, CT: Greenwood Press, 1986.

Roe, Sue and Susan Sellers, Eds. *The Cambridge Companion to Virginia Woolf.* Cambridge: Cambridge University Press, 2000.

Rokem, Freddie. "Catastrophic Constellations: Picasso's Guernica and Klee's *Angelus Novus.*" *International Journal of Arts and Technology* 1/1 (2008): 34–42.

Ronell, Avital. "Doing Kafka in the Castle: A Poetics of Desire." *Kafka and the Contemporary Critical Performance: Centenary.* Ed. Alan Udoff. Bloomington: Indiana University Press, 1987; 214–35.

Rossiiskii gosudarstvennyi arkhiv literatury i iskusstva (RGALI) [Russian State Archive of Literature and Art].

Roubinovitch, Jacques, and Édouard Toulouse. *La Mélancholie.* Paris: Masson, 1897.

Russolo, Luigi. "The Art of Noise." *Futurist Performance*. Ed. Michael Kirby. New York: Dutton Paperback, 1971. 166–74.

Sacks, Peter M. *The English Elegy: Studies in the Genre from Spenser to Yeats*. Baltimore: The Johns Hopkins University Press, 1987.

Sánchez-Pardo, Esther. *Cultures of the Death Drive: Melanie Klein and Modernist Melancholia*. Durham, NC: Duke University Press, 2003.

Santner, Eric. *My Own Private Germany: Daniel Paul Schreber's Secret History of Modernity*. Princeton: Princeton University Press, 1996.

Sass, Louis A. *Madness and Modernism: Insanity in the Light of Modern Art, Literature, and Thought*. Cambridge, MA: Harvard University Press, 1998.

Sayer, Derek. "The Language of Nationality and the Nationality of Language." *Past & Present* 153 (Nov 1996): 164–210.

Schleifer, Ronald. *Modernism and Time: The Logic of Abundance in Literature, Science, and Culture, 1880-1930*. Cambridge: Cambridge University Press, 2000.

Schwartz, Sanford. *Matrix of Modernism: Pound, Eliot, and Early Twentieth Century Thought*. Princeton: Princeton University Press, 1985.

Scott, Bonnie Kime. "The Subversive Mechanics of Woolf's Gramophone in *Between the Acts*." *Virginia Woolf in the Age of Mechanical Reproduction*. 97–113.

Sebald, W. G., "The Undiscover'd Country: The Death Motif in Kafka's *Castle*," *Journal of European Studies* 2 (1972): 22–34

Segal, Hanna. "Notes on Symbol Formation." *International Journal of Psychoanalysis* 38 (1957): 391–97.

———. *Psychoanalysis, Literature, and War: Papers 1972-1992*. Ed. and intro. John Steiner. London: Routledge, 1997.

Séglas, Jules. *Le Délire des négations; sémiologie et diagnostique*. Paris: Masson, 1897.

Seifrid, Thomas. *The Word Made Self: Russian Writings on Language, 1860-1930*. Ithaca: Cornell University Press, 2005.

Shaw, J. Thomas. *The Transliteration of Modern Russian for English-Language Publications*. Madison: The University of Wisconsin Press, 1967.

Sheringham, Michael. *Everyday Life: Theories and Practices from Surrealism to the Present*. Oxford: Oxford University Press, 2006.

Sheppard, Richard. "Kafka, Kierkegaard, and the K.'s: Theology, Psychology, and Fiction." *Journal of Literature & Theology* 5/3 (November 1991): 277–96.

———. *On Kafka's Castle: A Study*. London: Croom Helm, 1973.

———. "Modernism and Modernity: The Problem of Definition." *Modernism-Dada-Postmodernism*. Evanston, IL: Northwestern University Press, 2000. 1–30.

Shklovsky, Victor. "Bely and Ornamental Prose." *Theory of Prose*. Trans. Benjamin Sher. Elmwood Park, NJ: Dalkey Archive Press, 1991. 171–188.

Showalter, Elaine. *The Female Malady: Women, Madness and English Culture 1830-1980*. New York: Pantheon Books, 1985.

Shpet, Gustav. *Vnutrenniaia forma slova*. Moscow: Gosudarstvennaia akademiia khudozhestvennykh nauk, 1927.

Silver, Brenda R. Ed. "'Anon' and 'The Reader': Virginia Woolf's Last Essays." *Twentieth Century Literature* 25 (1979): 356–435.

Silverman, P. and J. W. Worden. "Detachment Revisited: The Child's Reconstruction of a Dead Parent." *American Journal of Orthopsychiatry* 62 (1992): 494–503.

Simmel, Georg. "The Crisis of Culture." *Simmel on Culture. Selected Writings*. Ed. David Frisby and Mike Featherstone. London: Sage, 1997. 90–100.

_____. "K voprosu o metafizike smerti" ("Zur Metaphysik des Todes"). *Logos*. Russian Edition. 1/2 (1910): 34–49.

_____. "The Metropolis and Mental Life". *Simmel on Culture*. 174–185.

Smythe, Karen. "Virginia Woolf's Elegiac Enterprise." *NOVEL: A Forum on Fiction* 26/1 (Autumn 1992): 64–79.

Sokel, Walter H. *Franz Kafka*. Columbia Essays on Modern Writers: 19. New York: Columbia University Press, 1966.

_____. *Franz Kafka—Tragik und Ironie: Zur Structur seiner Kunst*. Munich and Vienna: Langen and Müller, 1964.

_____. "Kafka und Sartres Existenzphilosophie." *Arcadia* 5 (1970): 262–77.

_____. *The Myth of Power and the Self: Essays on Franz Kafka*. Detroit: Wayne State University Press, 2002.

Solomon, Andrew. *The Noonday Demon: An Atlas of Depression*. New York: Simon & Schuster/Touchstone, 2002.

Spears, Monroe K. *Dionysus and the City: Modernism in Twentieth Century Poetry*. Oxford: Oxford University Press, 1970.

Spector, Scott. *Prague Territories: National Conflict and Cultural Innovation in Franz Kafka's Fin de Siècle*. Berkeley: University of California Press, 2000.

Spoo, Robert. *James Joyce and the Language of History: Dedalus's Nightmare*. Oxford: Oxford University Press, 1994.

Staten, Henry. *Eros in Mourning: Homer to Lacan*. Baltimore and London: The Johns Hopkins University Press, 1995.

Steinberg, Mark D. "Melancholy and Modernity: Emotions and Social Life in Russia between the Revolutions." *Journal of Social History* 41/4 (Summer 2008): 813–41.

Stocchi-Perucchio, Donatella. *Pirandello and the Vagaries of Knowledge: A Reading of "Il fu Mattia Pascal."* Stanford: Stanford University Press, 1991.

Stroebe, M. et al. "On the Classification and Diagnosis of Pathological Grief." *Clinical Psychology Review* 20/1 (2000): 57–75.

Suchoff, David. *Critical Theory and the Novel: Mass Society and Cultural Criticism in Dickens, Melville, and Kafka*. Madison: University of Wisconsin Press, 1994.

Sypher, Wylie. *Loss of the Self in Modern Literature and Art*. New York: Vintage Books, 1962.

Taylor, Charles. *Source of the Self: the Making of the Modern Identity*. Cambridge, MA: Harvard University Press, 1989.

Taylor, Michael Alan, and Max Fink. *Melancholia: The Diagnosis, Pathophysiology, and Treatment of Depressive Illness*. Cambridge: Cambridge University Press, 2006.

Trotter, David. *Paranoid Modernism: Literary Experiment, Psychosis, and the Professionalization of English Society*. Oxford: Oxford University Press, 2001.

Tsivian, Yuri. *Early Cinema in Russia and Its Cultural Reception*. 2nd ed. Trans. Alan Bodger. Chicago: Chicago University Press, 1998.

Turner, Victor. *Dramas, Fields and Metaphors: Symbolic Action in Human Society*. Ithaca: Cornell University Press, 1974.

Vishnevetsky, Igor. "Poetic Dominion in the Work of Andrei Belyi." *Symposion* 1 (1996): 75–91.

Walkowitz, Rebecca. *Cosmopolitan Style: Modernism Beyond the Nation*. New York: Columbia University Press, 2007.

Weinstein, Philip. *Unknowing: The Work of Modernist Fiction*. Ithaca: Cornell University Press, 2005.

White, Hayden. *The Content of the Form: Narrative Discourse and Historical Representation*. Baltimore: The Johns Hopkins University Press, 1987.

Widlöcher, Daniel. *Les Logiques de la dépression*, Paris: Fayard, 1995.

_____. Ed. *Le Ralentissement dépressif*. Paris: Presses Universitaires de France, 1983.

Wiley, Catherine. "Making History Unrepeatable in Virginia Woolf's *Between the Acts*." *Clio* 25/1 (Fall 1995): 3–20.

Wilson, Eric G. *Against Happiness: In Praise of Melancholy*. New York: Farrar, Straus and Giroux, 2008.

Winter, Jay. *Sites of Memory, Sites of Mourning: The Great War in European Cultural History*. Cambridge: Cambridge University Press, 1995.

Wollaeger, Mark, with Matt Eatough, ed., *The Oxford Handbook of Global Modernisms*. Oxford and New York: Oxford University Press, 2012.

Woodward, Kathleen. "Freud and Barthes: Theorizing Mourning, Sustaining Grief." *Discourse* 13 (1990): 93–110.

Woolf, Virginia. *Anon*. Typescript with the author's ms. corrections. Paginated 1–25, two pages paginated 22. November 24, 1940. Berg Collection, New York Public Library.

_____. *Between the Acts*. San Diego, New York, and London: Harvest Book and Harcourt Brace Jovanovich, 1970.

_____. *The Diary of Virginia Woolf*. 5 vols. Ed. Anne Olivier Bell. San Diego, New York, and London: Harcourt Brace Jovanovich, 1984.

_____. *The Essays of Virginia Woolf*. 4 vols. Ed. Andrew McNeillie. London: The Hogarth Press, 1986.

_____. *Holograph Reading Notes*. Vol. 21. Berg Collection. New York Public Library.

_____. *The Letters of Virginia Woolf*. Eds. Nigel Nicolson and Joanne Trautmann. 6 vols. London: The Hogarth Press, 1975-1980.

_____. "Modern Fiction." *The Common Reader*. Ed. and intro. Andrew McNeillie. San Diego, New York and London: Harcourt Brace & Company, 1984. 146–54.

_____. *A Passionate Apprentice: The Early Journals 1897-1909*. Ed. Mitchell A. Leaska. New York: Harvest and Harcourt Brace Jovanovich, 1990.

_____. *Pointz Hall: The Earlier and Later Transcripts of 'Between the Acts'*. Ed. Mitchell A. Leaska. New York: The John Jay Press, University Publications, 1983.

_____. "The Russian Point of View." *The Common Reader*. 173–81.

_____. "The 'Sentimental Journey'." *The Second Common Reader*. Ed. Andrew McNeillie. San Diego, New York, and London: Harcourt Brace & Company, 1986. 78–85.

_____. "A Sketch of the Past." *Moments of Being: Unpublished Autobiographical Writings*. Ed. Jeanne Schulkind. New York and London: Harcourt Brace Jovanovich, 1976. 64–137.

_____. "Street Haunting: A London Adventure." *Death of the Moth and Other Essays*. London: Hogarth Press, 1942. 19–29.

_____. *Three Guineas*. London: Hogarth Press, 1938.

_____. *Virginia Woolf's Reading Notebooks*. Ed. Brenda Silver. Princeton: Princeton University Press, 1983.

_____. *The Waves*. London: Penguin Books, 1992.

Woronzoff, Alexander. *Andrej Belyj's 'Petersburg,' James Joyce's 'Ulysses' and the Symbolist Movement*. Berne: Peter Lang Publishers, 1982.

Wussow, Helen. *The Nightmare of History*. Bethlehem: Lehigh University Press and London: Associated University Press, 1998.

Yoshino, Ayako. "*Between the Acts* and Louis Napoleon Parker—The Creator of the Modern English Pageant." *Critical Survey* 15 (Summer 2003): 49–60.

Young, James E. *At Memory's Edge: After-Images of the Holocaust in Contemporary Art and Architecture*. New Haven: Yale University Press, 2000.

_____. *The Texture of Memory: Holocaust Memorials and Meaning*. New Haven: Yale University Press, 1994.

Ulmer, Gregory. "The Object of Post-criticism." *The Anti-Aesthetic*. 83–110.

Ziehen, Theodor. "Die Erkennung und Behandlung der Melancholie in der Praxis." Halle: Alt's Abhandl. C. Marhold, 1896.

Zimmermann, Hans D. "Franz Kafka liest Božena Němcová." *brücken: German Language and Literature Studies Yearbook* 15 (2007): 181–92.

Žižek, Slavoj. *The Sublime Object of Ideology*. London: Verso, 1989.

Zwerdling, Alex. *Virginia Woolf and the Real World*. Berkeley: University of California Press, 1986.

Index